2892 19○○ 12/03

Inside the Klavern

LaGRANDE, OREGON
July II/23

Mr. W.M. Pierce;
Esteemed Klansman;

Last nights discussion in our Klavern brought forth the ;

Fact that the Criticism tendered youn by the Oragonian;

in behalf of the Pagent at the top of the Blue Mts. was ;

but a continuance of the Eneemy who never sleeps and that;
the oraginators of that epistle were none other than our;

Friends Namely Williams and Tooze; As to the general,census;

of opinion through the grande Ronde Valley ; we accept their

challenge relative to your Popularity ; and this Klan feels ;

highly honored to know that in accord to your Offical ;

Capacity as Gov. Of The Democrats as well as the Rebublicans

You tendered a real reception to our President such as a red

Big Hearted Western Governor should of done ; We want you to

Know that in this Community when they Say anything Against;
Walter Pierce and His Admistration ; they have dealt a blow;
against our Beloved Order ; When Jesus Christ came upon;
this earth he cleased but very few men ; Yes Bruce Dennis ;
says that with the power of his paper he can make or break ;
any local man ; But up to date he hasnt been able to solve ;
the election of two Klan School directors ; Going from this
I wish to state that the Petitions of Ed Reynolds and Huron;
will be in your office in the very near future ; and that ;
We are back of you to the limit ; We are enjoying on e clean
Administration and our appreciation of your efforts are ;
going to be recorded in the pages of History.

Yours in the Sacred;
And Unfailing Bond.

Harold R. Fosner
LaGrande Ore. I4.

PRINTED BY THE KU KLUX PRESS

Letter from La Grande Klan secretary Harold R. Fosner to Oregon governor Walter M.
Pierce, July 11, 1923. Courtesy of The Walter Pierce Papers, Coll. 68, Department of Special
Collections, University of Oregon Libraries

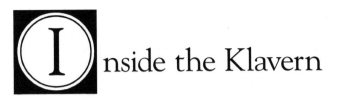

Inside the Klavern

The Secret History of a Ku Klux Klan of the 1920s

Edited by David A. Horowitz

Southern Illinois University Press

Carbondale and Edwardsville

Designed by Dennis Roberts

02 01 00 99   4 3 2 1

Library of Congress Cataloging-in-Publication Data

Inside the klavern : the secret history of a Ku Klux Klan of the 1920s /
edited by David A. Horowitz.
    p. cm.
Includes bibliographical references and index.
1. Ku Klux Klan (1915–   ). La Grande Klan No. 14 (La Grande,
Or.)—History—Sources. 2. White supremacy movements—
Oregon—La Grande—History—Sources. 3. La Grande (Or.)—
Race relations. 4. La Grande (Or.)—Social conditions.
I. Horowitz, David A. II. Ku Klux Klan (1915–   ).
La Grande Klan No. 14 (La Grande, Or.)
HS2330.K63I57   1999   98-30730
322.4′2′0979571—dc21   CIP
ISBN 0-8093-2247-1 (cloth : alk. paper)
ISBN 0-8093-2248-X (pbk. : alk. paper)

The paper used in this publication meets the minimum requirements
of American National Standard for Information Sciences—
Permanence of Paper for Printed Library Materials, ANSI
Z39.48-1984. ♾

To the memory of my uncle,

Milton ("Mickey") David Levine (1913–1996),

who never gave up the dream of universal social justice

ontents

cknowledgments

HISTORICAL SCHOLARSHIP IS AN INNATELY individualistic task that cannot be accomplished without the unselfish cooperation of others. This fortunate contradiction has never been more apparent than in completion of this work.

My initial exploration of the La Grande Ku Klux Klan Minutes of 1922–24 was facilitated by a summer scholar's stipend from the Oregon Council for the Humanities in 1983. Relevant background work and occupational studies on Klan members were undertaken in connection with publication of "Order, Solidarity, and Vigilance: The Ku Klux Klan in La Grande, Oregon," in Shawn Lay, ed., *The Invisible Empire in the West: Toward a New Historical Appraisal of the Ku Klux Klan of the 1920s* (Urbana: University of Illinois Press, 1992). The bulk of the task of compiling and annotating the minutes and producing the ancillary portions of this volume was completed during the spring of 1994, thanks to a partial release from teaching duties by the Portland State University Department of History.

The La Grande Minutes are housed in the Manuscripts Room of the Oregon History Center Research Library in Portland. The proper citation for the collection is Ku Klux Klan, La Grande, Or. Chapter, Records, 1922–1923, Oregon Historical Society, Mss. 2604. Permission to publish the documents has been granted by the Oregon Historical Society. Permission to reproduce the contents and letterhead of Harold R. Fosner's letter of July 11, 1923, to Walter M. Pierce has been extended by the University of Oregon. The document appears in The Walter Pierce Papers, Coll. 68, Department of Special Collections, University of Oregon Libraries.

The Oregon History Center's archival, library, and technical service staffs, led by Archival Collections Director Kris White, have extended themselves selflessly throughout the project. Manuscripts librarians Vicki Jones and Linda Long of the Department of Special Collections at the University of Oregon Libraries, and Patty Cutright, the reference librarian at Eastern Oregon University, also have been most helpful. I further wish to thank the staffs of the Multnomah County Public Library, the Tillamook County Public Library, and the

Portland State University Library. Mary A. Grant, director of the Office of Archives for the Archdiocese of Portland in Oregon, deserves special apprecia- tion for useful leads in filling out the story. Vital court records have been pro- vided by Needa Wilson, Union County Circuit Court trial clerk, and Eldon Slippy, finance director of the City of La Grande.

Jerry Bingner, Sister Margaret Meyers, and John T. (Jack) Evans were sources of important insight and background information. Evans, former library direc- tor at Eastern Oregon University, assisted in tracing the provenance of the min- utes, as did attorneys Willard K. Carey and R. Thomas Gooding. Former Judge Gooding provided me with a copy of the La Grande Klan Minutes. Former *La Grande Observer* reporter Jay Griffiths and current publisher Bob Moody also proved useful in describing the process by which the documents became public. Further assistance was extended by Edna Jones of the Union County Historical Society, Lowell Jensen of Bend, and Maryanne Davis of the Baker Diocese at Bend. Fellow Oregon Klan scholar Eckard V. Toy consistently has extended thoughtful encouragement and support over the years. The map of Oregon was produced by Jason Clark, a student in the Department of Geography, Portland State University.

I am grateful for the guidance of Susan Wilson, assistant director, and John K. Wilson, assistant managing editor, of Southern Illinois University Press. Kathryn Koldehoff served as a superb copyeditor. The wise counsel and unflag- ging support of Press Director Rick Stetter literally brought this project to life. Special thanks also go out to friend and colleague, Peter Carroll. Finally, the spiritual sustenance and strategic advice of Gloria E. Myers Horowitz once again proved indispensable.

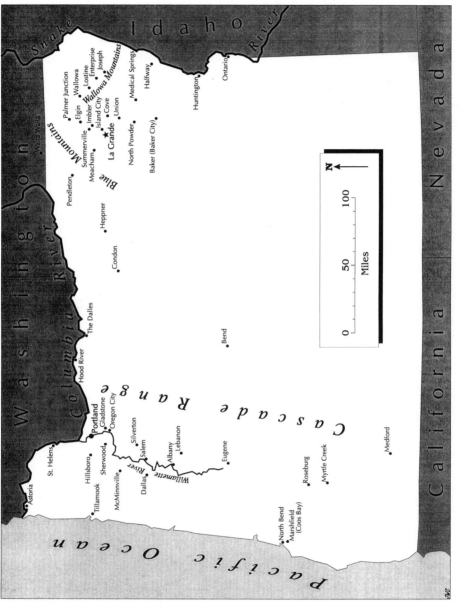

Locations of Ku Klux Klan Activity Described in the La Grande Minutes. Jason Clark, cartographer

Inside the Klavern

(I)ntroduction: Setting the Context

WHEN EIGHTY-SIX-YEAR-OLD Colon R. Eberhard, former state legislator, school board commissioner, and Masonic lodge master of La Grande, Oregon, was fatally injured by a car while crossing a street on an icy night in January 1968, a new chapter of U.S. social history began to unravel. As the contents of the prominent eastern Oregon attorney's safe were processed for probate, investigators discovered an unlabeled folder separate from the files of Eberhard's sixty-three-year professional practice. Inside the folder, a binder contained some two hundred typed pages of the secret minutes and commentary of the La Grande Ku Klux Klan for 1922 to 1924.[1]

Providing an inner view of a thriving KKK chapter of more than three hundred members, the La Grande documents comprise the most complete set of Klan Minutes ever to be uncovered. They focus on the secret order outside the South and cover a period in which the Invisible Empire was a nationwide organization of millions whose members fused purity reform and community activism with a controversial heritage of racism and nativism. Ample summaries of internal discussions and gossip in the klavern offer extraordinary insight into the rank and file of one of the largest social movements in U.S. history. In line with historian Leonard J. Moore's dictum that nonelite movements "cannot be understood by examining leaders and ideology alone," the Oregon minutes help to explain how the constituents of a powerful middle-class organization of the 1920s came to terms with the complexities of modern life.[2]

Since the 1960s, historians of the Jazz Age Ku Klux Klan have benefited from the discovery of chapter financial records, membership lists, and legal documents. Yet only Nancy MacLean's *Behind the Mask of Chivalry* (1994) has incorporated actual accounts of secret Klan meetings, and MacLean's use of the sparse minutes of a late-1920s klavern in Athens, Georgia, is necessarily limited. As scholars have focused on the Invisible Empire after World War I, an interpretive "cultural war" has taken shape. One view, rooted in the pioneer work of sociologist John Moffatt Mecklin and historian Richard Hofstadter and sustained by writers such as Wyn Craig Wade, David H. Bennett, and Nancy

MacLean, emphasizes reactionary racism and rural nativism as keys to the secret order. In contrast, a succession of "revisionist" historians since the mid 1960s have portrayed the "second" Ku Klux Klan primarily as a middle-class purity crusade directed against corrupt urban elites.[3]

The controversies of Klan scholarship are rooted in the KKK's tumultuous history. Attracting between two and six million members in the years after World War I, the Invisible Empire traced its roots to a secret Confederate veterans club formed in Tennessee in 1866. The original Klan expropriated *kuklos*, the Greek word for "circle," and *clan*, a Gaelic tribal reference suggesting "loyalty" and "service." It also initiated the use of the mask, hood, and robe and much of the language, ritual, and organizational hierarchy that would characterize its successors. Reacting harshly to post–Civil War threats to white supremacy and Democratic rule, Klansmen defied the law with acts of terrorism and intimidation against newly freed African-American slaves, Union army occupiers of the southern states, and white Republicans.[4]

By the time northern troops completed withdrawal from the South in 1877, the Ku Klux Klan long had disappeared. Yet the southern novelist Thomas Dixon idealized the order's legacy in *The Clansman* (1905), a romantic chronicle that pictured the Klan as protecting Victorian civilization against irresponsible blacks and manipulative Yankees. D. W. Griffith brought the racial and regional stereotypes of the book to the screen in his 1915 cinema masterpiece, *The Birth of a Nation*. Just as the controversial but popular motion picture premiered in Atlanta, Georgia, William Joseph Simmons, a southern Methodist and former circuit rider, reconvened the KKK in a ceremony featuring a fiery cross on nearby Stone Mountain.[5]

Simmons's emphasis on white supremacy took its cues from former Georgia Populist Tom Watson, whose demagogic newspaper editorials had sparked the lynching of a Jewish factory owner falsely accused of the 1913 rape and murder of a white female employee. The second KKK confined membership to white, native-born Protestant males. Expanding upon the Invisible Empire's ritual and hierarchy, Simmons borrowed from Masonic- and fraternal-order protocol to demand strict organizational loyalty. He designated an imperial wizard as national ruler; grand dragons as state leaders; exalted cyclopses as chapter, or klavern, officers; and terrors as the assisting officials of the local units. The new Klan's constitution required initiates to swear oaths to secrecy, obedience, fidelity, and Klannishness. The latter compelled Klansmen to support "100 percent" Americans instead of "hyphenated" ethnics in trade and public affairs. Significantly, new members were referred to as "naturalized aliens."[6]

Seeking enhanced recruitment in 1920, Simmons hired two Atlanta publicity agents who created a scheme that awarded a percentage of initiation fees to professional kleagles, or organizers. The movement soon made vast inroads in the booming post–World War I oil towns of Texas, Oklahoma, and Louisiana. In response, the *New York World* and the House Rules Committee of the U.S. Congress conducted exposés in 1921 that accused southwest Klansmen of whippings, brandings, tarrings, and other vigilante action against morals offenders. Yet when Klan leaders defused the charges, favorable publicity popularized the secret order. As a result, the organization's strength spread to the Middle West, Pacific Coast, and Northeast. By late 1922, when Dallas, Texas, dentist Hiram Wesley Evans wrested control of the Invisible Empire from Simmons, the Ku Klux Klan had become a national mass movement. At mid-decade, more than two-fifths of its membership came from Illinois, Indiana, or Ohio.[7]

Local klaverns worked closely with Protestant clergy, mainly nonfundamentalists in the Methodist, Presbyterian, and Christian churches. Although the Klan often tapped skilled manual laborers, it recruited heavily among chiropractors, dentists, real estate agents, auto dealers, and others of marginal middle-class status. Klansmen mirrored the casual racial and ethnic prejudices of national life after World War I, which included stereotypical views of African Americans, Roman Catholics, Jews, Asian Americans, and immigrants. Evans aligned the order with the broad coalition of reformers who successfully pressed for postwar national immigration-restriction legislation. On the local level, the movement's ideological emphasis on Nordic-American values often translated into economic boycotts, whispering campaigns, or political vendettas against Catholics, Jews, foreigners, and people of color.[8]

Yet the Ku Klux Klan of the 1920s went beyond mere racism and nativism to identify itself as the guarantor of traditional social morality. Evans consistently proclaimed the Invisible Empire's devotion to sacrifice, service, unselfishness, purity, and the interests of the common people. KKK publications promoted the flag, the Constitution, and the Bible as the movement's core symbols. Because it viewed education as the most important "Americanizing" agent of the nation's youth, the secret order made federal aid to public schools one of its main political demands.[9]

The Klan also established a dramatic identification with law enforcement, particularly in the implementation of national Prohibition, which took effect in 1920 as a result of the Eighteenth Amendment to the Constitution. Upholding the law was so important that local klaverns frequently ignored race and ethnicity when organizing against elites implicated in vice, crime, and political corruption. Evans extended such standards to Klansmen by threatening to discipline those tied to illegal vigilantism. The imperial wizard even attributed statistical declines in southern lynching to the order's restraining influence and growing power.[10]

By disassociating the Invisible Empire from its violent history and achieving political legitimacy, Imperial Wizard Evans converted a loosely administered fraternal order into a centralized political machine and lobby. Peaking in influence between 1922 and 1925, the postwar Ku Klux Klan helped to elect seven governors, three U.S. senators, and half the 1924 Indiana state legislature. Rumors even suggested that President Warren G. Harding had been inducted in a White House ceremony. KKK political power surfaced when opponents sought to unseat Texas Senator and Knight Earl B. Mayfield. One year after the 1922 elections, a Dallas law firm charged that Mayfield had used the Klan to intimidate voters, to take over county election machinery, and to violate Texas limitations on campaign spending. Adversaries insisted that the senator's open membership in the Invisible Empire provided additional grounds for unseating him. Once the Senate agreed to make an inquiry early in 1924, however, two key committees upheld Mayfield's election, and he took office without debate.[11]

KKK electoral power became an issue in Oklahoma in 1923 when a series of Klan-related whippings and floggings prompted Governor Jack Walton to declare statewide martial law. When Walton used the campaign against the secret order to attack legislative and political adversaries, however, he was impeached and removed from office. Outside the South, the Invisible Empire normally worked within the Republican Party. Yet Klan loyalists were sufficiently strong to defeat a resolution at the 1924 Democratic National Convention that condemned the order by name. The following year, more than thirty thousand robed knights and Klanswomen openly marched in a massive public demonstration on the streets of the nation's capital.[12]

The Ku Klux Klan found fertile ground in Oregon, a state whose population of fewer than eight hundred thousand in 1920 was 85 percent white, native born, and 90 percent Protestant. Kleagle Luther I. Powell crossed the California border to organize the southern Oregon town of Medford early in 1921. Forty-three years of age, the Missouri-born Powell was of Welsh and New England background. A Spanish-American War veteran, a Mason, and an Orangeman, he had organized the Louisiana Klan. Powell employed the familiar KKK tactic of recruiting from the membership lists of local fraternal organizations. A former Klansman later estimated that between 50 percent and 60 percent of Oregon's initial four thousand knights were Masons. By dramatizing the need for law enforcement against Jackson County bootleggers, Major Powell quickly attracted a founding group of twenty-five Medford Klansmen.[13]

A second kleagle, C. N. Jones, began to apply Powell's recruiting methods to the University of Oregon city of Eugene in the summer of 1921. By mounting a campaign to oppose the establishment of a campus branch of the Catholic Newman Club, Jones stimulated the rapid enrollment of four hundred Klansmen. Meanwhile, Oregon's capital city, Salem, boasted more than three hundred recruits. In the state's largest metropolis, Portland, Brad Calloway of Houston, Texas, distributed patriotic literature to police, firefighters, and fraternal groups before convening a founding meeting of one hundred Klansmen. The new klavern elected Fred L. Gifford as exalted cyclops at a six-hundred-dollar monthly salary. By 1922 Gifford had won Atlanta's endorsement as Oregon grand dragon and imperial representative in the Pacific states.[14]

A Minnesota native and active Mason in his early forties, Grand Dragon Gifford was a former telegraph operator, electrical workers' union official, and manager for a Portland utility. Both Powell and Gifford had a flair for publicity. Convening an August 1922 meeting with Portland's mayor, local law enforcement officials, and a special Prohibition agent from the Justice Department, the two Klansmen scored a coup when they donned full Klan regalia and staged a group portrait for the benefit of a newspaper photographer. Yet Gifford also lashed out at press adversaries by mounting boycotts of the hostile *Oregon Labor Press* and *Portland Telegram* and threatening action against the *Oregonian* newspaper. Portland's exalted cyclops helped to publish a *100% Directory* of Klan allies in the business community, organized a boycott of the Jewish-owned Meier and Frank Department Store, and recruited "Portland Police Vigilantes" to aid Prohibition enforcement and harass the radical Industrial Workers of the World.[15]

By offering a program of nationalism, law enforcement, and resistance to the alleged power of the Catholic Church, Gifford used his Portland base to recruit Klansmen across the state. Klaverns surfaced in small Willamette Valley towns, such as Sherwood, McMinnville, Gladstone, Lebanon, Dallas, and Albany. To the south, Klan representatives organized railroad and lumber workers in Roseburg and Myrtle Creek. On the coast, kleagles found receptive targets in the working ports of North Bend and Marshfield (Coos Bay). To the north in Tillamook, local dairy farmers, retail merchants, and professionals built a powerful klavern whose members dominated area politics for a full decade. In northwest Oregon's Astoria, KKK organizers exploited sentiment against Finnish Americans, Catholics, and bootleggers to elect a mayor, sheriff, four city commissioners, and two state legislators while building a Klan chapter whose membership peaked at nine hundred. Klaverns also appeared in the central and eastern Oregon towns of Hood River, The Dalles, Condon, Pendleton, and Baker (now called Baker City).[16]

By the spring of 1922, Gifford claimed that fourteen thousand Oregonians had joined the Invisible Empire, nine thousand from Portland. The *Oregon Voter* counted fifty-eight chartered klaverns and several provisional chapters by the end of the following year. Despite its secret membership, the Ku Klux Klan functioned in the open. Kleagles often inaugurated recruitment campaigns by arranging public lectures by anti-Catholic clergy in municipal auditoriums or downtown theaters. Klan leaders kept the secret order in the public eye by mounting dramatic nighttime parades and rallies. More than one hundred robed and hooded knights marched down the main street of the southern Oregon town of Ashland on July 4, 1922. The next year, more than fifteen hundred Salem Klansmen participated in an evening cross burning and initiation ceremony at the Oregon State Fairground's racetrack. Oregon klaverns also orchestrated "kavalkades" of the rank and file in ceremonial automobile processions that often passed by Catholic hospitals and schools.[17]

As the center of regional KKK power, Portland provided the most effective stage for the Invisible Empire's Oregon presence. Fiery crosses frequently were burned on such nearby hillsides as Mt. Tabor and Mt. Scott. The Klan's first outdoor initiation in Portland occurred in conjunction with the city's Rose Festival of 1923. Three months earlier, Oregon Governor Walter M. Pierce and Portland Mayor George L. Baker participated in a "patriotic" dinner honoring Grand Dragon Fred Gifford in which the Klan leader declared that the secret order was based on the highest Christian principles and national ideals. "It is here that we are to prove what the standards of true American citizenship . . . can accomplish," declared Gifford.[18]

Statewide Klan activity soon focused on politics and patronage. Yet KKK political ambitions were threatened by three night-riding incidents perpetrated by Medford Klansmen shortly before the 1922 Oregon spring primaries. Accusing an African American, a Hispanic Indian, and a white piano merchant of moral offenses against the community, six Jackson County knights staged three separate abductions, which resulted in "necktie hangings," terrorist acts that avoided death or serious injury by permitting the victim's feet to skim the ground. As the primary approached, Republican Governor Ben W. Olcott issued an executive proclamation denouncing "masked outlaws" who stirred up fanaticism, race hatred, religious prejudice, fraternal strife, and civil terror. "Oregon needs no masked night riders, no invisible empire to control her affairs," declared Olcott. The governor warned that the state could not be "turned over to some secret clique or clan, to be made the tool of invisible forces." The true American spirit resented bigotry, secrecy, and terrorism, he concluded.[19]

When Department of Justice officials rejected the governor's request for federal prosecution of the Medford case on jurisdictional grounds, Olcott asked the state attorney general to impanel a grand jury to press charges against the night riders. Accordingly, the Klan opposed Olcott in the Republican gubernatorial primary and supported Marshfield business leader Charles Hall. Appealing to nativist and anti-Catholic sympathies, Hall endorsed a Scottish Rite Mason proposal for compulsory education of all children in public schools instead of in parochial institutions or private academies. Oregon Masons soon gathered enough signatures to place the plan on the November ballot as a voters' initiative.[20]

Klan commitment to the school bill and hostility toward Olcott brought national attention to the Oregon election of 1922. The dual agenda pushed the secret order into a curious alliance with La Grande Democrat Walter Pierce. Yet state KKK leaders worked with nativist legislators in both parties. One result was the Garb Act of 1923. Directed at Catholic nuns, the law prohibited the wearing of religious habits by public school teachers. Another was the 1923 Alien Land Act, a measure that prevented Japanese and Chinese immigrants who were ineligible for U.S. citizenship from owning property in their own name. Klan-supported politicians also tried to eliminate Columbus Day as a state holiday, to prohibit the importing of sacramental wine, and to tax church and sectarian property.[21]

The Ku Klux Klan arrived in La Grande in the spring of 1922 when kleagles from Portland and Pendleton organized the nucleus of a new chapter. Located three hundred miles east of Portland in the Grande Ronde Valley of the Blue Mountains, La Grande lies midway between the eastern Oregon towns of Pendleton and Baker City. A commercial and construction nexus, as well as the Union County seat, the city functioned as a processing center and distribution point for regional fruits, grains, and livestock. In the years following World War I, La Grande hosted twenty manufacturing facilities. Its four lumber mills provided work for thirteen hundred people. With the second highest payroll and fourth largest public school enrollment in the state, the city experienced a population increase from seven to eight thousand in the 1920s.[22]

Much of La Grande's Jazz Age flavor and character was provided by the Union Pacific Railroad, which boasted eight hundred fifty resident workers, an annual local payroll of $1.8 million, and the second largest number of division maintenance shops and roundhouses in the state. La Grande owed its development to the Oregon-Washington Railroad and Navigation Company (O-WR&N), which first linked the milling and gold-mining center to distant markets. Once the frontier city was incorporated in 1885, local entrepreneurs convinced the railroad to use the town as a transportation division point. As the Union Pacific assumed management of the line in the 1890s, La Grande prospered, its main street soon featuring opulent Victorian homes. Another sign of self-confidence came in 1913 when voters emulated the spirit of Progressive reform and provided for the election of three at-large municipal commissioners and the appointment of a city manager.[23]

The Union County Chamber of Commerce portrayed the Grande Ronde Valley of the 1920s as the embodiment of the American Dream—a pristine but lucrative environment characterized by both moral traditionalism and economic progress. La Grande was a metropolis blessed by "a feeling of wholesome activity" and civic pride—"a clean, beautiful little city . . . an ideal place in which to live." Chamber boosters drew attention to the fact that railroad workers owned one-fourth of the city's homes.[24]

Despite such idyllic pretensions, La Grande residents of the 1920s faced contradictions between their cherished cultural isolation and the disruptive threats of the national market from which they benefited. By the early years of the decade, highway, air, water, and pipeline transportation contributed to serious declines in rail freight and passenger profits. Railroad managers also felt compelled to cut costs and increase earnings after the federal government relinquished administrative control of the depreciated lines following World War I. Resulting labor-management tensions exploded in the nationwide strike of four hundred thousand railroad shop-craft and maintenance workers in the summer of 1922. More than six hundred La Grande rail employees joined the labor action.[25]

Ethnic and racial diversity marked another consequence of the valley's ties to the national market. As a railroad and construction headquarters, La Grande attracted numbers of casual laborers and traveling workers. Chinese migrants originally had come to the area during the 1880s gold rush and railroad boom. Many had remained as merchants, laundry proprietors, restaurant owners, cooks, and gardeners. During the depression year of 1893, however, anxieties over job competition resulted in the burning of La Grande's Chinatown and the expulsion of its residents by a white mob. In 1917 a dispute among surviving tongs, or ethnic syndicates, led to an exchange of gunfire near the city's post office and the arrest of six men for the killing of a Chinese restaurant operator. Following an investigation of Chinese opium dens and a single house of prostitution by an official citizens' committee, an informal agreement between local officials and tong leaders spared the Chinese community from further reprisals by confining prosecution to the six Chinese gunmen for second-degree murder.[26]

Although the 1920 census listed only forty-six people of Chinese ancestry in Union County, concerns over the small community's ties to vice and crime persisted. In August 1922, a raiding party of federal officers, sheriff's deputies, and city police discovered a major opium distribution center in a Chinese home near the railroad yards. Concerned about the potential spread of opium use to the white community, local authorities stepped up efforts to uncover Chinese drug dealing and bootlegging. "[W]hen a Chinaman steps out and induces Americans to smoke opium or use dope," editorialized the La Grande Evening Observer in 1924, "away goes patience of real Americans who have permitted these descendants of Old Confucius to live under the stars and stripes." The census also listed seventy-five Japanese Americans in Union County.[27]

Racial anxieties extended to the manner in which local citizens viewed the small African-American quarter near the railroad yards. The 1920 census identified only fifteen La Grande residents as black. Nevertheless, the largest Prohibition raid in the city's history resulted in five arrests and the confiscation of 14.5 gallons of moonshine in the black district in late 1922. The following April, the arrest, conviction, and jailing of African-American bootlegger Dee Rogers received front-page treatment by the La Grande Evening Observer. In August 1923, the newspaper reported the apprehension of Pearl Fagin, a black woman who had been cited repeatedly for keeping a "disorderly house."[28]

Ethnic tensions among whites also influenced public perceptions of crime and vice. The 1920 census listed 425 foreign-born whites in La Grande and another 1,154 people with at least one immigrant parent. At mid-decade, the Catholic Church claimed 661 parishioners in Union County, mainly of Canadian, German, Irish, and Italian backgrounds. Of the ethnic groups, Italian Americans and Mexican Americans were most often linked in newspaper stories with public drunkenness or Prohibition violations.[29] Yet immoral behavior affected white Protestants as well.

Drunkenness at town dances "has got to be stopped," Municipal Court Judge R. J. Kitchen vowed early in 1923. Indeed, Prohibition offenses accounted for a substantial and growing percentage of crime in Union County. Of 101 arrests in 1922, twenty-six were for liquor-related offenses. Between August 1 and December 15 of that year, La Grande police arrested eighty-seven people and announced that liquor-related violations accounted for the great majority. To dramatize the alcohol problem in July 1923, Sheriff Lee Warnick poured nearly sixty gallons of confiscated brew into the sewer by the courthouse. Warnick also dumped several bottles of scotch and told the press that his officers had destroyed seventeen stills over the past year. The seriousness of Prohibition crime became evident in October 1923 when a banner headline in the *La Grande Evening Observer* reported the fatal shooting of the deputy sheriff of neighboring Baker County by J. E. "Dad" Griffith, an ex-convict "crazed with moonshine."[30]

Ethnic, racial, and cultural diversity served to heighten local tensions over changes in social values associated with the spread of early-twentieth-century consumerism. Two newspaper stories served as symptoms of the perceived decline of moral discipline, family responsibility, and social decorum. One reported that former La Grande Police Chief Roy Flexer had deserted his wife and children in the summer of 1922 to accompany a married woman on an auto trip across the country. A Portland federal court subsequently convicted the former officer for violating the Mann Act by transporting a woman across state lines for immoral purposes. The second story appeared under the September 1922 headline "Sold Booze to Children" and conveyed a report from the county prosecutor that a La Grande barber had peddled liquor to five boys under the age of eighteen. Three months later, the newspaper published police reports that forty teenage boys of school age habitually frequented local pool halls and card rooms.[31]

The La Grande City Commission had outlawed the possession or sale of intoxicating beverages in 1917, a supplement to the Oregon Prohibition Amendment of 1914. In November 1922, voters approved a city charter amendment requiring licenses for soft-drink establishments, card rooms, and pool halls and prohibited gambling on these premises. The following month, the city commission authorized municipal court search warrants for Prohibition raids as part of the effort to eradicate La Grande's vice rings.[32]

Difficulties in enforcing liquor laws amid the perceived moral decline of the postwar years and the ethnic diversity of La Grande helped set the stage for Ku Klux Klan organizing. Following establishment of the chapter in 1922, officers compiled the Charter List of all recruits. Although this document soon disappeared, a series of kligrapps, or secretaries, assumed the responsibility of maintaining typewritten records of weekly klavern proceedings, financial transactions, and conversations.[33] Each week's minutes were organized in a similar format, a task facilitated by the provision of official Klan stationery after the chapter received its permanent charter in March 1923. Information included meeting dates and time, the number of officers and attendees present, the names of visiting Klansmen, and summaries concerning the processing of new members. The occupations and home towns of initiates frequently were listed alongside their names.

The quality of the La Grande Minutes improved dramatically when a postal clerk, Harold R. Fosner, assumed the role of chapter kligrapp between October 1922 and September 1923. Twenty-four years old when he accepted the assignment, Fosner was the grandson of a German immigrant to Indiana in 1848. His father had served as the pioneer dentist of Enterprise, located sixty-five miles northeast of La Grande in the Wallowa Mountains; his mother, Isabelle Parrish, was an Enterprise native whose family had been active in the Church of Christ. Fosner's parents relocated in 1917 to Sherwood, a small town near Portland. Three years later, the young man took on temporary work as a La Grande mail carrier and received permanent employment at the post office in 1922.[34]

As chapter secretary, Fosner dutifully recorded klavern procedural motions, summarized budgetary decisions, described the details of Klan ritual and initiation ceremonies, replicated formal addresses by klavern leaders, and dutifully listed occupational data for new initiates. Each week's minutes indicated whether any Klansmen were sick or in need of "fraternal assistance." The written record also noted which members of the order endorsed new applicants. But the most remarkable feature of the La Grande documents appeared in the extemporaneous comments and gossip that Fosner occasionally volunteered for the record.

Assuming that the proceedings of a secret society would remain confidential, the youthful mail clerk attached a series of supplemental exhortations, observations, and meditations to selected entries. These personal musings provide unprecedented insight into the manner in which Klansmen defined and sought to address organizational and community problems. Both the procedural minutes and Fosner's asides offer readers a uniquely rich guide to the inner workings of a 1920s Ku Klux Klan at the grass roots.

Coming across the La Grande Klan records in 1968, attorney Willard K. Carey was surprised to learn that the KKK had thrived in Union County and that distinguished Masons, such as Colon Eberhard and law partner George T. Cochran, had been members. Since the records had nothing to do with the administration of Eberhard's estate and were unclaimed property, however, Carey kept the documents in his personal files. Sometime in 1980, Portland attorney Edward R. Sullivan suggested that the minutes be turned over to the Oregon Historical Society (OHS) to preserve a record of the Union County

Klan and an account of its activities and leaders. OHS records list March 17, 1980, the fifty-seventh anniversary of the granting of the La Grande Klan's permanent charter, as the date of Carey's donation.[35]

R. Thomas Gooding, Carey's law partner, also found the Klan Minutes of interest. Gooding, a Roman Catholic familiar with La Grande's history and past Klan activity, made a photocopy of the documents within a year of Eberhard's death and turned them over to James B. McLaughlin, a fellow Catholic who had been a railroad telegraph operator and dispatcher in the 1920s. Fearing for the survival of the records after his death, McLaughlin described the nature of the documents to John T. Evans, then library director of La Grande's Eastern Oregon College. When McLaughlin died in 1983, his widow returned the minutes to Gooding, by then Circuit Court judge of Union County.[36]

Two years after McLaughlin's death, the *La Grande Observer* obtained access to the Klan documents. Gooding acknowledges that a newspaper reporter "may have borrowed" his copy, but he does not remember the writer, does not recall the article, did not know that the journalist had a copy of the minutes, and has no recollection of lending the documents to anyone. Evans, however, remembers reading over the records at the journalist's request and attesting to their apparent legitimacy. A two-part series on the La Grande KKK appeared in the *Observer* on November 29–30, 1985. The feature highlighted the Klan Minutes and presented the results of an interview with a former knight who said he had been in his mid twenties when participating in the local chapter after 1922.[37]

Although the subject of the newspaper story withheld his name, he was undoubtedly Carl Eugene Millering. Born in 1895, Millering was a Mason, Elk, and Christian affiliate who had served as manager of Klansman C. W. Bunting's Caterpillar franchise in the 1920s. Millering had identified himself as a former member of the La Grande KKK in a 1970 interview with Arthur H. Bone, the biographer of former Oregon governor and Union County rancher Walter Pierce. Although Bone incorrectly described Millering as the chapter's "number two man" and a Klan-supported city commissioner, klavern minutes substantiate Millering's active membership. When the former Klansman died in 1990 at the age of ninety-five, there were no longer any survivors of La Grande's brief encounter with the Ku Klux Klan of the 1920s.[38]

Carl Eugene Millering's interview with Arthur Bone contained the claim that the La Grande Klan of the 1920s reached 650 members. Indeed, local newspaper coverage of the receipt of the klavern's permanent charter in 1923 noted that chapters were required to reach one thousand initiates before gaining permanent status. Yet the KKK Minutes provide far more modest figures. A count of all names mentioned in the La Grande records produces a total of 326 knights. Of these, 264 can be identified by occupation through chapter records and period business directories. Ninety-seven (nearly 37 percent) of these worked for the Union Pacific Railroad. This figure is considerably lower than the two hundred fifty described in a 1922 article in the *Salem Capital-Journal* but certainly constitutes a significant number.[39]

Using a system of occupational classification developed by the U.S. Bureau of the Census and incorporated in Robert A. Goldberg's work on the Colorado Klan, an economic and class profile of the La Grande klavern can be constructed. Such an analysis shows that 30 percent of the chapter's Klansmen with listed occupations were of middle nonmanual status; 22 percent were of low nonmanual rank; 21 percent were skilled workers; and 16 percent fell into semiskilled and service levels of employment. Over 90 percent of La Grande knights with known occupations, therefore, could be described as working class or lower middle class. Similarly, 41 percent of Klan railroad employees were skilled manual workers; 28 percent were in the low nonmanual category; and nearly 25 percent turned out to be semiskilled or service workers.[40]

Beyond offering data on the class background of the klavern rank and file, the La Grande Klan Minutes provide tantalizing detail on the controversial relationship between Walter Pierce and the Invisible Empire. Scholars previously have offered rumors concerning Pierce's alleged induction into the KKK during the summer of 1922. La Grande klavern records document neither Pierce's initiation nor his donation of dues or financial contributions. But the minutes do reveal two visits by the Island City native to the La Grande Klan chapter in November 1922 and June 1923 and a close working relationship between this powerful Oregon figure and the KKK. Evidence of Pierce's ties to the Klan surfaces in a July 1923 letter to the politician from La Grande chapter secretary Harold Fosner, although Pierce's biographer chose to read the kligrapp's reference to a "discussion in our klavern" as "a discussion in the La Grande K Tavern" (see the frontispiece). Significantly, Fosner signed the communication with the salutation, "Yours in the Sacred and Unfailing Bond," a closing repeated in a subsequent letter to Pierce from self-acknowledged Klansman Lem A. Dever.[41]

Even more important than matters of klavern composition and political alignment, the La Grande Minutes provide crucial insight into the internal workings of a 1920s Ku Klux Klan. The documents explain how a KKK chapter exercised requirements for admission, how officers were selected, and how Klansmen encountered difficulties in enforcing the moral standards of their order. The minutes document the importance of ritual, symbolism, and ceremony in the klavern and illustrate the manner in which the KKK functioned as a fraternal organization providing assistance to needy members. While the records attest to the Invisible Empire's strong relationship with local Protestant clergy, they also point to the importance of economic solidarity, a concept rooted in the oath of Klannishness. Vocational networking can be observed in support of "100 percent" merchants and in efforts to achieve job protection for members in the local railroad industry.

The La Grande Minutes further reveal the nature of the klavern's impact on the community. They demonstrate ongoing ties to several Protestant churches, sponsorship of lectures by visiting religious figures, support for political candidates at all levels of government, involvement in issues concerning the public schools, backing for patriotic and other fraternal groups, assistance to civic institutions and organizations (like the Young Men's Christian Association [YMCA] and Red Cross), and participation in law enforcement campaigns and other purity activities.

EDITORIAL NOTE

Each entry of the minutes in this volume is preceded by the date of the relevant meeting and, when necessary, by introductory material designed to facilitate an informed reading of the installment. Occupational information not contained in klavern records has been derived from period business directories (see note 22 of this chapter). Minutes were composed several days after the weekly meetings. Klan secretaries wrote in the vernacular of the 1920s and conformed to fraternal group rhetoric. While preserving such expression and the abbreviations used by Klan secretaries, I have corrected the numerous spelling, typographical, and punctuation errors of novice typists and aligned capitalization and hyphenation with modern usage. Minor adjustments essential to clarity are marked by brackets. Ellipses denote the elimination of tedious or redundant passages. The entire minutes of a few meetings have been omitted.

# The Minutes

MAY 11, 1922

THIS IS THE FIRST RECORD of La Grande Ku Klux Klan proceedings, although the existence of officers suggests previous organization. Lodge leaders credited a Portland organizer, or kleagle, with convening the chapter. The exalted cyclops was the klavern's presiding officer; the klaliff was vice president; and the kligrapp was secretary. The Board of Klokans served as the investigatory arm of the chapter. James E. ("Ed") Reynolds was president of the Union County Farm Bureau and later an undertaker. Dr. J. L. McPherson was a dentist and Claude Emerson Cooper a watchmaker at a downtown jewelry store.

Meeting called to order by the Exalted Cyclops Reynolds.
The following changes made in officers—Dr. McPherson takes W. G. Sawyer's place as klaliff, C. E. Cooper taking Earl N. Doane's place as kligrapp, and C. E. Cooper taking Earl Doane's place on the Board of Klokans.
Motion made and seconded that the report of the committee of fifteen Klansmen appointed to investigate the candidates for political offices [i]n the primaries be accepted. Carried.
Motion made and seconded that the Committee of Fifteen on political investigation be given a vote of thanks. Carried. . . .
Thirteen candidates were initiated into the Invisible Empire.

MAY 18, 1922

Four days after the first recorded Klan meeting in La Grande, an audience of nearly one hundred men paid fifty-five cents each to attend a local theater to hear Portland minister Reuben H. Sawyer discuss the secret order and its mission. Sawyer, a former Christian Church pastor, joined local Klansmen in marching onto the cross-lit stage in full KKK regalia. The fiery speaker espoused "100% Americanism" and questioned the moral values of Roman Catholics and the foreign-born. Intensive activity inside and outside the klavern preceded the next day's Oregon state primaries.[1]

. . . General discussion of the political situation coming up at the primaries on May 19th, 1923, by members of the Klan.

Thirteen candidates were naturalized into the Invisible Empire.

May 25, 1922

Alliances with Protestant ministers—particularly evangelicals from the Baptist, Methodist, Christian, and United Brethren churches—were an important part of Klan strategy nationwide. Reverend Stanton Lapham was a graduate of Oregon's Linfield College, a former YMCA activist, and a supporter of Portland Mayor Harry Lane's antivice crusades before World War I.[2]

. . . Motion made and seconded that a donation fund for a needy and deserving Baptist preacher, Stanton Lapham, be started. Carried.

Motion made and seconded that the kligrapp keep a record of those donating to this fund. Carried.

Motion made and seconded that donation fund campaign be brought up at next meeting. Carried.

General discussion by Klansmen of the various situations around town. . . .

May 31, 1922

It is not clear whether the date for this session should read June 1 or whether the klavern met on Wednesday instead of Thursday. Klansmen continued their discussion of the fund for Rev. Lapham.

. . . Donation fund campaign brought before the Klan and discussed by the Klansmen present.

Suggestion made that the amount of the donation should be twenty-five dollars.

Sixteen candidates were naturalized and became citizens of the Invisible Empire.

General discussion of the school question by the Klansmen present. Definite action suggested for next meeting. . . .

JUNE 8, 1922

The La Grande KKK initiated forty-two members between May 11 and May 31, rented the local Eagles Hall for meetings, and paid for the construction of a klavern cross.

"K of C" referred to the Knights of Columbus, a Roman Catholic fraternal order, which the Klan viewed as its main adversary.

Klan leaders placed a great deal of organizational focus on political alliances, but the May 1922 Oregon Republican primary brought disappointing results. Pendleton's James H. Gwinn lost a bid to unseat Nicholas J. Sinnott, a Catholic from The Dalles who was a five-term member of the House of Representatives. Even more troubling for Klansmen was the fact that Charles Hall, a Marshfield (Coos Bay) banker and utility operator, failed to defeat incumbent Republican Governor Ben W. Olcott, who had publicly condemned the KKK as a secret society days before the election.

A list of thirty Klansmen donating to the fund for Rev. Stanton Lapham appears at the conclusion of this installment. Most donations were one dollar.[3]

. . . Motion made and seconded that the amount of the donation to Stanton Lapham be twenty-five dollars. Carried.

Motion made and seconded that school director nominee[s] be left in the hands of the political committee of fifteen. Carried. . . .

Motion made and seconded that kligrapp write to Portland headquarters to get information regarding the race for governor of Oregon. Carried.

Motion made and seconded that officers now in chairs get busy with their parts or their offices be declared vacant at next meeting. Carried.

Motion made and seconded that the exalted cyclops be notified that a K of C delivers his mail and makes remarks regarding same and that the Klan suggests the rental of a post office box. Carried. . . .

JUNE 15, 1922

The klavern continued to focus on housekeeping matters.

. . . Motion made and seconded that a P.O. box be rented at the La Grande Post Office. Carried.

Motion made and seconded that the Klan go on record as favoring a paid organizer to enter La Grande and continue our organization and put us in a working condition. Carried. . . .

JUNE 22, 1922

Klan leaders used this meeting to fill the remaining slots for klavern officers. The new appointments included the kludd (chaplain), kladd (conductor of ceremonies), klabee (treasurer), klarogo (inner guard), klexter (outer guard), and night hawk (custodian of the fiery cross and supervisor of preinitiation recruits). The officers of the La Grande Klan were an occupationally diverse group. Dallas Green was a railroad employee; Clyde E. Bunting worked at the family Caterpillar tractor and Maxwell automobile dealership; Ralph E. Byers was a railroad timekeeper; C. D. Stansfield was a lumber company driver; C. Kenneth McCormick was the county clerk; Tellus K. Bellamy was an insurance agent; and Victor Melville owned a plumbing service.

> . . . Class of twenty-four initiated into Invisible Empire. . . .
> Report of nominating committee as follows:
> Kludd—Dallas Green, Kladd—Clyde Bunting, Klarogo—Ralph Byers,
> Klexter—C. D. Stansfield, Night Hawk—Mood Eckley, Klokans—
> C. Kenneth McCormick, T. K. Bellamy, Victor Melville. . . .

JUNE 29, 1922, TO JULY 20, 1922; AUGUST 10, 1922, TO AUGUST 24, 1922

[omitted]

AUGUST 31, 1922

By the end of August, the La Grande klavern had inducted thirteen more members, voted to push for a paid organizer, and decided on weekly readings of lists of knights in local business. The chapter also contributed forty-one dollars to the Public Defense League of Oregon, a political lobby organized by the state Klan.

Following Charles Hall's allegations of illegal Catholic primary voting in the towns of Mt. Angel and St. Paul, fourteen La Grande Klansmen donated $49.50 to fund a suit to force a recount. Members also contributed to Rev. Lapham's initiation fee, a gift the KKK often extended to Protestant clergy.

The *Western American* was an official Oregon Ku Klux Klan weekly founded in Astoria in 1922 by Lem A. Dever, a Tennessee-born journalist and publicist. The publication moved to Portland the next year.

Elgin, the target of chapter recruitment, is fourteen miles northeast of La Grande.[4]

. . . Motion made and seconded that a sum of $.25 be assessed each member to finance convention of exalted cyclops[es] to be held in Portland some time soon. Carried. . . .

Motion made and seconded that our kleagle ascertain cost to run small ad in local or Elgin paper which appeared in the *Western American*. . . .

SEPTEMBER 14, 1922

The La Grande Klan sought to offer job protection and a sense of dignity to those of its members employed by the Union Pacific Railroad, often referred to as the Oregon-Washington Railway and Navigation Company (O-WR&N, also as O.W.), its regional subsidiary and predecessor. Such support received a severe test when six hundred local shop-craft workers joined a nationwide railroad strike initiated by the American Federation of Labor in the summer of 1922. Although most Klan rail employees belonged to the nonstriking railroad brotherhoods, Glenn H. Forwood, a Klansman and shop-craft blacksmith, served as vice chair of the local strikers' committee. KKK sympathy for the walkout resonated with negative views of racial minorities.

Charles Hall's recount effort in the governor's race failed in August when state courts upheld the right of voters to change party registration on Election Day. Accordingly, the Klan's Public Defense League called for Hall to run as an Independent. Yet as the statewide KKK moved to back Democrat Walter M. Pierce, the *Western American* opposed any effort to split the anti-Olcott vote with an Independent candidacy.[5]

. . . Motion made and seconded that committee be appointed to investigate case of four Klansmen who are strikebreakers and who are teaching Negroes and Japs to take places of strikers. Klansmen Cochran, Cooper, and myself appointed.

Motion made and seconded that we write letter to Public Defense League and ask them to reimburse us for expenses of Exalted Cyclops McPherson['s trip] to Portland some time ago, and further, that if they do not pay same, to take the $8.50 we have on hand for them into our own funds. Carried.

Motion made and seconded that a resolution [be drafted] denouncing the stand now taken by Hall, copy to be mailed to all Klans in the state. Carried. . . .

SEPTEMBER 21, 1922, TO SEPTEMBER 28, 1922

[omitted]

OCTOBER 10, 1922

On September 21, the La Grande klavern elected Carl Eugene Millering, a former railroad accountant, as klexter, or outer guard. The following week, the Klan decided to meet on Tuesday instead of Thursday evenings. With a vacancy in the kligrapp's, or secretary's, position, postal clerk Harold Fosner began to compile the minutes on October 10.

Klan chapters often used anti-Catholic speakers from outside the organization to assist recruiting. Sister La Precia undoubtedly was Sister Lucretia, a former nun and seventeen-year floor supervisor at Portland's St. Vincent's Hospital, whose name was Elizabeth Schoffen.

KKK chapter meetings emulated those of other fraternal groups by employing precise ritual, symbolism, and ceremony, including the use of passwords, handgrips, and secret signs.[6]

. . . No. of Klansmen present: Twenty. . . .

In regards to unfinished business our kleagle reported that he would get in touch with Sister La Precia at once and find out just when she could be here. Klansman Fields then reported that the Star Theater would be at our disposal on Oct. 21/22/23. This matter was left pending.

Suggestions

That members be required to show their cards before entering klavern.

That all Klansmen conduct themselves in a militant order and avoid confusion.

That all Klansmen be properly instructed on how to enter the klavern.

That officers and as many Klansmen that can, meet in the klavern on Sunday afternoon and learn the work. This will hasten our charter.

That secrecy still remains the chief motive for our progress.

That we all have facts enough. What we need most is the heat that dissolves the facts. . . .

OCTOBER 17, 1922

In September, Democratic gubernatorial candidate Walter Pierce endorsed the Oregon compulsory public school initiative first popularized by Charles Hall in the Republican primary. The *Portland Telegram* accused Pierce of agreeing to back the bill in exchange for state Klan influence in discouraging an Independent candidacy by Hall. Whatever the case, the Oregon KKK now swung its support behind the anti-Catholic school proposal and rallied to Pierce, a Union County rancher, tax-reform activist, and former state senator.

As the target of Klan animosity, Governor Ben Olcott elicited a fitting KKK response on nearby Table Mountain when he delivered a campaign address to a large gathering in La Grande on October 18. Meanwhile, the klavern pushed Klansman C. M. Humphreys for a city commission slot. Humphreys, a former leader of La Grande's Knights Templar, a Masonic order, served as an officer of the local Brotherhood of Locomotive Engineers. Retired rail worker and Klansman William W. Kinzie sought to be elected justice of the peace as an Independent. The klavern also endorsed Baker Knight and realtor James Harvey Graham, the Democratic candidate contesting U.S. Representative Nicholas Sinnott's seat.

Chapter political adviser and La Grande attorney George T. Cochran was a partner in eastern Oregon's leading law firm and an Episcopalian, Rotarian, Elk, officer of the Knights Templar, and active Mason.[7]

. . . Klansmen present: Thirty-three. . . .

Our kleagle then reported that Sister La Precia could be with us on Oct. 23 and 24.

Two Klansmen were dispatched at once to rent the hall for those two nights after the motion was carried to have her speak. The committee returned shortly and reported that we could have the hall these two nights for the sum of $110. This seemed a bit high owing to our financial report so a motion was made to this effect: that a committee of three be appointed to canvas the business district for funds to defray the expense. Should they fail to attain the necessary amount, the balance would be draw[n] from the treasure. This motion also stated that the sum of twenty-five dollars be drawn from the treasure to bind the bargain and assure us in obtaining the hall.

Klansmen Vade R. King and James A. Bugg were taken through the ceremony of naturalization, our progress in this due to the fact that all officers were present is well worthy of mention.

Klansman Cochran gave a very interesting talk regarding the opinions of the people and Klans throughout the state where he has traveled. He reports the city of Salem will go strong for Pierce and that the school bill is coming in for its share of the credit. In conclusion, he wished to impress upon our minds that now is the time to get our shoulder to the wheel and do everything in our power to elect Klansmen Humphreys and Kinzie in the coming election. Get the spirit. Think and talk these issues and make them a part of your daily obligations. . . .

Two communications were read, one from Klansman S. S. George of Eugene, who told us where to send for literature and tickets in regards to our candidates for the coming election.

The other comm[unication] spoke in regards to a new issue known as Klan Komfort. This will be a beneficial fund as well as a protection to each individual and is to be paid at the rate of one cent a day for a year. No action was taken regarding this, however, as we desire more information regarding same.

General Business Discussion

That the kligrapp write to Hdq. in regards to candidate tickets and literature on the school bill.

And signifying our intentions to support Klansman Graham of Baker in the coming election.

That we obtain some of his tickets for distribution in this jurisdiction.

That all Klansmen turn out to hear Ben in his last triumphant speech before we close the portal doors of his political career forever.

That the rays of the Fiery Cross lighten the pathway of his Majesty and remain a symbol of welcome in his memory forever.

That a notice be placed on the outer door stating our next meeting would be held at the Star Theater, unless the hall would be opened for a few minutes discussion.

Klansmen Rhodes, Nichols, and Webb were appointed by E.C. for our new Board of Klokans. . . .

For the good of the order our E.C. commented most favorably upon our renewed spirit and general progress. . . .

OCTOBER 24, 1922

The kleagle, or organizer, played a central role in preparing the klavern for official chartering by the national organization in Atlanta.

. . . Our new kleagle gave a short but very interesting talk on Klan advancement.

Mr. Carter wishes to impress upon our mind that in numbers there is strength.

Meeting then adjourned to hear Sister La Precia speak.

OCTOBER 31, 1922

Sister La Precia held forth for two nights at a downtown theater, although the klavern was charged three nights' rent.

. . . Klansmen present: Thirty-seven.

Visiting Klansmen present: Four, representing Pendleton and Portland Klans respectively. . . .

Motion made and carried that a letter of appreciation be sent to Sister La Precia.

Eight applications . . . for citizenship were read and approved by assembly. Five men were taken through the ceremony of naturalization. . . .

The Finance Comm. appointed to raise funds for the rent of the Star Theater report:

Total amt. of rent for the three nights and afternoons—$140
Total amt. raised by subscription and collections—$135.33
This left a balance of $4.67 to be drawn on treasure.

Motion made and carried that letter be sent to Klan hdq. in regards to what stand the J. C. Penney Co., Inc. with hdq. at New York City has advised their employees to take in affiliation with the Knights of the Ku Klux Klan.

Closing ceremony in short.

NOVEMBER 14, 1922

No Klan meeting was held on Election Day, November 7, an event that produced mixed results for the Invisible Empire. Klavern members Humphreys and Kinzie failed in their respective bids to become city commissioner and justice of the peace. Klansman and attorney Colon R. Eberhard lost the senate seat to which he had been elected in 1918 by fewer than one hundred votes. Republican Representative Sinnott, moreover, easily defeated Baker Klansman and Democrat James Harvey Graham. Nevertheless, the state KKK triumphed when the school bill passed and Walter Pierce won election to the governorship by a 57 percent plurality. La Grande knights boasted that they had distributed school bill literature in towns forty to sixty-five miles across the Grande Ronde Valley.

Notwithstanding the dual victory, local Klan leaders continued to be frustrated over perceived Roman Catholic influence in town, especially through the "K.C.," or Knights of Columbus. One target was insurance agent Charles H. Reynolds, the school clerk and board member whom the KKK castigated for being less than "100 percent." Another was insurance practitioner and political activist Chester Newlin, whose wife, Evelyn, recently had been fired from her post as a public school teacher. One of Chester Newlin's sisters had married Frederick L. Meyers, another Klan adversary. Meyers was the Catholic and Canadian-born cashier (financial executive) of the La Grande National Bank. Census records show that his father was German and his mother Irish. Meyers should not be confused with a well-known contemporary of a similar name, Portland variety store entrepreneur Fred Meyer.

Increased Klan political activity may have prompted Kligrapp Fosner to attach an extemporaneous essay to the recorded minutes in which he mocked klavern enemies. Klansmen paid particular attention to John ("Jack") H. Peare, the Irish-born Catholic chair of the Union County Republican Committee. Peare was proprietor of a La Grande jewelry shop in which his son, William, served as optometrist. Fosner's barbed reference to J. C. Murphy may have been a flippant jab at the state's Irish Catholics. A *coon*, in turn, was a prevalent and racist term for an African American.

The minutes for this date describe two sets of fireworks because the Klan burned a cross on Saturday night, Armistice Day, November 11, the same day that La Grande hosted a much-heralded veterans' parade and fireworks display.

Republican state senator Bruce Dennis, the owner, publisher, and editor of the *La Grande Evening Observer* since 1910, was a frequent Klan target. Although local KKK activities seldom received coverage in the *Observer*, one of Dennis's editorials had attacked the influence of "secret societies" in state politics.

"Sister" Newlin referred to Evelyn Newlin, the fired Catholic schoolteacher who found employment in the city's parochial academy. George Noble was a continual subject of KKK allegations concerning Prohibition violations.

Klavern leaders were eager to recruit local businessmen. Such enthusiasm led to allegations of coercion. *Salem Capital-Journal* Managing Editor Harry N.

Crain charged in a Klan exposé that the La Grande lodge had employed economic pressure and the threat of potential boycotts to ensure that town businesses were "right."[8]

> . . . Klansmen present: Fifty. . . .
> A letter was read by our E.C. from Headquarters in regards to a prize
> which is being offered to the Klansman who writes the best essay on
> "Why I am a Klansman." This essay must be sent to Portland before
> November 27th.
> Motion was made and passed that kligrapp send to the E.C. at Oregon
> City our letter of proxy stating our desire to have him be our representative
> at the national meeting of the Klan in Atlanta, Georgia within the near
> future. . . .
> Klansman Tull volunteered to have the cord ready for our cross at the
> next meeting night.
> Motion made and passed that our small cross be attached with a battery
> and globes and money drawn from treasury for the same.
> Recommendations given by E.C. to our Fiery Cross Comm.
> Twenty-four applications read and passed.
> All dues read and passed by body and ordered paid.
> Number of Klansmen naturalized: twenty-three. . . .
> Kleagle Carter volunteered to talk to our school board and find out if
> in the near future that it may be possible for the position of school clerk to
> be filled with a 100 Percent American. He also stated that he would get in
> touch with the directors of the La Grande National Bank and advise them
> in regards to our feelings for their present cashier, F. L. Meyers.
> Kleagle Carter reported that the Baker Klan would be here fifty strong at
> our next meeting.
> Motion made and passed that we endeavor to entertain these Klansmen
> in a most sumptuous manner.
> Klansmen Tull, Lindsay, Snider, and Bunting were appointed on the
> Entertainment Comm.
> Klansmen Ben Decious, Hopkins, and Fields were appointed on the
> Lunch Comm.
> Suggestion made by E.C. that Klansmen Bunting and Kligrapp Fosner
> see Governor Pierce in person and extend to him a cordial invitation to
> attend our next meeting and welcome our visitors from Baker.
> Meeting closed in short order.

Klansmen and Their Work During the Last Two Weeks

Thirteen Klansmen journeyed to Baker where they received a royal welcome by that esteemed body who added to their membership twenty-eight 100 Percent Americans. Our klaliff, Mr. Johnson, made a short and very spirited talk before that assembly on Klan edification and its encouragement.

Kleagle Carter reports that during his stay in Baker he has more than doubled the Klan. We are proud of his recent achievements. They are well worthy of our highest praise and may this incentive be an inspiration to us all.

Having witnessed the officers of the Baker Klan in action, I have many words of praise to offer to give our officers. I do not wish to criticize[—] only in the light that will be a benefit to all Klans' spirit and pep, with the idea supreme that our mission is the most worthy of them all. Our work is hardly begun. Remember your oath at the foot of the fiery cross and let not the spell of timely emotions lie buried in the ashes of our sacred pledge.

Following down the long line of generations that have came and gone before us, we find these issues have come up before the people time and time again. Its comparison is like the spirit of war[—]quickly forgotten once the objective has been reached. It is true, indeed, we have tasted the first fruits of victory at the last election but that fact is but a small part of the great fundamental plan that we must ever consider ourselves engaged in battle until we or those to follow behold the downfall of Catholicism buried in the ruins of its own iniquity.

That the Democrats and Ku Klux Klan held an election.

That the Republican party outnumbers the Democrats three to one in the state of Oregon.

That we never realized the school bill would pass. But that we have three Klansmen who had nerve enough to bet it would.

That if K.C. Peare would of had enough coons whom he swore to have known for thirty days, Walter Pierce would have to farm for many years yet to come.

That J. C. Murphy finally admitted there was thirty thousand more Klansmen in the state than he ever realized.

That the fiery cross burned as our signal of victory.

That the kligrapp wrote a masterpiece regarding same which our friend Bruce has so far failed to publish.

That even if our school bill fails to materialize as a true one, we well know how the majority of the people stand.

That twenty-three new applications were placed in the hands of the kligrapp.

And that these men have been notified to appear tonight for naturalization.

That many members are still riding the fence in fond hopes of obtaining their share of glory no matter how the wind may blow.

That the fireworks were good on Armistice Night. Both of them.

That the kligrapp has been a busy man mailing receipts, sending letters of thanks, and trying to give each and every member his personal attention.

That the night before election twenty stalwart Americans placed under every door in this town a straight American ticket and a copy of the school bill. Our work was not in vain.

That Governor Walter has been sent a personal invitation to attend our next meeting.

That one man walked six miles to obtain an application to join our Klan.

That another Klansman has ordered his robe. May a few more soon follow in his footsteps.

That we put up a good fight for Klansmen Kinzie, Humphreys, and Eberhard. But Rome was not built in a day.

That school literature was sent to the following towns: Lostine, Wallowa, Joseph, and Enterprise.

That we still have a few Klansmen who do their business at the La Grande National Bank. Don't forget you are Klansmen.

That a petition is now being circulated in our village asking that Sister Newlin be reinstated as a teacher in our public schools. This issue is thoroughly un-American, a direct insult to the school bill, and something that the Klan will not under any consideration tolerate if in their power to do otherwise. This woman not only sends her children to the parochial school but her influence with the pupils in her charge is not born of Old Glory. Neither is it symbolic of the fiery cross. I have taken particular pains to find the originator of this petition and it is no other than her husband, Mr. Chester Newlin, the esteemed gentleman who sat at the polls and told our worthy citizens how to vote the right way.

I sincerely believe that this town could run very well without citizens by the name bearing the title of Newlin, for I can find no record of accomplishments achieved by them that are written in gold on the pages of its history. The petition for signers was taken from house to house by a lady of the Mormon faith who bears the name Lyman.

That a list bearing approximately 125 names of businessmen who should be in this organization was sent to each of the fifteen members appointed to solicit these men for membership in this order. At the expiration of one month we hope to obtain at least a few of these. Klansman Last started the ball a-rolling; let's keep it in motion.

That as far as I know there has been no change in our municipal judge, R. J. Kitchen. Let's keep a-blaze that which we have kindled.

No doubt you have all heard or seen the petition being circulated in behalf of the King of Bootleggers, namely one George Noble. If ever a case needed our hasty action it was this one and I am glad to say we were on the job and that immediately we started a petition counteracting this hypocrisy. It went up.

NOVEMBER 21, 1922

Walter Pierce's populist gubernatorial campaign built upon his endorsement of the public school initiative, support for prohibition of landownership by foreign-born Japanese, and a demand for tax reform to benefit property holders instead of urban income receivers. Kligrapp Fosner's lyrical recitation of the Pierce homecoming provides a classic example of the gushing cadence and literary contrivances associated with fraternal order prose.

La Grande Klansmen continued to concern themselves with alleged Roman-ist penetration of the order's security and the tenure of the Catholic director of the town's leading bank. Rev. O. W. Jones, an influential klavern leader, was a minister of the local Christian Church, an evangelical sect derived from the nonsectarian Protestant preachers of the frontier.

Meeting called to order at 8:15 by E.C.
Number of officers present: 100%
Number of Klansmen present: Ninety-six.
Number of visiting Klansmen present: Twenty. . . .
Motion made and carried that all Klansmen who could swear to the fact that they saw Raymond R. Garrity in the hallway of our lodge room or at the foot of the stairs between the hours of seven and nine on the meeting night held Nov. 14, 1922, report to Kleagle Carter at the Club Cigar Store on Saturday, November 25, 1922, at 4 P.M. to swear same before our postmaster of this city.

Owing to the fact that our last meeting was held for the purpose of entertainment only the opening ceremony and general business was held in short form. . . .

The motion to adjourn was made at 12 P.M. and lasted until 1:45 A.M.

The Bitter and the Sweet

That our last meeting held Nov. 21, 1922, shall go down on our records as being one of the best ever held in the state of Oregon.

That the music rendered by our 100% Orchestra was excellent and its appreciation was justly proven by the response of all that were fortunate enough to be present. Let's boost these talented members by attending their dances.

The honorary members in attendance were Klansman Walter M. Pierce, governor-elect, of La Grande, Oregon, and Klansman Harvey Graham of Baker, Oregon, our nominee for representative in Congress of this district, of whom we believe by a little more effort on our part and by a few speeches like he delivered before our body could of very easily won the election.

Following our very delightful musical program our kligrapp read the applications of seven men who are desirous of obtaining citizenship in the Knights of the Invisible Empire. These men were all passed on and turned over to the Board of Klokans for further investigation.

Also, two weekly letters from Atlanta, Georgia, were read. They contained messages full of fire and encouragement, especially the one which stated that the governor of Kansas was going to run all the Klansmen out of that state. No doubt within the near future we shall be called upon to provide room for these banished refugees.

Next came a short and very interesting talk from our E.C., who endowed upon our visiting Klansmen from Baker the spirit of welcome to our klonklave and in one accord all Klansmen arose and gave the sign of welcome.

Following this came short talks of appreciation from Klansman McLaughlin and Klansman Johnson. Their remarks in regards to our organization brought much applause and they were duly welcomed into our Klan.

The Klansmen from Baker were then called upon to express their ideas in general and we found them full and running over at the brim. Should I even attempt to relate the least part of their concentrated and soul-inspiring outbursts, I would have to keep you here 'til morning. But

I must call to your attention at this time a few remarks from Klansman Graham. His first notes of appeal came in regards to our practice of secrecy: keep your thoughts and strength of number from the camp of the enemy; t'is the facts they don't know that keep them ever on the warpath and their ceaseless efforts in this behalf only tends to strengthen our cause. For the good of all Klans he suggested that a board of at least seven men be appointed to dictate the final action of all important issues that may arise before that respective Klan. After these suggestions followed his sense of humor which brought down the house and left a warm spot for him in the hearts of all. His final declaration is the true manifestation of our desires. For he said "next time I shall run and a winner I shall be."

By this time the red blood in our veins had reached the point of boiling and we lived realizations which we never thought would see the dawn of reality.

And did you hear Klansman Cochran in his speech entitled "True Klannishness" and the climax which ended in the story about the lamb dyer? Oh yes, and there was Rev. Klansman Jones, who during his speech told us that in the beginning his opinion was that the Klan was just the expression of the day and that in a very short time, like all other organizations, it would die. But he says, "when I gaze upon this noble body of citizens from every calling and profession I must confess that my judgment has surely been construed and I am proud and happy to say that I am a member of this organization whose purpose I trust is sanctioned by the Savior above who guides our every movements." May the order ever be worthy of men like Klansman Jones and may the principles for which he stands be an inspiration to us all.

And behold the next decree arrayed in the form of one Walter M. Pierce, governor-elect by our combined efforts, now arose to express his full gratification for the noble support that all 100% Americans had tendered in behalf of his election. His vital thoughts and sincerity of expression cleansed from our minds all thoughts of political selfishness. And as truly as he has spoken we shall know that when he is summoned to join that immovable band that whatever he did came from the abundance of his heart. May we ever cherish these memories and hold them sacred in the cause for which we are striving. Let us bid Klansman Pierce God's speed in his new undertakings to come and continue to support him as we have done in the past.

Meanwhile, in the kitchen without, five stalwart Knights of the Invisible Empire were busily engaged in providing for us a very delightful repast.

Its abundance was sufficient to justify the demands of all and I wish to
thank them for their continued efforts which lasted until the last dish
was cleansed and laid to final rest.

T'is beyond my power of expression to relate the harmony and fellowship
which reigned supreme during this lunch. Suffice to say that these were the
golden moments of our lives.

That discussion regarding the cashier of the La Grande National Bank
led to many facts that before had never been revealed.

That we found on the first showdown of true Americanism regarding
the case of Garrity many Klansmen who for some reason or other had not
the courage of their own convictions. I would suggest that these facts be
retraced and sufficient evidence be collected before any hasty action leads
to our committal.

NOVEMBER 28, 1922

Communication from state and national Klan leaders comprised an important part of the secret order's meetings. King Kleagle Luther I. Powell, chief
KKK organizer for the Pacific Northwest, was the author of the salty prologue
to George Estes's *Old Cedar School*. The pamphlet mixed nostalgia, populism,
anti-intellectualism, and anti-Catholicism in an emotional defense of public
schools and patriotism. Estes was a Troutdale, Oregon, attorney and former railroad union organizer.

School bill opponent John S. Hodgin, the object of klavern suspicions, was a
former Union County district attorney who had prosecuted the 1917 Tong case
in which Klansman George Cochran had acted for the defense. Hodgin's law
office was located in the La Grande National Bank Building.[9]

. . . Klansmen present: Forty.

Applications read for citizenship: Eight

Number of men naturalized: Fourteen

Opening ceremony held as given by instructions.

The robes that had been ordered for some time arrived and were used at
this meeting.

Amount of dues collected during week: twenty dollars

Communication was received from Major Powell regarding the little
books entitled *The Old Cedar School*, which gives the reason why the
school bill became a law in the state of Oregon. He suggests that we buy as
many of these as possible and give them a wide circulation in this territory.

A motion was made to the effect that we send for two of these whereby we may be more able to judge as to how many we could dispose of.

Communication from Major Powell asking that this Klan send a check for not less than twenty-five dollars and if possible fifty [dollars] to the E.C. at Oregon City who is our representative at the national convention in Atlanta, Georgia. This money is to be used in defraying his expenses while in that city. A motion was then made and passed that the kligrapp send the sum of twenty-five dollars to this man at once.

Communication received from Huntington, Ore. regarding the speech made by attorney Hodgin of this city against the school bill. This man desired to know if Mr. Hodgin had not at one time in his life been a Catholic priest. This information your kligrapp has promised to impart.

Our E.C. is in receipt of a check from the Public Defense League for $29.20 refunded to him for expenses while attending a conference held in Portland at a recent date.

No Klansman or Klansman's family was reported sick or in need of fraternal assistance.

Meeting closed in full ceremony.

DECEMBER 5, 1922

After approving the membership of City Manager Oscar A. Kratz and six others, the klavern inducted ten new Klansmen. Beginning with this date, Kligrapp Fosner recorded the occupations and places of business of all new knights. One new member turned out to be the bookkeeper of the U.S. National Bank, the rival to the institution directed by Frederick Meyers. The other nine included three auto mechanics, the high school athletics coach, a Standard Oil employee, a railroad brakeman, a produce dealer, a dry-goods merchant, and a farmer.

The La Grande klavern took pride in the fact that it recruited members from the far reaches of the Grande Ronde Valley and surrounding countryside. This included Imbler, eight miles northeast of La Grande; Union, eleven miles southeast; Island City, two miles northeast; Palmer Junction, eight miles northeast of Elgin; and Halfway, fifty miles northeast of Baker. Note that disaffected Klansman W. G. Sawyer, owner of a feed and fuel concern, had been the chapter's first klaliff (vice president).

The "Roach" Garage, the employer of the three recently inducted mechanics, was an auto dealership owned by Marcus Louis Roesch, the son of Julius

Roesch, a German-Catholic pioneer who operated a local brewery between 1880 and the first full year of Prohibition in 1921.

Attorney John Hodgin continued to be a target of Klan concern. Hodgin's opposition to the school bill tied him in Klan eyes to "Pope" Jack Peare, the Catholic leader of the local Republican Party.

Tanalic, the subject of a lighthearted reference, was a vegetable pill widely advertised in the era's newspapers with personal testimonials.

The first page of the supplement to the minutes for this date is missing. Klansman Richardson appears to have been describing a conversation with Grand Dragon Gifford. La Grande's municipal judge, of whom the Klan disapproved, was R. J. Kitchen.

The reference to tax referenda sent to voters by the legislature is confusing. The Oregon Grange had proposed a 1922 voters' initiative dedicated to a graduated income tax. Despite the support of Walter Pierce and tax-reform groups, however, the measure was kept off the ballot when state courts found fraud in the collection of signatures. A constitutional amendment legalizing a flat-rate income tax failed in the November election by a 2–1 margin.

As one of the four secret oaths, Klannishness lent itself to economic campaigns against Catholic-, Jewish-, and foreign-owned businesses. Klansman Jasper ("Jap") M. Choate owned the town pool hall. In contrast, Herman's Lunch Counter, located a half block from the railroad depot, was off-limits because its German-American and Catholic proprietor, Herman Roesch, was the nephew of former brewery operator Julius Roesch.

Heppner, the site of a minor indiscretion by a prominent Klansman, is sixty miles southwest of Pendleton. School board member James A. Russell was subject to pressure from both sides of the Newlin controversy because he owned a meat company and could be boycotted.[10]

. . . Klansmen present: Thirty-two.

Visiting Klansmen: Mayor Robinson and Klansman Courtney from Lostine, Oregon. . . .

E.C. McPherson recommended that the kligrapp send a letter to Atlanta, Georgia and have the weekly letter addressed to either the E.C. or the kligrapp of this Klan.

Nat. ceremony was held in full and ten noble Americans were made Knights of the Invisible Empire. . . .

In regards to unfinished business our E.C. appointed the following

Klansmen whose purpose is to give the final decision on all important actions that may come within the jurisdiction of this Klan. Their first obligation will be to make a list of our businessmen who are right:

Klansman Geo. T. Cochran, chairman. . . .
Klansman Rev. O. W. Jones
Klansman J. G. Holm, merchant
Klansman Frank Turner, employed by O-WR&N Co.
Klansman Ben Decious, retired restaurant man of this city
Klansman Ed Reynolds, our former E.C.
Kligrapp Harold R. Fosner, P.O. Dept., City

General Business

We now have 207 naturalized members.

Twenty-five applications read and passed and three held for further investigation.

Of these 207 members, 178 are from La Grande, eleven from Elgin, nine from Imbler, four from Union, two from Island City, one from Palmer Junction, one from Halfway, Oreg., and one from Idaho Falls, Idaho.

No. of deceased members: one Klansman, Marion Davis, of Union, Ore.

No. of Elgin Klan members naturalized in La Grande: Eleven

No. of Klansmen desiring to be dropped from this Klan: Two. They are Klansman C. E. Short, present manager of the J. C. Penney Co., and W. G. Sawyer, produce dealer of this city. Their consent to withdraw from this Klan is now under consideration and further actions will take place in the near future.

That Marcus Roach stood without our portal doors and beheld in dire astonishment the multitude of Knights that passed within. Sometimes I wonder what he would think or do if he knew that his garage was nearly 100 Percent.

That investigation of attorney John Hodgin revealed the fact that he is an evolutionist, that is he means to say that he firmly believes that man and monkey are true kindred spirits. So our research of the missing link has not been in vain. At least we know that his motives are ruled by the Pope of this village and that he needs a little fixing over.

Numbers of members who have not paid their dues—Seventy-eight. One of these has passed in the valley and shadow of death. One is sick and unable to pay. Two are financially embarrassed but have promised to pay in the near future. Five have left this vicinity and the balance have either forgotten their oath or else they are seemingly neglectful. . . .

With a little vim, pull, and Tanalic we can make ourselves a Christmas present of three hundred members. Let's go.

Number of Klansmen who have ordered robes up to date: Six. . . .

For the encouragement and edification of the Klan our E.C. suggests that all Klansmen order their robes as soon as possible. He also told us that in the near future the musical program would be featured. . . .

UNTITLED SUPPLEMENT TO THE MINUTES OF DECEMBER 5, 1922

. . . [That] he would be in our city within the next week and that he would bring pressure to bear upon the offices of our municipal judge, whom we are trying to relieve. The porter on the train coming home happened to spy his Klan pin and the world was his as regards accommodations. At the breakfast table one of the dear fathers came in and sat directly across the table from him, and after making a few short remarks about the weather and conditions in general, also spied the pin, and without further adieu beat a hasty retreat for more congenial surroundings.

Klansman Richardson reports that our grand dragon, Fred L. Gifford, has been called to Atlanta for reasons unknown. All in all his trip was a decided success and we wish that every Klansman going to Portland from this community would take the same interest in regards to this Klan's welfare.

Last Friday morning we received from Kligrapp St. Claire of the Pendleton Klan six referendum petitions relative to the state income tax passed at the last legislature. The purpose of these petitions, I believe, is to give the voters of this state a chance to vote on this bill, in which event it shall be either accepted or rejected by the citizens of this state. I regret that owing to lack of time . . . only two of them were filled. One was circulated by Klansman Kinzie to the general public and the other by myself, bearing the names of Klansmen only. We have no direct bearing of the Klan in relation to these petitions but it is generally understood that the Klan as a body was backing their circulation. We shall hear more concerning this in the future.

Some time ago we had under discussion the fact that our nat. ceremony should be held every Tuesday instead of every other Tuesday and Kleagle Carter and Klansman Evans of the Baker Klan both made brief talks in this behalf, both sincerely believing that while applications are coming in so fast that we do nothing that will stem the tide of advancement.

That there are many Klansmen yet remaining who have not paid their charter dues. Don't delay any longer and remember that promptness is the keynote of all industry.

Klansman Frank Turner has departed for the City of Portland in search of work and in this behalf we wish him luck.

Number of men notified to report for naturalization tonight: Ninety-three.

Klansman Earl Silvis is now confined in the local hospital, having underwent a slight operation from which he is doing nicely. Flowers have been sent to cheer his ward and Klansman Jap Choate has started to raise money in which to pay his doctor and hospital bills. Any Klansman who feels he can donate a dollar in this behalf shall be greatly appreciated, I'm sure. What more in this world or what greater pleasure can we have than giving to those in need? That little touch of brotherly love sets aglow a new fire in our hearts and makes the whole world akin.

That the Endeavor social held at the Christian or Klan Church was a decided success, there being a goodly number of Klansmen in attendance, both to the joy of Rev. Jones and our E.C., Dr. J. L. McPherson, chairman of the evening.

That Klansman Colon Eberhard stayed in a K.C. hotel during his visit at Heppner.

The following items were too late for classification at the last meeting: Klansman Tull was seen buying meat at the Dutchman's shop in Fir Street; Klansman Fred Huffman deals with Thorn's Grocery; and Klansman Kenneth McCormick still eats at Herman's Lunch Counter.

Last Saturday I paid a visit to the school clerk to find out what members of the School Board voted for the reinstatement of Mrs. Newlin. The vote is as follows: Eberhard, no; Reynolds, no; Russell, no; Hill, yes; Black, yes.

There is some talk that Russell has been reconverted and that another meeting will be called and another vote taken. Jack Peare and Fred Meyers informed that worthy gentleman that unless he voted to reinstate Mrs. Newlin they would boycott him. Same old line.

Amount of dues collected during week: eighty-five dollars. . . .

Any Klansman who may have something of interest to add to these columns shall be greatly appreciated.

December 12, 1922

New inductees at this session included a tailor, laborer, railroad employee, engineer, Standard Oil agent, retail clerk, bookkeeper, and popcorn vendor.

The Knights of the Invisible Empire saw themselves as purity crusaders concerned with family stability and community standards. The man accused of irresponsibility at this meeting, E. J. Schilling, was listed in a city directory as a railroad worker.

Klansmen insisted that their rituals, ceremonies, and costumes symbolized devotion to spiritual values. Note the reference to the cross burning commemorating the election of Walter Pierce and passage of the school initiative.

George Cochran frequently advised the klavern on strategic decisions. Cochran's political lessons on this date focused on the central committees of both political parties.

. . . Klansmen present: Thirty-two. . . .

Visiting Klansman Youcum from Walla Walla, Wash. gave us a very interesting talk touching on the constructive methods that many other Klans use in regards to Klansmen attending meetings and that every Klansman should take an active part in all the deliberations of this klonklave. . . .

Mrs. Clyde Bunting, wife of Klansman Bunting, was reported sick. Following this announcement a motion was made and passed that some flowers be sent to her in the Klan's name together with our message hoping her a speedy recovery. . . .

Motion made and passed that a standing comm. be appointed in case of emergency to send flowers to the sick and assist those who are in need of financial support. . . .

Number of naturalized members: 216.

No. of applications read and passed and ordered to report: Twenty-four.

No. of Klansmen who have ordered robes: Fifteen.

After much discussion all Klansmen gathered around the altar and our parting devotion was held in full.

Discussion

For the third time it has been reported that E. J. Schilling, who resides at 1203 U. Ave., has three children by his first wife who are being neglected most shamefully and several Klansmen have advised that we take this matter up and see if the present conditions cannot be adjusted. Acting on this suggestion, I found that his particular case should come under the jurisdiction of the county health nurse.

Discussion arose to the fact that many more citizens would join our organization if they were properly approached and a number of names were mentioned and turned over to Kleagle Carter, who will endeavor to convince them that this organization is one worthy of their support. . . .

Arguments in defense of the Klan brought to light these facts: that this is the only organization that you go into with your eyes open and that concerning the robes, the K.C. wear the black and the Klan wear the white. As for the mask, t'is but a symbol, like in comparison to creeds in the different churches. We are ashamed of nothing, neither have we anything to hide for we are proud of the fact that we have nerve enough to express in word and action our true convictions.

Only a short time ago our beloved friend, Senator Bruce Dennis, made a talk against the Klan at a meeting of the Elks held in Heppner, Oregon. He spoke of us Klansmen as being breeders of trouble and from all reports there were several there who were looking for trouble. Consequently, he has made for us a few more Klansmen. Keep the good work up, Bruce. We all know that you are a 100%, Bruce, and were you walking on our side of the fence and had some selfish achievement in view, we know in what behalf all your efforts would be centered. It has been rumored that he would like to sell his paper. Klansman Cochran has expressed his desire to be the manager and nothing would please me more than to help tell the world in print how Jack Peare became acquainted with thirty Negroes on the day of election and why he refused to print that stirring epistle your kligrapp wrote regarding one beautiful cross we put upon the hill.

Klansman Cochran gave a very interesting talk in regards to who elects our officers and where we must strike the blow in order that 100% Americans may be placed on guard. He informs us that place is what is known as our central comm. This is a small group of men representing that particular party—Republican, Democratic, and all others. They guide and direct the votes of the people as well as choosing what men they desire to fill the offices. And so to carry out our full desires we must have a majority of Klansmen in this central comm.

That Kleagle Carter wrote a letter and requested the kligrapp to send same to Klansman C. E. Short, charging that his actions of late were being questioned by this Klan and that he appear in person at the next regular meeting night to prove his right to hold the title of Klansman.

That in the future we must place another cross upon the hillside to keep a-blaze our purpose in the hearts of all.

Exalted Cyclops and esteemed Klansmen, a Merry Xmas I extend to each and every one of you.

DECEMBER 19, 1922

This meeting proceeded after the rank and file approved the applications of six railroad workers. City Manager Oscar A. Kratz was one of three men receiving induction. Klannishness encouraged an economic solidarity designed to promote the vocational and business interests of the membership. Ironically, Klansman C. H. Tull's speech on the subject came only two weeks after he had been chastised for buying meat at "the Dutchman's" shop. Nevertheless, the automobile business was the most competitive retail field in many small towns and cities, and salesmen required the commercial advantages of membership in fraternal orders.

J. C. Penney manager C. E. Short may have told the Klan that company policy forbade membership in the secret order. The letter sent to him was not included in surviving klavern records.[11]

... Klansmen present: Fifty-one. ...

A recommendation was made to the effect that all Klansmen desiring to address the chair will do so according to the ritual and not according to their comfort. ...

Our E.C. suggested that the Board of Seven Directors meet during the following week and make a list of our businessmen who are right.

After this suggestion Klansman Tull of the Roesch Motor Co. was given the floor and what he didn't tell us about practicing real Klannishness needs not be recorded. He advises that when you go to Pendleton you want to watch your step or the chief of police might ask you why you didn't eat your meals in an American restaurant. And be sure when you trade at the Roesch garage that the man waiting on you is a Klansman. ...

Our letter of reply received from National Hdq. regarding how the J. C. Penney Co. stood on the Klan question revealed the fact that they are for us and a motion was made and passed that Klansman Short of the local Penney store and Klansman W. G. Sawyer be banished from our Klan. ...

We are in receipt of an application blank used by the Pendleton Klan which covers in full detail man's history from babyhood up and when we get our charter we shall have some printed as they are a big help to the Board of Klokans. . . .

Until our E.C. so orders there shall be no statement made regarding our strength in numbers. It may be possible that we have a leak in this organization.

Klansman St. Claire, kligrapp of the Pendleton chartered Klan, was our distinguished visitor and he brought us some very cheerful news as well as many suggestions that will help to keep us in the straight and narrow path. Those desiring a detailed account may obtain same from our E.C. His statements reveal the following:

That we shall receive our charter when we can put our work on according to ritual, when every man has paid his dues and signed the Charter List, and when we have the required amount of robes. The date of our charter depends on you. Get the fellow next to you moving.

After our charter is granted the E.C. will reign supreme. The La Grande Klan shall be the only chartered Klan in this county. For under one head only can any organization function in perfect harmony.

Our charter will not only enable us to do away with a lot of red tape but will be a financial help, keeping a certain percent of the money in our own treasury which now goes to Hdq.

In the future there will be a number of officers and noted speakers visit our klavern. Let's strive in every effort to leave an impression on the minds of these men. Be constant in attendance. If you've got anything on your chest, get rid of it while you are here assembled and don't tell it to the wind on the street below. Klansmen, we have all shirked responsibility in the past and practiced our Klannishness in a very loose manner. And in the future when you fail to attend at least one out of every three meetings you are going to have to tell your E.C. why in the presence of this klonklave.

That May the 6th is the date set for the election of all national officers.

Klansman Randall, our missionary, gave a short talk and asked if anyone had any anti-Catholic literature, he would be glad to dispose of same.

For the encouragement of the Klan:

That flowers be sent to the home of Mrs. Decious, who is the mother of three noble Klansmen in this order.

That our robes be ordered as soon as possible, as it takes a long time to get them from Hdq.

That our kligrapp receive a recompense for his service to this Klan.

That all men who have not signed the Charter List do so at once.

That we get our hair cut in the Ellis and Meyers Barber Shop, where Klansman Winn works and [ask] the others to become Americans. We want that place 100%. Why take a chance? . . .

The following is a copy of the letter sent to Klansman C. E. Short, who is now banished from our Klan. Klansman Sawyer's letter was held up by order of our E.C. and his case will be given further consideration.

Meeting closed in full ceremony. Klansmen, don't forget the opening hour is 7:30, not 8:30.

December 26, 1922

This session began with approval of the applications of a barber at the Ellis and Meyers Shop and the owner of a competing concern. However, klavern attention soon turned to organizational controversy over Oregon Grand Dragon Fred Gifford. A rift had begun in September when a KKK faction in Salem had accused the official of dictatorial methods and misappropriation of funds. After a representative of the grand dragon had seized the records and books of the Salem klavern and had sought to reorganize the chapter, two hundred members had withdrawn and formed their own movement. Note the ambivalent response of the La Grande klavern.

The reference to Edward Young Clarke as former imperial wizard is incorrect; Clarke had served as imperial kleagle and was awarded the honorary post of imperial giant, or past imperial wizard, when he resigned. The commemoration of Clarke, Elizabeth Tyler, and second KKK founder William Joseph Simmons disguised an internal coup by which Hiram Wesley Evans took control of the Invisible Empire as imperial wizard in December 1922. La Grande Klansmen learned of the election of new national officers in an Atlanta communication, which Kligrapp Fosner reported in this session's minutes.

Elgin, which had its own Klan gathering under the leadership of Dr. George R. Vehrs, is twenty miles north of La Grande.[12]

. . . Klansmen present: Twenty-eight. . . .

Recommendations for the good of the order: that all Klansmen come early and thus avoid unnecessary confusion. . . .

There was no ceremony of nat. due to the fact that candidates notified failed to appear at the appointed hour, 8:15. . . .

In regards to Standing Comm., Kligrapp Fosner reported that Chairman Cochran of the Board of Directors had ordered him to notify all members to meet at his office on Thursday evening at 7:15 sharp for the purpose of classifying all our members. . . .

Communication from Major Powell notifying this Klan that after Jan. 1, 1923, all communication of any nature whatsoever will be made direct to the grand dragon's office, who is F. L. Gifford, 433 Pittock Block, Portland, Ore. He also stated that the propagation of which he is the head is now located in Seattle, Wash. His closing remarks bid each and every Klansman a Merry Xmas and a Happy New Year.

Comm[unication] dated December 11, 1922, from S. S. George of Eugene, Ore. announced the fact that it is imperative that our E.C. attend a meeting held at the Multnomah Hotel, Portland, Ore. for the purpose of collecting all data that will lead to the prosecution of one F. L. Gifford, our present grand dragon. This letter also informs us that our letter of proxy was not honored at the national meeting held just recently at Atlanta, Georgia. Our E.C. did not reply to this letter. Nor was he a representative at this meeting.

Comm[unication] dated Dec. 23, 1922, from Eugene, Ore. and written by S. S. George states the following: that on Jan. 7th at 1 P.M. at Salem, Ore., Room 224, Oregon Bldg., a meeting shall be called by the organization now known as the Associated Klans, Realm of Oregon, for the purpose of protecting this organization and [to] determine upon a course of action to meet future contingencies. This Klan shall be entitled to one representative with proper credentials but will have no vote.

A copy of the letter sent to Nat[ional] Hdq. by the Pendleton Klan contains the following: "we wish to assure you of our absolute loyalty to both national and state officers and that we wish to go on record as absolutely opposed to any move of this nature made by disgruntled political aspirants whom we consider unworthy of the high honor of being Klansmen."

We are also in receipt of the official banishment letter used by the Pendleton Klan and now being used by this Klan until we obtain our charter and construct one of our own.

A local comm[unication] addressed to Klansman Rhodes contains this information: that Mrs. Jennie Byer, who resides at 1806 East Penn Ave., City, and who is a widow, is in need of financial assistance. Investigation of this brought to light the fact that just at present she was in no dire needs as the Elks Comm. had not forgotten her. Klansman Jones then volunteered to keep us in touch as regards her future welfare and action shall be taken according to his report. This letter bore no signature except to say that "I am writing this to you," meaning Klansman Rhodes, "because I halfway believe you are a KKK."

Another letter dated Dec. 20, written by S. S. George of Eugene, Ore. in behalf of the new organization known as the Associated Klans, Realm of Oregon, and asking that we pledge our support to this movement. The names of twelve Klans appeared on this letter as being supporters of the movement charging the faithfulness of our grand dragon, Fred L. Gifford. . . .

Comm[unication] reporting the disappearance of one William Peed, Klansman, who was last seen leaving the city of Indianapolis, Indiana, in his Buick Car. He had on his possession a large sum of money and is thought to have met with foul play. Keep this name in mind for we know not the day nor the hour and the restoration of this man will bring happiness to a saddened family.

Our retired Imperial Wizard, Edward Young Clarke, commended all Klansmen most highly on the work achieved in the past year and asks that this cooperation still continue. And above all he begs the pledging of our sacred loyalty to our officers and our noble cause so that perfect harmony may reign supreme and light the pathway of our future destiny. Klansman Clarke has been voted our national thanks and given a life membership certificate in the Klan. His parting words are the inspiration of the day: "though I am leaving you from active service the fulfillment of my dream lies in the final dawn of all things Klannish."

National honor and gratitude was paid to the following at the national meeting just recently held at Atlanta, Geo.: William Joseph Simmons, Edward Young Clarke, H. W. Evans, Fred L. Savage, and Mrs. Elizabeth Tyler. These five human beings served and sacrificed and made possible Klancraft for America and the world.

To those of you who were unfortunate enough not to be present at the last meeting and hear the Weekly News Letter from Atlanta, Georgia, I am all sympathy. For its glowing account of national proceedings are vital thoughts flowing in the veins of all 100 percent Klansmen. Are you one of them? . . .

Klansman C. E. Short was banished from this Klan Dec. 26th, 1922.

Moved and seconded that Klansman W. G. Sawyer of this city be banished from our Klan for ninety days. After the expiration of this time, provided he has not filed for a new application, his name shall be reported to all Klansmen and to National Hdq., which shall mean for them banishment forever from the Knights of the Ku Klux Klan.

Motion made and passed that a letter be sent to each of the twelve Klans in the state of Oregon asking for an official statement regarding their affiliation with the new organization known as the Associated Klans, Realm of Ore. The following is a letter written in this regard:

Esteemed Klansmen:

In regards to the letter being sent out to all Klans in the state of Oregon excepting Klans No. 1 and 2 respectively by S. S. George of Eugene, Ore. in accusations against one Fred L. Gifford, our grand dragon, we are very desirous of knowing officially from your Klan if you have gone on record as favoring and pledging your support to the new organization known as the Associated Klans, Realm of Oregon. Up to the present date this Klan has taken no stand regarding our feelings in this matter.

. . . The following letter by order of E.C. has been sent to Klansman Vehrs of Elgin, Oregon:

Esteemed Klansman:

By virtue of the status officially declared at the national Klan meeting held at Atlanta, Ga. just recently and by order of E.C. Dr. J. L. McPherson, I am sending to your Klan two charter blanks, which we earnestly desire to have signed by all members of the Elgin Klan as well as those of the La Grande Provisional Klan at the earliest possible date so that we may obtain our charter. Basing our authority given by Kligrapp St. Claire of the Pendleton Klan that there shall be but one chartered Klan in a county, we trust you will cooperate with us wholeheartedly in this decision and that no enmity shall be derived from same.
Yours in the sacred and unfailing bond, Kligrapp

Motion made and passed that a ton of alfalfa hay be sent to Mr. J. W. S. Johnson, a poor man of this city, who was about to sacrifice his cow due to the lack of feed. . . .

Motion made and passed that we notify our grand dragon, Fred L. Gifford, that this Klan wishes to go on record as being entirely unsympathetic in regard to the new organization known as the Associated Klans, Realm of Oregon. . . .

Motion made and passed that a letter bearing credentials be given to J. E. Reynolds of this city who has volunteered to be our representative at the meeting of the Associated Klans, Realm of Oregon, to be held in Salem, Oregon on Sunday, Jan. 7th, 1923. . . .

Motion made and passed that a reply be sent to Mr. S. S. George of

Eugene regarding our stand for future affiliation with the Associated Klans, Realm of Oregon:

Dear Sir:

In regard to your letter dated Dec. 20th desiring the affiliation of this Klan with the new organization now known as the Associated Klans, Realm of Oregon, I wish to inform you that our past exalted cyclops will be present at the meeting . . . for the purpose of investigation before we take any stand regarding same.

Motion made and passed that a night letter be sent to Atlanta, Ga., pledging our loyalty to all state and national officers.

Motion made and passed that all members who have not paid their dues be notified to do so at once.

Standing notifications ordered to report for nat[.]: Sixteen.

New applicants ordered to report: Nine. . . .

That just as soon as a few more members pay for their robes we can send for same.

Klansman Tull suggested that some flowers be sent to the home of Klansmen Harry Clyde and Ben Decious, whose mother . . . has been ill for some time and . . . has now departed from this shore to join that inevitable band wherein reigns peace and harmony, the fulfillment of this life. Our condolences we offer to these brother Klansmen in their bereavement and a tribute in gold do we pay to a well loved mother.

Despite the tremendous amount of business we transacted our meeting was closed in full ceremony at an earlier hour than usual. Exalted cyclops and Klansmen, I sincerely hope that the coming year will bring to each and every one of you an abundance of happiness and a large helping from the horn of plenty and a sincerity for our noble purpose that shall mark an epoch in the history of our lives.

January 2, 1923

This meeting provided the opportunity for the klavern to resolve its ambivalence toward the move against Grand Dragon Gifford. It also featured motivational speeches by officers that dramatized the foundations of Klan fraternalism and Protestant solidarity. The Klavern's vice president, Alfred J. Johnson, was a railroad accountant and a member of the Christian Church.

The reference to the Portland exalted cyclops was to Dr. James R. Johnson, a virulent anti-Catholic and former pastor of the city's Sellwood Christian Church.[13]

. . . Klansmen present: Thirty-two. . . .

Klansman Ben W. Noyes, a barber of this city, was taken through the ceremony of nat. and is now one among us.

The Standing Comm. on investigation of one Salvation Army captain of this city and by name, J. M. Buchanan, fell down on their mission but they guaranteed us a report on the next meeting night.

We received a telegram from Nat[ional] Hdq. relative to the trouble which some Klans are brewing, charging the faithfulness of our grand dragon, F. L. Gifford, which reads to this effect: just sit calmly in the boat for this is but a riffle on the waters of life.

Three comm[unications] read from four different Klans placed them as going on record as favoring the investigation of our grand dragon, F. L. Gifford, and the other one expressed the same loyalty as we have pledged.

Following Kleagle Carter's talk on this subject we became sorry that we ever permitted its discussion in our klonklave. . . .

Our E.C., Dr. J. L. McPherson, arose at this occasion with a frown on his brow and a sparkle in his eye and from this talk that followed I would say that some of us are not worthy of the high honor of being called a Klansman. Klansmen, your E.C. has been very lenient with you in the past. Very few of you have denied yourselves any time apart from your daily lives for the promotion of the noblest cause in all the world. The final realization of this cause must mean the sacrifice of each and every individual of time, money, and devotion to your officers, both national and local. Have you given up one night's pleasure to pay your dues? Have you attended at least one out of every third meeting? And how many men have you convinced that it is the sworn duty of every Protestant to be leagued in this cause for righteousness? You have pledged yourselves to the fulfillment of these duties and when your kligrapp gets down to true working form so that each Klansman gets his store of personal attention, you are going to account for the title you wish to defend. . . .

In regard to unfinished business a motion was made and passed that the sum of twenty-five dollars a month be paid to the kligrapp for services rendered in behalf of this Klan.

That a letter be written to our former kleagle, T. M. Whitmore, who now resides at The Dalles, Ore., asking him concerning the whereabouts of our original Charter List, which up to date we have been unable to locate.

Following this rose a heated discussion from our klaliff, Alfred J. Johnson. His talk started the red blood flowing in our rusty veins and the desire to launch a membership campaign in behalf of this cause. He suggested that we purchase a mimeograph machine for the purpose of advertising but general conclusion of the body based upon expense and results failed to make it an order and in some other way we must seek the key that shall unlock the hearts of others. The least to say we enjoyed his enthusiasm to the fullest degree and he voiced the sentiment of us all.

Motion made and passed that our Charter List be completed and sent to H.D.Q. at the earliest possible date.

Our E.C. then informed Klansmen Eberhard, Jones, and Chester Thompson to be prepared at the next meeting to make a talk on any subject they may choose.

We have a free library in this town and many topics worthy of recognition. So Klansmen get prepared for you may be the next in line and as this organization stands for the up-building of character we might just as well turn out a few orators to help the good cause along.

Klansman Eberhard told us that within the next few meeting nights . . . we should get some official reports on the doings of our legislature which convenes very shortly. These reports will add interest to our meetings. Klansmen, we are far stronger in this town than are the K.C. Let us take advantage of every opportunity and gain complete control of all local affairs. We demand the right to place 100 Percent Americans on guard. Americans for America, Romans when all others fail.

Klansman Green gave a splendid report of the meeting he attended while in Portland announcing that things are done there to the complete joy of a Klansman's heart and that twelve hundred men were made citizens of the Invisible Empire. The E.C. of the Portland Klan is a Christian minister and owing to the fact that his office requires him to travel a great deal, he is paid a salary of four hundred [dollars] a month.

Final discussion was relative to a number of prominent [men] of this city who should be approached in regard to becoming citizens of this empire. Your kligrapp has sent to each of these an application and some literature in regards to the purpose of our organization.

January 9, 1923

La Grande Klan ties to the railroad were evident in recruitment. Three of the five applicants approved for induction at this meeting were rail workers. Two other employees of the railroad were suggested as "good material for knight-hood." In addition, a railroad engineer joined a meat-company employee and a traveling salesman as new initiates at this meeting. August Stange's inquiry concerning potential membership was significant since Stange was a prominent business and civic figure in the community.

Minutes for this date illustrate the energy KKK officials put into recruiting new members. Fraternal rhetoric concerning self-improvement and social uplift played a major role in such efforts. Note, in contrast, the casual mockery of Irish, Jewish, and African-American adversaries. The book received from second Klan founder William Joseph Simmons probably was *The Klan Unmasked* (Atlanta, Ga.: William E. Thompson, 1922).

Klansmen were angered at banker Frederick Meyers's ties to brother-in-law Adolph Newlin, a fellow German Catholic and local pharmacist. Newlin had been convicted in 1915 of disorderly conduct on a charge stemming from late-night activities in the drugstore that bore his name. Although the allegations led to a retrial in Union County Circuit Court, no subsequent documentation of the prosecution appears in legal records.

By September 1917, six months after the United States entered World War I against Germany, the Newlin Drug Store had changed its name to the La Grande Pharmacy, although Newlin was listed as store manager. Difficulties continued to mount when city police arrested the pharmacist on September 12 for allegedly selling a two-dollar pint of liquor, thereby violating a five-month-old municipal Prohibition ordinance. Convicted two days later, Newlin appealed to the Circuit Court. Meanwhile, the beleaguered druggist sold the business. On November 10, a Circuit Court jury found Newlin innocent of municipal and state liquor charges. Eighteen days later, his name reappeared as shop manager in newspaper advertising for the pharmacy.

Newlin was arrested on a second Prohibition charge in September 1918. Found guilty of keeping liquor at the drugstore, the defendant received a $150 fine and thirty days in the city jail. While he appealed the second conviction to the Circuit Court, Newlin's name once again disappeared from pharmacy advertising and did not resurface until 1923. By then, prosecutors presumably had dropped the charges since no subsequent record of proceedings against Newlin survive.[14]

. . . Number of Klansmen Present: Forty-two. . . .

Several new faces both local and from the surrounding country were to be seen and it's a real pleasure to have them here and learn something of our growth and progress. . . .

The names of twenty-three applications who have been read and passed some time ago and ordered three times each to report for nat. were reread and checked up as to their present location. Most of these men were found to be working on extra gangs out of town and I have notified them that they are ready for nat. and to appear on the first Tuesday night at their earliest convenience. We have the credentials here to make them Americans and we don't like to see them struggling along on the too well beaten path any longer than they have to. . . .

The Standing Comm. reported favorably on the reputation of one Salvation Army Captain, Jesse Buchanan, formerly of this city. And this information was forwarded at once to the Pendleton Klan. . . .

Communications

Note of thanks received from the Decious family for our floral gifts during their sickness and bereavement.

The weekly newsletter from Atlanta, Georgia, contained a little book, the official message of our emperor, one Col. William Joseph Simmons, read before the most noble band of men ever assembled and for the noblest cause in all the world. To my firm belief this book is the leading masterpiece of our day and age. It is an inspiration to half-baked Klans and a just reward for those who have pledged their lives and taken an active part in the greatest constructive and character building organization the world has ever known. It is my earnest desire and prayer that every Klansman read this message. For it dwells on the origin of the Knights of the Ku Klux Klan as well as for its purpose toward the destiny of all mankind. Seven short but eventful years ago begins the foundation of our Klan. From sixteen original members it has grown to hundreds of thousands. Only by the truest and firmest of fundamentals could we have grown to be such a powerful factor that in but a short time to come all judgments shall be guided and directed by the combined efforts of real Americans who are profoundly conscious of the tremendous importance of this hour. Klansmen, our motto is "Lord God of Hosts be with us yet, lest we forget, lest we forget."

I wish to call your attention to this paragraph written in the weekly newsletter. Upon motion of the Council of the City of Chicago the following men were appointed to a comm. to investigate the activities of the Klan in that city: one Irishman, one Jew, and one Negro. I wonder if this mixture could be termed Irish Stew. Their report to our knowledge has not been recorded.

Comm[unication] read from Kligrapp St. Claire of the Pendleton Klan stating that our grand dragon, F. L. Gifford, had granted to the Elgin Klan a separate charter of their own. He also stated that the Baker charter had been sent in and was approved and that he would be glad to receive this Klan's charter and send it in at the earliest possible date. Klansmen, our Charter List has been completed and I hope is now merrily rejoicing on its way. Also, your kligrapp has sent in an order for sixteen more robes.

A local comm[unication] was received from August Stange of this city who asked to become a member of this organization and his praise for the Klan and its purpose in general was exceptionally high and we are very glad to find out the senses of opinion by local citizens who yet have not joined our ranks. Our actions and just deeds shall in time rally these men to our support.

Kleagle Carter received a comm[unication] from Major Powell, who recommended him most highly for his efforts centered in behalf of the Klans within his jurisdiction and I think he voiced the opinions of us all.

Klansmen Jones and Eberhard, who were ordered at our last meeting to have a speech prepared for us, fell down on the obligation and the other Klansman, Chester Thompson, also ordained to give a short talk, gave a clean confession of his lack in oratical ability, and after giving a splendid report of the Newlin case was allowed to be seated with the goodwill of all.

General discussion then brought forth the issue of former Klansman W. G. Sawyer being elected on the board of directors for the La Grande National Bank and Fred L. Meyers's visit to the chief of police, at which time he told that official that his efforts centered in the arrest of Newlin were anything but pleasing, and I wonder if he would do as much for you or I.

Motion made and passed that at our next meeting there would be no nat. ceremonies and the evening would be given up to general discussion of topics along the main drag and that after the conclusion of our business the comm. thus appointed would serve us with a delightful repast.

Motion made to adjourn at a very late hour.

Klansmen, those of you who accept the responsibilities of today shall receive the rewards of tomorrow.

JANUARY 16, 1923

Recruitment continued to be a major priority of the La Grande klavern. Union County Circuit Court Judge J. W. Knowles was a prime object of such efforts. Minutes for this date record membership applications of a railroad brakeman, fireman, pipe fitter, and clerk, as well as a filling-station proprietor, lumber-company worker, and bookkeeper.

Readers should note the subtlety of George Cochran's counsel regarding klavern adversary Frederick Meyers and the La Grande National Bank. The powerful eastern Oregon attorney appeared to be restraining the potential disruption of Klannishness to the regional economy. Significantly, two months later nearly two hundred people joined guest-of-honor Governor Pierce in a celebration of the bank's thirty-sixth anniversary. Among speakers at the New Foley Hotel were the chief officer of the rival U.S. National Bank, the president of the city commission, and County Treasurer Hugh McCall, a former employee of the honored institution. The Cochran and Eberhard law firm, moreover, was located in the La Grande National Bank Building, while the former made his home around the corner from the family of Frederick Meyers. Also observe Cochran's ambivalence toward school clerk Charles Reynolds, whom the Klan considered an unsteady ally in its attempt to purge perceived Catholic influence from city public schools.

One day after his induction, Klansman Oscar A. Kratz announced his resignation as La Grande city manager and soon assumed the same post in Astoria. Meanwhile, the klavern responded to the appointment of Kratz's replacement.

Klavern speaker Ed Fields was a railroad maintenance foreman whom the *Salem Capital-Journal* described as La Grande kleagle, or organizer, although the minutes do not substantiate that claim. Note the emphasis of speakers Fields and auto salesman Tull on purity work, common for Klan organizers of the 1920s. Yet how is one to take Fosner's seemingly humorous reference to the attractions of "moonshine?"[15]

... Klansmen present: Sixty-two. ...

Comm[unication] from our grand dragon read to the effect that he would visit our klavern on the last of the month.

Comm[unication] from Kligrapp St. Claire of the Pendleton Klan stated that he would rush our charter through at the earliest possible date.

Comm[unication] from the *Western American* from Portland, Ore., our Klan paper, requesting that we subscribe for as many copies of this paper as possible and get it circulated in every home in eastern Oregon.

Comm[unication] read from Judge Knowles commending this organization for its stand behind the law, but owing to the fact he must not show any prejudice in any case he may try, he desired not to affiliate with the Klan at this time.

In regard to unfinished business, the case of Fred L. Meyers and Edwin Pryke, our YMCA director, and Chas. Reynolds, our school clerk, was well covered by Klansman Geo. T. Cochran, who in a most sensible and forceful talk convinced us of these facts:

That if Fred L. Meyers was to lose his position at this time it would in all probabilities mean a loss of fifty thousand dollars to the bank. You may use your own discretion in dealing with this bank but this man shall continue in his position until we convince the men who have placed him there for another year that his methods are detrimental to this community and to the further building of that institution. We desire to force Meyers from his position and still have that institution retain its full value in the commercial world. And when our strength is sufficient and our purpose endorsed by the community at large we can gain this victory in the twinkling of an eye. To this end must we labor.

As to your YMCA director, Klansman Cochran states that his talk with Mr. Pryke convinced him that he stood right and that within a short time this matter would work out to the satisfaction of this Klan.

In regard to our school clerk, Klansman Cochran states that it would not be a feasible thing to release him at this time as it is about the middle of the term and no man can step into that position and immediately make all things harmonize. Thus our work in this behalf will be to defeat him in the coming June election. First of all we must establish a reputation in this comm[unity] and prove to these natives that we are behind the laws to the fullest extent and that we are the only truly patriotic organization existing in this community today.

A motion was made and seconded that these matters be tabled for a period of ninety days.

Motion made and passed that a comm. be appointed to choose our candidates for all coming elections in which we are concerned.

That our new city manager, who comes from Pendleton, is a K.C. and quite naturally opposed to this organization. We must support this man to our fullest capacity until such a time when we are in a position to put all 100 Percent Americans on guard.

Klansman Fields and Klansman Tull gave two very interesting talks on intemperance in this community and this organization has gone on record to the extent that ten men have volunteered to be deputized and so help our local officials make a clean sweep of all unlawful proceedings that take place in our village.

After this discussion Klansman Gar Holm, chairman of the Food-for-All Comm., informed us that that repast now awaited our consumption. Thus we forgot our crave for moonshine for the time being and took up the issue of more subtle things. We had dogs and hot dogs, Ku Klux Klan cake and all other kind of cakes, thick Klannish cream for our Niggar soup, and apples from the Garden of Eden. So impressed were all by this delightful repast that a rising vote of thanks was tendered this comm.

While we were gorging down these delicacies the old tin pan was passed around and all contributed from the abundance of his heart except Stiles and he even gave a dime. Anyway, by compressing the tin we were able to realize twenty whole dollars and forty-nine cents, of which six dollars was profit going into the treasury, $11.70 going to Chairman Gar Holm, and two dollars given for the use of the dishes.

Our exalted cyclops then commanded that within the next two weeks he expected every member to bring in at least two new applications. Failure to do so will mean a penalty given at a future date. It was then suggested that we have a card index of every man in this town and your kligrapp stated that he would start work upon this immediately. . . .

Kleagle Carter will place in this Klan's treasury the sum of one hundred dollars providing one hundred paid members are taken in this Klan by Jan 31st. Can we do it?

Klan adjourned in short form at the hour of 11:30.

January 23, 1923

Five of the eleven applicants approved for membership at this meeting were railroad workers. The others were a jeweler, farmer, cook, barber, clerk, and deputy sheriff. New inductees included a bookkeeper, farmer, lunch-counter operator, barber, plumber, service-station proprietor, railroad trainman and foreman, and two railroad clerks.

Readers should note Fosner's use of the epithet *red neck* to discredit Oregon Klan critics of Grand Dragon Gifford. The term incorporated an apparent reference to the red collars of Roman Catholic cardinals.

The Hooverized Grocery, the object of Klan concern because of the ethnic background of its proprietor, was a low-priced food store. The term originated during World War I when Food Administrator Herbert Hoover promoted the curtailment of demand as a means of preventing commodity inflation. Advertisements of the early 1920s proclaimed that La Grande's two Hooverized groceries were supported by local investors and designed to fight "monopoly." A contemporary business directory listed one of the store's operators as Samuel Harris.[16]

... Klansmen present: Sixty-five. ...

One recommendation was made to the effect that in our membership campaign we start with the names of citizens beginning with the letter "A" and so continue 'til every man in this community is placed on one side of the fence or the other.

Our E.C. then informed this body that at the conclusion of the nat. ceremony he would declare a five-minute recess. Kindly smoke in the hallway or anteroom and so relieve klonklavish congestion. ...

Kligrapp Fosner's Standing Comm. of One reported favorably on index system being prepared for our membership campaign. ...

Financial report from our klabee gave us a total of $180.33 in treas[ury].

One comm[unication] was read from the Enterprise Klan giving the name of one of their temporary banished Klansmen who desired to affiliate himself with that red neck gang charging the loyalty of our grand dragon.

Under the topic of unfinished business Klansman Rev. Jones, who has been quarantined in his home, made the talk our E.C. ordered him to make some time ago.

And we haven't forgot that Klansman Eberhard up to date has failed to fulfill his obligation of a twenty-minute speech.

Announcements were made to the effect that in the very near future the Roach Garage would be no more and that we would have Americans running that place of business. That the American Legion Comm., Postmaster R. R. Huron, has rumored about the town that the Klan is opposed to the American Legion. I wonder what he would say if he knew most of the American Legion men in this city were Klansmen.

Also that this Klan would hold a special meeting Friday evening, Jan. 26th, in honor of our grand dragon, Fred L. Gifford.

It is reported that the new manager of the local J. C. Penney store is a good Mason and in sympathy with our organization. ...

To you Klansmen who have been trading at the Hooverized Grocery: don't insult this organization anymore. They are 100% Jews.

Motion made and passed that a vote of thanks and a recompense be paid to the order that consented so willingly to let us use the lodge room for this special meeting.

Klansmen Brinker, Kline, and Andrews were appointed upon a comm.

to investigate the feeling that the local American Legion has for this organization.

For the encouragement and edification of the Klan we had a number of short talks on Klannishness, illicit places of business, law enforcement, harmony in our klonklave, and better attendance at our meetings.

Motion made to adjourn at a late hour with ceremony closed in full.

Special Meeting Held January 26, 1923

Oregon Grand Dragon Fred Gifford appeared at the La Grande klavern as the state and national KKK faced major disruptions. Three days earlier, a Salem meeting of representatives from thirty of the state's Klan chapters had voted to discontinue the payment of dues until Gifford was removed from office. The rebel klonklave charged the grand dragon with fraud and Catholic ties. Gifford soon faced additional fire for attempting to merge the Ladies of the Invisible Empire (LOTIES), which Oregon Klan leaders had incorporated in July 1922, with Atlanta's Women of the Klan.

Oregon's KKK had a complex relationship with newly elected Governor Pierce. The grand dragon claimed that a plot to subvert the Klan's alliance with Pierce had been hatched on Portland's Burnside Street, the skid row of the downtown waterfront. Yet state Klan leaders were dissatisfied with the governor's appointments at the state penitentiary, hospital, and highway commission and demanded replacement of the state Prohibition director. Meanwhile, Pierce was finding it difficult to shepherd tax reform and government consolidation measures through a Republican legislature.

A further source of adverse publicity for the Klan involved allegations of a KKK branding of a twenty-nine-year-old woman in Tillamook, a coastal dairy center seventy-two miles west of Portland. Mrs. Nevada Standish, who recently had been acquitted on appeal of a Prohibition charge, claimed that two masked men with sheets over their heads branded her breast with a hot metal cross while she was home alone in late November 1922. Standish's husband, ill at Portland's St. Vincent's Hospital, charged that the Ku Klux Klan was implicated. Yet it turned out that the woman and her mother were members of the LOTIES. As the story broke in mid-January 1923, the victim forcibly denied Klan involvement. One week before Gifford's La Grande appearance, the pro-Klan *Tillamook Headlight* chortled that "by the time all the trimmings are taken from the story it doesn't amount to very much." After an intensive investigation, the Tillamook County Grand Jury found insufficient evidence to prosecute.

Grand Dragon Gifford also felt compelled to respond to accusations against the KKK outside Oregon. Federal investigators insisted that Klansmen in the northern Louisiana town of Mer Rouge had abducted five local opponents in August 1922, mutilating and killing two. Despite considerable evidence, a local grand jury refused to indict anyone.

A great irony underlay Gifford's anxiety over the assignment of Father Dominic O'Connor to Bend in December 1922. Klan leaders feared that the Franciscan priest had been sent from Ireland to contribute to the campaign to overturn the Oregon school bill. But Rome had "exiled" O'Connor to protect him from reprisals for his role in the recent Irish uprising. Carl A. Johnson, manager of a Bend pine mill and liaison to the statewide Catholic Civil Rights Association, was the key figure in local efforts to overturn the school initiative.

The Klan senator from Texas to whom Gifford referred as McFall was probably the recently elected Earl B. Mayfield.

The national school legislation described by Gifford was the Towner-Sterling Bill, which the Atlanta leadership supported. This proposal called for the establishment of a department of education with cabinet status and federal aid for schools, Americanization and literacy programs, and teacher training. The Klan also pushed for compulsory use of English in grade schools. Note how Gifford used discussion of the school issue to portray the Invisible Empire as opposed to the institutional power of the Church not to Catholic worship.

Oregon's KKK endorsed D. C. Lewis's proposal to tax church property. Lewis, a Republican state house member from Portland, served as an officer in the Federation of Patriotic Societies, a consortium of Protestant fraternal orders in which the Klan controlled a major faction. Despite Klan support, the measure went down to defeat in early February 1923. At the same time, Eugene poultry farmer Ben F. Keeney introduced a bill to tax sectarian hospitals, colleges, schools, and other institutions. Keeney's proposal passed the state house but died in the senate.

Lodge discipline over members sometimes proved difficult. In a case to which Fosner made apparent reference, Klansman Leonard J. Smith was arrested for bootlegging in June 1922. A second conviction in December 1923 would lead to a thirty-day jail sentence. In another instance, police arrested Klan aspirant Jay Conley for public drunkenness three days after klavern authorities held up his application for further investigation.

"KOTOP" signified "Klansman obey their oath persistently" and could be featured as an automobile sticker or other sign to convey Klan membership.

Three of the six applications read at the special meeting belonged to railroad employees—an engineer, fireman, and switchman. Nine new inductees included a garage man, restaurant owner, factory worker, jeweler, barber, farmer, and three railroad employees.[17]

. . . Klansmen present: Seventy-two.

Opening ceremony held in full.

With pleasure I notice that some of our officers are learning their parts and can commit them to memory. This includes our E.C. Did you notice on the wall behind the E.C. chair two beautiful American flags? They were hung there by our Klansman decorator, W. A. Richardson, and we wish to thank him very kindly and commemorate him on his great presence of mind so appropriate for that occasion.

Klansman Morris from the Portland Klan was a visitor in our klavern. He told us that he had been in our city for six weeks and up until just a few days ago had failed to find a KOTOP man in town. I guess it's about time we put out our shingle. We have got a show that I think is well worth a little advertising.

Kleagle Carter informed us at this time that our guest and grand dragon, Fred L. Gifford, would arrive on No. 18 and every man began to count his Q's and P's and snap right into line.

I noticed at prayer service that Klansman Green, our parson, did not refer once to his book. I would like to advise that a few more find out from him what kind of tonic he uses. . . .

The application of Jay Conley was turned over to the Board of Klokans for further investigation. His application states that his parents were Catholic.

That the new manager of the J. C. Penney Co. has promised to seriously consider joining this organization.

Our klabee's final report left us with a balance of $186.83 now in our treasury.

After this report I beheld standing in within the entrance of our klavern a stranger, and like the two men at the Lord's feast he was not dressed as the others in a robe of white, but arrayed in a garment of exquisite beauty and color and dotted like the feathers of a peacock. And surely me thinks as all arose to greet him, this must be our guest of honor. And like the little tyrant of the fields withstood, he strode into the klavern.

Thus we behold our grand dragon, Realm of Oregon, one Fred L. Gifford. Many times in my subconscious mind I had tried to picture this great man to whom we have sworn our allegiance, and he more than fulfilled the dream. After the glory of God he is a man of meekness, richly endowed with a warm friendly smile that touched the hearts of us all, and spiritually enthused in the great constructive program of which he is a vital part. The many accusations against him have turned to ashes. He is worthy to serve and the biggest thing of all, political aspirations he has none. Following close in his footsteps came Kligrapp St. Claire, a familiar figure in the klonklave.

There were no Klansmen or Klansmen's families reported sick or in need of financial assistance.

The Standing Comm. appointed to investigate the feeling of the local American Legion toward this body told us they would turn in a report within the very near future.

One comm[unication] was read from Kligrapp St. Claire of the Pendleton Klan which stated that our new city manager was very much opposed to the Klan and that he would advise that this organization refuse to accept his application should it be presented.

A bill for the sum of one dollar spent for a typewriter ribbon was read and ordered paid. Also a check for twenty-five dollars was paid your kligrapp for attempted services rendered.

Motion made and passed that kligrapp find out the amount of expense the Royal Neighbors incurred by giving us their meeting night and check be drawn to pay same.

Next we behold Klansman Cochran making a supreme effort to reach his chair after coming in late, but his effort was all in vain for Klansman Fields called his hand and smilingly he saluted the flag and the chair and went his way in peace.

Klansman Eberhard has not made his speech yet. Klansman Choate has got the grease of [f] his shoes and Klansman Butler has promised to quit trading at the Hooverized as soon as they pay him what they owe him. Something accomplished, something done to earn a life's repose.

Nine worthy citizens burned their bridges behind them and became masters of their own convictions[—]thus added to our list of Knights. . . .

Klansmen, after giving the sign of greeting to the candidates, most of you failed to return to Klan loyalty[—]Boner No. 1.

And Klansmen in robes who formed the lines through which the candidates passed forgot to take their seats promptly[—]Boner No. 2.

And when the candidates were given the clasp there was too much confusion[—]Boner No. 3.

Grand Dragon Gifford then informed us that the weekly newsletter had been discontinued.

Our E.C. then called on Kleagle Carter for a few remarks and he passed the buck to St. Claire and that esteemed Klansman did likewise to our grand dragon, Gifford. And this is a summary of his speech:

"Klansman, first of all I wish to say to you that you people have the only real kleagle in the state of Oregon. I wish to impress upon your minds that his work has been carried on with marked attention and that he has educated the Klans as they should be." These statements brought forth much applause and Kleagle Carter lost four buttons.

"Now in regard to the Ladies Organization I wish to state that Dr. Sawyer has begun a reorganization of that body and that their work is to be along the same order as the Klan. The Ladies of the Invisible Empire are not an auxiliary of the Klan and no men are allowed to become members of that order. Possibly within the next ninety days their new program will be outlined so that they can get down to a working basis. They are going to play an important role in regard to upholding the morals of our young women. Let us give them our full support in this community and see that they grow in grace and numbers."

Mr. Gifford next took up the political situation, telling us that the Louisiana affair was just a political issue which has not gone to the next grand jury and in all probabilities this is the last we shall ever hear of this bluff.

Relative to the case at Tillamook, Ore., Mr. Gifford had this lady come to his office and give an explanation of these alleged accusations. "On her left breast you could see a large red spot and by drawing the skin tight you could trace a very dim cross, probably put on by a very light acid and is rapidly disappearing. This woman held the position of a bootlegger and had trouble with the authorities to the extent that they desired to get rid of her and this is the means they used. Klansmen, the chief of police and his assistant put on the cross and though the papers refused to publish this, our Klan paper, the *Western American*, will eventually do so. We want the whole world to know that they can't put this over on the Klan."

Mr. Gifford informed us that the Pope has one of his representatives at Bend, Oregon. "I don't recall the good Father's name. Anyway, we may expect some trouble from this bird as we know him to be a big man politically and that he isn't in Bend for no special good. A large amount of money is to be raised to fight the validity of the school bill and in all probabilities it will be raised under the name of some Protestant institution so beware of dropping any chance remarks that may help in aiding the enemy in this issue.

"Within the next three months we expect to double the Klan membership in this state and we expect the next general election to be a cinch." He particularly stated that "Democraticism and Republicanism didn't mean anything to us. Let's forget it and see that the right man gets in. The next president of the United States is going to be a Klansman. And we now have sixteen United States senators who are Klansmen and a large number of representatives. Senator McFall of Texas is a Klansman and an exceptionall[y] brilliant man. He hails from a Klan which is 120,000 strong, practically five times the strength of Oregon. But we took first place in the eyes of the nation when we put over the school bill. This will be an epoch in state history and a battle long remembered. Many governors and practically all states have wired for a copy of this bill and all literature that helped to put it over. In the very near future this will be a national law instead of a state law."

Governor Pierce told Mr. Gifford that all appointments he made would be given to men who are right. "Owing to fact that Olcott's office force started to pack and leave at his appearance he has made some K.C. appointments. But bear in mind that they are but temporary and as soon as the governor's legislative troubles are over with" he shall take his list of appointments to Gifford's office "and together they will go over the list and weed out the culls. Gov. Pierce and the Klan are now on trial in the state of Oregon and by our loyalty to him and our efforts to keep out all Bolshevism, we will succeed.

["]When you hear a rumor on the street, squash it for its origin comes from Rome, which never sleeps. Gov. Pierce's success means our success. If ever you were a good citizen, be one now. Get behind this administration and let's give the people of the state of Oregon something in the line of true Americanism that they have never had presented before."

Mr. Gifford told us that when we find a poison spreader in our ranks to get him out. "If one man gets by with a little of this bunk there will be no limit to what he may try next." Mr. Gifford told us the fight and many insults he and his family had to take while trying to clean up this state and that he went on trial before his Klan and before a special investigator from Atlanta, Geo. and was duly acquitted. Somebody had to be the goat during the campaign and the principles of our organization were defended most nobly by our grand dragon. Olcott and his elements thought if they could kidnap Gifford they would give Hall the nomination and thus elect Olcott. This job was given to a labor leader on Burnside Street. But a body guard composed of Klansmen and Klan police officers broke up the attempt and Gov. Pierce and the school bill went over with a bang. Mr. Gifford told us that not at any time was Hall the Klan's choice for governor. We were simply backing the action taken by the Patriotic Societies and when they failed we took the matter in our own hands and brought about Gov. Pierce's election.

"We were never in favor of the recount and when we found that a few supposedly good Klan lawyers were looking for a killing, we stopped our donation at once. This organization is very interested in some of the bills now before the legislature but in no way are we trying to put over anything just because we have the power to do so." Gifford has not been near Salem and does not intend to. "We do not intend to dictate [to] this administration but we . . . intend to stand behind Walter Pierce and any measure he tries to put over.

"Klansmen, this order does not boycott anybody. We just practice Klannishness. Don't forget that.

"We are not against the way the Catholics worship but we are against the Catholic machine which controls our nation. We believe in the separation of church and state and through our public school system we hope to break up their propaganda. Thus the national school bill is our strongest hold and when it claims attention in Washington, D.C. we know it shall be a lawyers' battle from start to finish."

Let us keep hitting the ball for membership. Remember our charter will be here within the next six weeks and that will fall about St. Patrick's Day. Baker will have their charter about the same time and Gifford will be either here or at Baker to present same. Mr. Gifford's talk in conclusion was all praise and I think our attendance and work pleased him very much.

Along the Main Drag

That the Baptists are against church taxation.

That our Christian minister, Klansman Jones, is in favor of this bill.

That the Catholic schools or property owned by them is not taxed and they own a lot of taxable property in this state, including a good many lots in our own city.

People who send their children to Catholic schools have to pay for their keep and tuition and for each child there the state pays a specified sum for learning things contrary to our beliefs. This money comes from our pockets indirectly. But it goes for the building of institutions and fostering of ideas contrary to all American ideals.

If any of you Klansmen get invited to a K.C. party do not fail to go and keep your eyes open as the raising of funds to defeat the school bill is the social object centered in their behalf.

Not long ago we had two pupils in this city who wrote an essay on the Knights of the Ku Klux Klan and the teacher refused to read them. We will some day give her an education on Americanism some day and sing her the little song, "If You Don't Like the Hand That's Feeding You Then Go Back to Ireland Where You Belong."

The Klan now has a new constitution which will be sent to us in the very near future. It differs from the old one only in the respect that it [is] more rigid and militant but to every man who has the courage of his convictions it will be a joy to live up to.

That we have two Klansmen in this order by the name of Smith Bros. who are bootleggers and if this is true we are going to get rid of them as fast as the mail can carry the notification.

That one of the head Masons of this town says the Klan members tell all they know. This is not true but propaganda from the other side. They do all the talking and wonder what we have to add to it that will make the topic more interesting. Tell them nothing.

To help further our interests in the public schools we must convince the members of the Parent-Teachers Association that we are right. They can do a lot of good if they are thoroughly convinced in what they think is right. If you believe in anything search its depths and be born again.

That a good Mormon cannot be a Klansman for first he owes his allegiance to his church. But if he can live up to our oath he is accepted by this organization.

Meeting closed in short at a very late hour.

FEBRUARY 6, 1923

Of the thirteen applicants approved for membership at this meeting, three were farmers, two were insurance agents, and two were skilled railroad employees. Newly inducted members included a secondhand-store proprietor, butcher, mill employee, and two railroad workers.

The Garb Bill mentioned by Klansman and former state senator Colon Eberhard passed the house without opposition in January 1923. Endorsed by Walter Pierce in the gubernatorial campaign, the measure was introduced by Republican William F. Woodward, the anti-Catholic director of the Portland School Board. It passed the senate and received the governor's signature in mid-February. The measure remains Oregon law. Note Kligrapp Fosner's taunting of "Old Black Crows," a reference to the fact that the legislation would impact Catholic nuns who taught in the state educational system.

The law partner of George Cochran, Eberhard had moved to La Grande in 1909, been elected to the town's first city commission, and subsequently served as Union County district attorney, city school board member, and state senator.[18]

Meeting called to order by our E.C. at 7:40 P.M.

Klansmen present: Fifty-two. . . .

Ceremony opened by singing "America"

Standing Comm. ordered to report on the feeling of the American Legion toward this organization reported they would have a report for the next meeting. . . .

After the reading of . . . applications all Klansmen's attention was called to observe more closely the correct way to enter the klavern. Klansmen, this is a militant organization and we ask you to perform this ceremony in a military manner. Approach the altar with a little pep in your step and salute the flag and not the exalted cyclops. And to you officers, [do] not take your respective places until so ordered by our E.C.

Naturalization ceremony was held in full and the following men forsook the world of iniquity and pledged themselves to the sacred rites of Knighthood. . . .

Our E.C. then declared a five minute recess and ordered that no Klansman leave the hall[—]only in a case of emergency.

The business part of our meeting is the best part and we desire to have you stay and affiliate in its achievements.

During the recess all Elks held a conference and although they made no report I think they wish to head that institution with a 100 Percent secretary.

Senator Eberhard, who was called upon some time ago to make a speech, was present and fulfilled his obligation well. He told of his many visits to different Elks lodges throughout the state and that he found that a large majority of Elks were also Klansmen and that they accorded him a splendid reception wherever he journeyed.

He also informed us that the legislature had passed a bill prohibiting all teachers in robes to teach in our public schools. This bill will hit the Mennonites and the Old Black Crows.

In 1920 there were only nine nuns teaching in the state and today we know of two counties that have nineteen nuns alone.

Kleagle Carter informed us that at any time we now desired we could obtain a public speaker by giving them the proper amount of time to so accord their dates.

Your kligrapp has sent for a hundred copies of the *Western American* for which we hope shall continue a permanent circulation. We shall rather have these sold on the street or have them in some store where you may go and obtain same.

Upon suggestion of Kleagle Carter and by vote of this body the Board of Seven Men now acting in the capacity of chief advisers for this Klan were duly appointed to function as a grievance board, should one be called upon to meet questions of this nature.

One comm[unication] was read from Gifford publishing a list of banished Klansmen in the state of Oregon.

Klansman Rev. Jones announced that on the Sunday following he would take as his topic, "Why I am a Protestant." He extended each and every Klansman a hearty invitation which met with a glad response. . . .

After several Klansmen had expressed the fact that they didn't know who was right to trade with, our E.C. made a splendid talk in which he stated if Klansmen were seriously enough concerned in practicing real Klannishness they know how to find out if a man is right before purchasing an article from him.

A motion was then made and passed that the kligrapp make a list of the business houses who are right and read same at every meeting under the topic, "For the good and edification of the Klan."

That our charter will be here on or about St. Patrick's Day.

That the election and installation of officers in all Klans takes place on the 6th of May.

Three Klansmen from Elgin were visitors in our klavern, the spokesman being the chief of police, and he paid a tribute to our initiation work and invited us all to attend their meetings held Monday evening of each week. . . .

FEBRUARY 13, 1923

The names of seven Klan applicants, including a train engineer, were read at this session. Ten others were inducted, including an insurance salesman, hotel proprietor, taxi driver, meat cutter, grocery clerk, farmer, locomotive inspector, insurance agent, game warden ("Be sure that you have a Klan card marked paid in full before you go fishing"), and deputy sheriff ("Don't forget if you have to be arrested that he is the man to do it"). Fosner equated chapter membership with participation in an "Honor list."

The ailing Glenn H. Forwood, the object of Klan fraternal concern, was a former railroad blacksmith who had served as vice chairman of the shop-craft strikers' committee during the summer of 1922.

An even greater challenge to solidarity arose with the impending threat to the survival of Klansman J. Garrison ("Gar") Holm's grocery. The issue hit home since Holm catered the klavern's buffets. W. K. Gilbert, a dry-goods merchant; George B. Richardson, a clerk at Holm's grocery; and Rube J. Zweifel, the town tailor and member of the Board of Klokans, were appointed to explore the situation.

> Meeting called to order by E.C. at 7:30 sharp.
>
> Klansmen present: Forty-eight. . . .
>
> Comm. investigating on feeling of American Legion for this organization reported that they were unable to get an organized statement and they advised that all men who are eligible get behind this post and make it a 100 Percent organization as far as possible. . . .
>
> After the reading of . . . applications we held an open discussion relative to obtaining a speaker. But owing to the fact that weather conditions would keep many from attending it was decided to obtain one at some future date.
>
> That we now have a standing order for one hundred copies of the *Western American*. They may be obtained at the lodge hall on Tuesday nights, at Birney's Jewelry Store, or at your kligrapp's Hdq. at 1602 Sixth Street.
>
> That if any Klansman is out of work or enters a new field of business kindly notify the kligrapp that he may publish same, thus keeping Klansmen's money in Klansmen's pockets.
>
> For the good of the order it was suggested that Klansman Dr. Vehrs see Mr. Glass, proprietor of the Glass Drug Store, and find out what is wrong with him for up to date his name has not been recorded on our Honor list.
>
> One bill amount to the sum of $40.50 for hall rent was read and ordered paid.
>
> That Klansman Jones's sermon last Sunday on "Why I am a Protestant" was highly appreciated by all who attended and I wish a few more of you

Klansmen would get the habit of going to church more often. Klansman Jones not only needs our support but your bodies can well stand a little more spiritual development.

It was reported that Klansman Glenn Forwood is in the Tubercular Home at Salem and your kligrapp has sent a letter to the Salem Klan asking that they visit this Klansman and see that he has all the comforts money can buy. . . .

Klansman Bennett from Walla Walla was a visitor in our klavern and a real he-man, the kind that goes without a meal unless he can buy it from a Klansman and his talk on Klannishness put a bug in the ear of a good many of us.

Motion made and passed that the kligrapp write to Portland and get a list of all articles that man uses that are 100%.

One of the most vital questions that has ever arose before this klavern and one that should be a real test of Klannishness came from Klansman Gilbert's report that Klansman Gar Holm has been forced to make a consignment. We believe our Klannishness toward Klansman Holm has been very lax and it has been a good lesson to some of us who have been trading at the Hooverized or the place that seems the handiest. Popular sentiment showed a strong desire to open up Klansman Holm's store again and show this village that we are strong enough to support our members, and by a little practice of Klannishness this can very easily be done. A motion was then made and passed that a comm. composed of three men make a thorough investigation of the case and report same at the next meeting so we may be able, if possible, to give him the backing that will put him on his feet once more.

The men appointed on this comm. are as follows: Klansmen Gilbert, Richardson, and Klansman Zweifel.

Motion made to adjourn at 12 P.M.

FEBRUARY 20, 1923

A record breaker in attendance, this meeting drew visitors from Walla Walla, just north of the Oregon-Washington boundary; Tillamook; and nearby Baker. New initiates included a merchant and farmer, as well as a locomotive fireman, conductor ("Be sure your dues are paid when you ride on his train for that will be your means of transportation"), electrician, and crane engineer ("Don't tell this man the Pope is O.K. unless you want to get licked"), all of whom worked for the Union Pacific.

The slightly paraphrased biblical quotation presented by a visiting minister was improperly cited: it should be Judges 20:16.

> Meeting called to order by Klaliff Johnson at 7:35 P.M.
>
> Klansmen present: 102. . . .
>
> Our 100 Percent Orchestra rendered the music for opening ceremony, which was the most impressive one ever held in this klavern. If those musicians only knew how large a place they held in our hearts and what a real inspiration they are to our meetings, they would never fail to attend our meetings regular[ly].
>
> I wish to state at this time that Klaliff Johnson, who held the E.C. chair during the absence of our exalted cyclops, started the show off with a rush and a bang. We are proud to know that we have a man who can step into the harness when the pilot of our ship is gone and continue the good work, being a pleasure in the sight of the master when he again returns again to our midst. As my official capacity grants me this privilege of telling every man both his good and bad features, I now state that Klaliff Johnson's work was highly recommended by all. One correction I would like to make is relative to his recognition of Klansmen entering the klavern. This must be done with alertness and with a real spirit of welcome.
>
> Klansman Shorty Perkins of the Baker Klan was then asked to tell us what he thought of the La Grande Prov. Klan. He commended us very highly and in conclusion stated that the Perkins Motor Co. of this city had a vacancy for a 100 Percent man to work nights. This is a sample of the kind of Klannishness that we all can enjoy.
>
> Klansman Youcum of the Walla Walla Klan always has something worthwhile on his chest and he told us in a very pleasing manner what was going on in the old home town.
>
> Klansman Rev. [J. T.] Keating from Tillamook. Known there as "the Fighting Klan Parson" and one who championed the cause of Sister La Precia by setting on the steps of the church with a gun in both hands while she told the world about the Pope and his machine and advised all citizens of Tillamook to join the Klan in its great movement at the earliest possible date. He also told us about the bunk connected with the lady who was branded. And something of the origin of the Klan which dates as far back as the days of Christ. Listen to the Sixteen[th] chapter of Judges and the twentieth verse: "Among all the people there were seven hundred chosen men lefthanded and every one could sling stones at an hair breadth and never miss."

Klansman Keating unfortunately has nearly lost his eyesight but there is always a place for the right kind of man. Consequently, he is now taking subscriptions for our Klan paper, the *Western American*.

Next I behold Klaliff Johnson surrendering the chair to the exalted cyclops of the Baker Klan and I am here to tell you that the esteemed gentleman knows his eggs. He puts out a very snappy program and instills within all Klansmen to do likewise. He knows the work by heart and he believes in the word Klannishness from shoe strings to radios. We wish to thank him for taking an active part in our nat. ceremony and we hope someday to be able to return the favor.

Marching into our klavern to the strains of one of the sweetest marches I have ever heard came these six noble citizens who desire to cleave from a world of selfishness and accept the divine lineage that our forefathers would have us do. Greetings to these. . . .

That sixteen more robes have arrived, giving us a grand total of thirty-nine. These robes make our ceremony much more impressive and I wish more Klansmen would make an effort to put their order in as soon as possible. . . .

Motion made and passed that the shelves be taken out of the robe locker and a more satisfactory arrangement made to keep the robes in better condition.

In the future kindly put on your robe before entering the klavern. This not only avoids a lot of confusion and time but it is far more impressive.

That on March the first Rev. [W. A.] Gressman, pastor of the Christian Church in Pendleton, Ore., will speak in the Union Theater at Union, Oregon on "The Truth About the Ku Klux Klan," and on the night of March the second he will speak at the Star Theater in La Grande, Oreg. on the same subject. Time 8:15 P.M. The La Grande Prov. Klan is promoting this speech and I want every Klansman to attend and let's put this over with a lot of vim and enthusiasm. We have got to wake this old town up and show the natives that we are just as strong for the issue today as we were at Election Day.

The comm. reporting on Klansman Holm's financial condition and what we can do as a Klan to restore him to his former prosperity was very favorable and the plans they have presented shall not cause any Klansman any unnecessary expense or involve him in any future complications whatsoever. All we have to do is practice what we stand for and none of our businessmen need go broke in this city.

Motion made and passed that flowers be sent to the funeral of baby

Parsons, the son of Klansman Parsons. And our sympathies we extend
to the family during their bereavement.

Klansman Rev. Jones reported that a lady by the name of Cantrell who
lives on Madison St. and works at the laundry for the sum of twelve dollars
a week has a sick husband in Portland and is trying to support several
small children. This report went home and the dollars began to fly thick
and fast upon the carpet until twenty-six of them were gathered to buy
her a ton of coal. With the balance we can buy her a coupon book on
what will be the new Holm Grocery.

That Homer Leffel got his shoes shined at the Greeks.

The wife of Klansman P. E. Wyrick was reported sick and flowers were
ordered sent to her home immediately.

The E.C. from Baker then gave a very interesting talk, thanking us for
the honors we extended him and inviting us all to attend his domain at
any time and be accorded a royal welcome.

FEBRUARY 27, 1923

As requested, Dr. George Vehrs recruited the proprietor of the Glass Drug Store
and managed to add two of the shop's clerks to the nine Klan applicants approved at this meeting. Other Klan aspirants included County Treasurer Hugh
McCall, a fuel distributor, construction contractor, bookkeeper, farmer, train
conductor, and railroad clerk. Sensitive to questions concerning moral and religious background, however, the klavern proceeded cautiously in embracing
potential recruits. Note Fosner's humorous realism concerning the behavior of
lodge members. New Klan initiates included a creamery employee, lumber
worker, auto mechanic, farmer, and butcher ("You will find him in the Jews
Block . . . [on] Fir St.").

The Royal Riders of the Red Robe, to which the La Grande Klan promised assistance in recruiting, had been organized in Oregon by Grand Dragon
Gifford as a KKK auxiliary for foreign-born non-Catholics not eligible for membership in the Invisible Empire. Portland physician Dr. Martin W. Rose presided
over the organization, whose name Fosner garbled. Significantly, the klavern
failed to show interest in promoting the group.

Note that George Cochran once again advised restraint in Klan activity.[19]

. . . No. of Klansmen present: Seventy-two. . . .

The applications of Arnett and Rogers were laid on the table pending
further investigation as to their character and religion.

Mr. William Keefer, who resides at 2008 North Fir St. and is a grocery store manager by profession, reported for naturalization but was asked to retire until further investigation was made concerning his character. It is reported that he was seen in the company of a Klansman's wife and in an intoxicated condition. We want you to practice Klannishness but don't pull this fraternity stuff with another man's wife.

Our exalted cyclops then told us that at Baker, Ore. they have the Klan songs printed in large letters and hung upon the wall where everybody could see to sing them. This report was considered an excellent idea and our E.C. appointed Klansman Zweifel and Klansman Tull to see that we had the songs printed by the next meeting night.

The Baker Klan is also promoting the Order of the Red Riders of the Red Rose and this matter was discussed relative to our progress in this behalf. The applications may be obtained from Major Carter, who also has the authority of giving the oath, and any men you may find eligible to join that organization, please report their names to Kleagle Carter or to your kligrapp. . . .

Klansman Earl Griffith of the Baker Klan was reported sick at Hot Lake, Oregon. Also Rev. Lapham is there, so Klansmen, if you pass there don't forget to visit these unfortunate brothers, remembering at all times that real friends are the greatest inspirations of life.

Klansman Brentneau, who hails from Denver, Colorado Klan, was a visitor in our klavern and he gave a wonderful account of the trials that his Klan were passing through and finished by telling us he thought Oregon just about the livest state in the Union.

Klansman Leffel told us why the Pope shined his shoes and Klansman Cochran told us of the danger of jumping to our first conclusion of any scandal which we may hear. Your kligrapp read a piece written by the Catholics telling us that America would be Catholic in 1924 and that the next president would be a Catholic. Klansman Humphreys reported a fine time while visiting in the East. The Klan then stood in silent honor for one minute in respect of those gone before us—Mrs. Ed Reynolds and Mrs. Fitzgerald. Meeting closed at the hour of twelve.

MARCH 6, 1923

Ten new applications were turned over to the Board of Klokans at this meeting for investigation, while the klavern approved another fourteen for membership. Meanwhile, eight men were initiated, including a construction contractor ("Don't forget this man when you build your new garage or home"), bookkeeper, railroad clerk, shoe shiner ("If you don't think this man can't beat the wops [derogatory term for Italians] shining shoes just step in and look him over"), fuel distributor, and three pharmacists ("chief pill rollers, all from the Glass Drugs, finally snapped out of the dope and woke to nobler and higher aspirations"). Rube Zweifel, the town tailor involved in a humorous klavern incident, distributed Klan robes through his shop.

By ordering the reading of Romans 16:17, Grand Dragon Gifford may have sought a fitting characterization of attacks on his leadership within the Oregon Klan: "Now I beseech you, brethren, mark them which cause divisions and offenses contrary to the doctrine which ye have learned and avoid them."

Klan ties to the Protestant ministry were very strong. Fosner used an announcement concerning organizational privileges for the clergy to enunciate the high moral tone by which the Invisible Order liked to describe itself. The facetious reference to "Father Quigley" involved G. H. Quigley, minister of La Grande's United Methodist Church between 1919 and 1920.

The Sommer Hotel, the object of unspecified Klan concerns, was located close to the railroad depot in the heart of central La Grande.

Meeting called to order by E.C. at 7:50 P.M. . . .

Klansmen present: Seventy-six.

Opening ceremony held in full and I noticed for the good of the cause that Klansmen put on their robes before entering the klavern. Our robe room has undergone a period of reconstruction and our E.C. will appoint some worthy Klansman who will be in attendance at the locker door to hand you your robe.

Klansman Denning, formerly of the Walla Walla Klan and now express agent of this city, and Klansman Wall of the Pendleton Klan, were visitors in our klavern. Klansman Wall, who is a brother of our Klansman A. W. Wall, commented on the spirit in our order and appreciated the fact that he was able to sit in klonklave with so many of his old friends. As for Klansman Denning, he got away before being called upon to speak but we have got him booked for a twenty-minute speech. We consider this as a special courtesy to all new Klansmen.

Oh yes, I nearly forgot to state that along the early part of the evening Klansman Zweifel came staggering up to the desk with his arms loaded with robe hangers and when asked what the compensation fee would be, replied as follows: "Er. Ahem. Do you remember that at the last meeting Klansman Tull and I were put on a comm. to have the opening song printed in large letters and hung on the wall where all could see to sing? Well, it didn't come to pass as we were too busy and furthermore, we greatly desire that someone else be duly appointed to function in that capacity." Well, I was forced to be bribed not only because we needed the hangers but I was afraid he might not do the job if I refused.

Anyway, we sang the opening song as best we could and the kligrapp will see that in the very near future we have the song printed.

Minutes of last meeting read and approved. Thank you.

Our treasurer's report left us with a balance of $56.68 now on hand in the treasury. We are getting a little financial embarrassed but I think we can worry along very nicely until our charter arrives. . . .

Klansman Rev. Jones read before this assembly as was ordered by the grand dragon the Sixteenth chapter of Romans and urged that all Klansmen study this chapter that we may in no wise be ignorant of the principles of which this glorious organization has been founded.

I wish to announce at this time that from this date all ministers of the gospel may be admitted free of charge into this organization. Let's see if we can't make Americans out of every preacher in this town, including Father Quigley. We are giving them more honor without compensation than any other organization of today has to offer them. This organization was created for Protestants and if you are an honorable citizen and believe in a strict enforcement of the law, then you owe your support to this Klan whether you are able to take an active part in its meetings or not.

Mr. John Hodgin, our former prosecuting attorney, told me just the other day that when this Klan could prove to him that they held the key to law enforcement in this town, . . . he would consider it a high honor to have his name placed on the roll of honor. Klansmen, practically all our time has been spent in the organization of our local Klan and will continue so 'til the granting of our charter. After our charter is granted we shall discontinue the nat. ceremony every meeting night and our meetings shall outline a constructive program of real law enforcement such as has never before been seen in the little village God forgot. By the ballot and by the personal touch of every Klansman are the two means by which we [are] to realize the final object for which we have started out to accomplish. So continue to be Progressive both in word and deed and what you are is what the Klan is to be.

The kligrapp of the Salem Klan has assured us that personal attention shall be given to Klansman Forwood, who is sick in the state tubercular home of that city.

During the lull of waiting for the Glass Drug Store to become Americanized our orchestra rendered some exceptionally fine music and we certainly wish to thank these generous Klansmen for the inspirations they add to our nat. ceremony.

Our worthy and esteemed subs[titute] klokard [klavern lecturer] then informed us that the following men stood knocking at the portal door imploring his Majesty to let them enter, imploring mercy as sinners of the outer world, and asking that their good intentions bring to them this night the dawn of a more nobler life. And thus it came to pass we now pay homage to the following: . . .

I noticed at the last meeting that many members came in late and that during the time just before the initiation ceremony there is too much confusion. If you want to have the goodwill of the E.C. try and keep your seat. Also remember only in case of extreme necessity will you be allowed to leave the klavern and when you do wish to retire, kindly go with the proper signs.

Comm. reporting on the Holm Grocery was very favorable and within the next few days we hope to have a real 100 Percent store backed by Klansmen who firmly believe we are now strong enough to support and complete any and all movements which has the sanction of this Klan.

Discussion relative to Klansman Ben Decious leasing the Grill Room at the Sommer Hotel held our attention only long enough to sanction the rights of Klansman Decious in relation to the Klan, then was dropped. Further discussion to be taken up by the Grievance Board. . . .

Klansman W. W. Kinzie was duly appointed by the E.C. to act as a guard to the side door and ascertain the reason for Klansmen who desire to go into the adjoining rooms. This is to avoid so much confusion.

We were then informed that our school clerk, Mr. Reynolds, took his first communion on last Sunday. The Ladies of the Invisible Empire are quite indignant at this. In the very near future we shall treat him as we did Mr. Peare. We have not forgotten, either, that Fred L. Meyers is a member of the Board of Directors at the Y.M.C.A. and that Jack Peare is the big gun as the head of our local Red Cross. Oh yes, and Bruce Dennis was reported to have made light of Klansman Pierce's letter read recently at the Ad Club luncheon. But soon the dark clouds shall be turned to silver and History shall tell how these battles were won.

MARCH 13, 1923

As the La Grande Provisional Klan prepared to receive its formal charter from Atlanta, Kligrapp Fosner summarized the klavern's year-long history, although he made a minor error when he noted that Dr. J. L. McPherson had replaced W. G. Sawyer as klokard instead of klaliff.

The last meeting of the La Grande Provisional Klan sent the applications of ten potential initiates for final approval to the Board of Klokans. Sixteen new members were sworn in, including five railroad employees, three laborers, three barbers, an insurance agent, a sales manager, a merchant, a grocery employee, and a waiter.

The twelfth chapter of Romans read by Rev. Jones was a favorite of the Ku Klux Klan, described by the *Imperial Night-Hawk* as the "Law of Life for Klansmen" because of its presentation of "so many of the sacred principles which the Klan seeks to inculcate." Among such virtues were character, purity, and sacrifice.

Knight Eberhard's references to the Medford trials involved not-guilty verdicts delivered the previous day for three Klansmen accused of night-riding atrocities. The southern Oregon proceedings were marred by the fact that a newly elected and Klan-supported judge presided over the trial. Membership in the KKK was ruled irrelevant in the selection of a jury whose foreman turned out to be a cousin of one defendant. In a second trial three days later, the state asked for dismissal of the charges against three other knights.

Leonard C. Smith, a La Grande Klan adversary, was proprietor of the local Buick dealership and repair shop.

The kligrapp closed this first chapter of the klavern's history with a reference to the Klan-designated calendar.[20]

> La Grande Provisional Klan we bid you a fond farewell. . . .
> Klansmen present: 103
> Just ten months and six days ago today there came to this city a stranger.
> Now little did we know or dream of the purpose of this man's mission.
> But tonight I behold in the fullness of its glory his motive for being in our village and since his departure I have many things which I desire to impart to you.
>
> This stranger was no other than Kleagle Warner, who in all probability must be given the credit of organizing the La Grande Prov. Klan. The minutes of the first meeting were dated May the 11th and the following officers were installed: exalted cyclops, Klansman J. E. Reynolds; Dr.

McPherson taking Klansman Sawyer's place as klokard; Klansman C. E. Cooper taking Klansman Doane's place as kligrapp. At this meeting a comm. of 15 men were appointed to investigate the candidates for political offices on the primary tickets and check the names of those being 100 Percent. Also thirteen men became Knights of the Invisible Empire at this meeting.

All meetings held in the immediate future were held for nat. of many large classes, and chief under discussion was the coming election, and little did that body realize that the Klan was to play such an important part in the affairs of our state, for those were the days of our infancy.

On May the 25th under discussion for the Good of the Order, the Klan donated to Rev. Lapham, a very needy preacher though not a Klansman, the sum of twenty-five dollars. Shortly after this Rev. Lapham became one of us, and the inspiration he has brought to those who know him fully realize our continued efforts in his behalf have not been pledged in vain.

On June the 8th the school question held the attention of the Klan and a comm. was appointed to find out just what plan the Klan would adopt in regard to its progress.

On the meeting held on June 22nd a motion was made and passed that a box be rented at the P.O. and thus avoid tempting a Catholic mail carrier. Also the following officers were elected to office: Kludd Dallas Green; Kladd Clyde Bunting; Klarogo Ralph Byers; Klexter C. D. Stansfield; Night Hawk Mood Eckley; and for the Board of Klokans, the following: C. K. McCormick, T. K. Bellamy, and Klansman Victor Melville.

At the meeting held on July 7th Kligrapp Cooper submitted an itemized statement of all Klan transactions and then turned in his resignation as his work kept him from giving the Klan work the proper attention.

On July the 20th the Pendleton warriors came over in their full war paint and naturalized sixteen braves from the La Grande tribes. Kleagle Powell and Kleagle Simonton were present at this meeting and both delivered a splendid address in behalf of Klannishness and its practice.

On August the 10th Kleagle Whitmore arrived to take charge of our membership campaign and instruct us in the ways of the klavern. On August the 17th Klansman F. S. Lyons was unanimously elected as kligrapp and the following motions were made: that applications be laid on the table for at least two weeks and that a list of Klansmen who were in business be read before the klavern at each meeting.

All meetings held in September were for the purpose of nat. more citizens and arranging a constructive program for the coming election.

Also, the first of August found us without a kligrapp, Klansman Lyons having to resign on account of work. While the E.C. was looking for a brilliant man to function in that capacity Klansman Rhodes stumbled over your present kligrapp, who volunteered to fill the vacancy until someone was found to fill the place. Well, it's been a long hunt but if my work has pleased you Klansmen as it has pleased me to do it, I shall always feel duly paid for service rendered.

At the meeting held on October the 10th a motion was made and passed that all dues and other Klan obligations be straightened out so that we could get down to a working basis. Also, Kleagle Whitmore reported that Sister La Precia would speak in La Grande should the Klan desire to have her, and immediate plans were made to have her speak in this city providing we could obtain the consent of the town bosses, Peare and Meyers.

We canvassed the town for funds and met with very good success as all businessmen seemed very interested in the startling invasion the Klan was making in every town. Thus the Star Theater was obtained, a Fiery Cross Comm. appointed, and great was to be the fall thereof. You know the rest.

Immediately after Sister La Precia's fiery talk, which did much to build up our membership, we started in earnest to help put over the school bill in eastern Oregon and put Klansman Walter Pierce in the governor's chair in Salem. We wired for 100 Percent tickets and all kinds of school bill literature and immediately upon its arrival we placed under every door in town a copy of the school bill and a 100 Percent American ticket. Along about this stage of the game Big Ben made his last triumphant speech in this village before we closed the portal doors of his political career forever. A fiery cross greeted him on his arrival. It served to lighten the pathway of his Majesty and serve as a symbol of welcome in his memory 'til the end of time.

On the night of October 24 we beheld at the meeting our new kleagle, namely Kleagle Carter. We liked his first appearance very much and from that night on until the present our Klan has undergone a great period of reconstruction thanks to Kleagle Carter.

Do you remember when the Democrats had an election assisted by the Knights of the Ku Klux Klan?

Do you know we have three Klansmen who bet the school bill would pass?

That the fireworks were good on Armistice Night, both of them.

That we put up a fight for Klansmen Kinzie, Humphreys, and Eberhard, but Rome was not built in a day.

That if Jack Peare would of had enough coons whom he swore to have known for thirty days our Walter would have to farm for many days yet to come.

That the cashier of the La Grande Nat[ional] Bank held our attention at this time and many Klansmen withdrew their money and placed it in the other bank. This is still a very advisable thing to do.

On November the 14th your kligrapp was ordered to send a letter of proxy to the E.C. at Oregon City, our appointed representative at the Nat[ional] Convention to be held at Atlanta [i]n the very near future. Also Klansman Walter was extended an invitation to attend our next meeting and the Baker Klan, headed by Klansman Graham, told us they would be here one hundred strong. Well, Klansmen, you who had the pleasure to attend that meeting know that it was one of the greatest Klan meetings ever held in the state of Oregon. Governor Pierce made the speech of the hour and Klansman Graham finished a closed second. We had the best only-Klan orchestra in town followed by a most delightful repast.

Following this meeting our membership began to grow in leaps and bounds. We began the practice of real Klannishness and planted the seed that in time we hope shall bear the fulfillment of a most rigid law enforcement and a cleanup of the state in general. Our E.C. appointed the following men to act as a Board of Directors and Grievance Board: Klansmen Geo. T. Cochran, O. W. Jones, J. G. Holm, Frank Turner, Ben Decious, J. E. Reynolds, and Kligrapp Fosner, clerk of Board.

We have but one Klansman who has departed on the journey to a 100 Percent heaven, that being Klansman Marion Davis of Union, Oregon.

Klansman C. E. Short and Klansman W. G. Sawyer were banished temporarily from our Klan on December 19, 1922, for a period covering ninety days. As their time shall soon be up I would advise that they be interviewed for they knew not of where they spoke. Who will return with the prodigal sons who have strayed from the paths of righteousness? We live to forgive and forget.

The grand dragon, Fred L. Gifford, invaded our klavern about two months ago and gave a most splendid talk on what the Klan had accomplished in the past year and what we hoped to do in the future. With him came Kligrapp St. Claire of the Pendleton Klan, who has been a wonderful help to this Klan and we wish to thank him very kindly for past services rendered.

To give in detail a full account of both our little troubles on the waters of life and our victories and accomplishments I would have to write a whole book. But I wish to say in conclusion that we have built up an organization of men whom we consider the cream of our nation. As for an exalted cyclops, well, they never made them any better. And our kleagle, Mr. Carter, is the best kleagle in the state of Oregon, and the warm words of his appreciation for our kindness during his sojourn in this city shall long be remembered by the Klan. In parting he urged that we continue to build up our Klan. For only by strength of numbers can we accomplish the final victory and the ultimate desire of every true Klansman.

The following names are Klansmen who have been the real promoters in this cause by obtaining members for the organization: Klansman Dallas Green heads the list with seventeen, Klansmen Doane and Fields are tied for second place with sixteen, Klansman Rhodes being third with ten. Klaliff Johnson, Earnest E. Vehrs, and Klansman Tull are tied for fourth honors, each having nine; Dr. G. R. Vehrs and Mood Eckley tied for fifth honors, each having six. Other members who have been very active are as follows: Klansmen exalted cyclops, Gilbert, O. S. Humphreys, Chester Thompson, John Allen, Pearl Stiles, Frank Nelson, Zweifel, Clyde Bunting, L. W. Weeks, Rev. Jones, Eugene Millering, and Harley Smith.

What Happened at Our Last Meeting

Opening service began by singing of "America."

Talk by E.C. in reference to opening ceremony and a snappy practice of the signs that go to show we are on the job and worthy of having our charter.

Rev. O. W. Jones read the Twelfth Chapter of Romans as ordered by our grand dragon, Fred L. Gifford. . . .

Our nat. ceremony reached the height of perfection. Not a single discord was brought to light and the following aliens became citizens in their own native land. . . .

Klansman Tull's lessons of instruction to the new candidates was the best ever given in this klavern.

The E.C. then announced that on next Saturday evening at the hour of 8:30 sharp we would hold a special meeting for the purpose of receiving our charter. This announcement gave rise to a high tide of grateful feeling.

One comm[unication] was read from Atlanta stating that the Klan Tailoring Co. were taking away from all Klansmen dealers the privilege of selling their clothes. Comm[unication] from Gifford stated that hereafter in a chartered Klan three negative votes would be sufficient to reject a man from becoming a member of the Klan.

Klansman Vincent McKay was called upon the carpet to explain why he permitted a red neck to cut his hair. The Grievance Board finally settled his case to the pleasure of all concerned.

Klansman H. H. Hopkins was reported to of had his hair cut also by alien barbers, and he, too, will have a chance to explain.

If you were in attendance at the last meeting you heard Klansman Hamilton explain why he didn't study to be a priest.

Klansman Bradford made a stirring address in which he stated he had been a Klansman all his life but didn't realize its fullness until he had been naturalized.

Klansmen Knight, Tapp, and Metcalf were visitors in our klavern from the Elgin Prov. Klan and Klansman Bucknell was a visitor from the Baker Klan.

Klansman Cochran was then called upon to explain what the sword stood for and this he did in the most charming manner.

Klansman Gilbert then announced that the Klan Holm Grocery Store had been duly opened and ready for the dispatch of business. The comm. consisting of Gilbert, Richardson, and Kligrapp Fosner, who were instrumental in opening the Holm Grocery, were tendered a rising vote of thanks.

Klansman Eberhard then added his usual inspiration to the cause by stating that Bruce Dennis forgot to announce in the paper that the Medford night riders had been acquitted.

Some Klansman then announced that L. C. Smith was very bitter against this Bolsheviki organization. Will some good prodigal convert this misinformed man?

Our E.C. then appointed a Feed Comm. and requested that all Klansmen who could, attend church on Sunday, and that the K.C. wouldn't show us up too bad on St. Patrick's Day, the 17th of Ireland.

Officers now in chairs will continue 'til further notice.

Comm. appointed to select future officers are the following: Gilbert, Zweifel, Eberhard, O. W. Jones, and L. W. Weeks.

Klansman Holm then thanked us one and all for our timely assistance.

Red Cross drive topic put off 'til future date.

Kleagle Carter then tendered us his final speech and we adjourned at a very late hour on the Terrible Minute of the Woeful Hour of the Howling Night of the Mournful Week of the Desolate Month of the Sorryful Year of our Lord P.H.B.V.D.

Last minutes of the La Grande Prov. Klan.

MARCH 17, 1923

The St. Patrick's Day klonklave provided the culminating experience of the La Grande klavern's history. The *La Grande Evening Observer* reported that Klansmen burned a red and white cross on nearby Table Mountain to celebrate acquisition of the chapter charter.

Former city manager Kratz, the object of Klan derision, had displeased Grand Dragon Gifford by refusing to cooperate with patronage appointments in his new position in Astoria.

"Father O'Hario" was no doubt a reference to Rev. Edwin V. O'Hara of Eugene, superintendent of Catholic schools and a leading activist in the Catholic Civil Rights Association of Oregon. O'Hara's published address, "Freedom of Education," summarized the argument against the public school initiative. The fictitious Mike Leviniskii and Rastus Richardson represented Klan caricatures of Jews and African Americans, respectively.

These are the first minutes to be recorded on official KKK stationery listing the presence of all terrors, or officers.[21]

Klansmen present: over Two hundred.

Special meeting held for purpose of receiving charter. Exalted Cyclops Gwinn of Pendleton and former E.C., C. H. Conroy, and Kligrapp St. Claire were the honorary members at our meeting, and E.C. Gwinn presented us with our charter, La Grande Klan No. 14.

Minutes of former meetings read and approved number of applications read for citizenship. Eleven Klansmen reported sick. . . .

E.C. McPherson reported that Klansman Kratz, city manager at Astoria, was not living up to his oath.

Naturalization ceremony was held in full and sixteen men became Knights of the Invisible Empire.

Local visitors in our klavern, one priest, Father O'Hario; one Jew, Mike Leviniskii; and one coon, Rastus Richardson.

Officers now holding chairs in the La Grande chartered Klan No. 14 will so continue until May 6th, next general election K.K.K.

One comm[unication] read from Gifford stating his sincere regrets that he was unable to deliver charter as was promised.

Our E.C. thanked the Pendleton visitors for their work in behalf of the La Grande Klan and all Klansmen retired to the banquet room and were served a delightful lunch.

Meeting closed in the early hours of the morning.

MARCH 20, 1923

Klavern discussion about the Ladies of the Invisible Empire may have related to Grand Dragon Gifford's controversial attempt to merge the state organization with Atlanta's Women of the Klan.

Having vowed to step up involvement in civic affairs once they received their charter, La Grande Klan leaders sought to energize the rank and file to complain to city authorities about Municipal Court Judge R. J. Kitchen. They also recommitted the organization to financial support for the local Red Cross despite the fact that Klan adversaries Jack Peare and Bruce Dennis served as officials of the La Grande chapter. Dennis's *La Grande Evening Observer* reported the Klan's donation to the charity on March 23. The newspaper's earlier account of the charter reception and ensuing cross burning were attributed to a Klan source, apparently railroad foreman Ed Fields.

Klansman Millering's Cross Committee report may have referred to alleged voter fraud by residents of the Foley Hotel.

W. Bollons, mentioned in passing, was a Union Pacific superintendent.[22]

No. of Klansmen present: Eighty-three.

After the opening ceremony our E.C. officially declared this meeting the first to be held after the granting of our charter. . . .

No. of applications read for citizenship: twenty-five. They are to be reread at the next official klonklave before being passed on.

Motion made and passed that Board of Klokans publish before the klonklave the names of applicants who are rejected.

E.C. then announced that we would continue with our ceremony of naturalization for next Tuesday evening.

Mrs. Ellen Strickler, wife of Klansman Strickler, was reported sick. Flowers were ordered to her home.

Klansman Fields of the Social Comm. made his report at this meeting.

Motion made and passed that only Klansmen who have robes may wear them. . . .

Motion made and passed that Grievance Board appoint at least fifteen men to approach businessmen of the city relative to joining this order.

Motion made and passed that Board get in touch with Short and Sawyer and get them to reconsider their intentions.

Motion made and passed that all Klansmen whenever possible drop in and see commissioners relative to our present municipal judge, R. J. Kitchen.

Motion made and passed that donation of fifty dollars be given to Red Cross.

Motion made and passed that Board decide charter dues and cards be shown at outer door.

A Klansman from the Corvallis Klan was a visitor in our klavern and made a very nice talk.

Discussion held relative to the Ladies Organization.

Motion made to adjourn.

Along the Main Drag for the Past Two Weeks

That on the 17th of March we were presented with our charter. We will be known from now on as the La Grande Klan No. 14.

That our membership is growing very fast and that from Saturday night until Tuesday night we obtained twenty-five applications.

That Klansman Harry Last be mentioned in orders for his valorous work during the past week and that his name be changed to Harry First, which I think by a careful count would make him our foremost Klansman in obtaining citizens for this Empire. . . .

That the latest dope on Dr. Vehrs's appointment for city health officer is very encouraging. It is not a very good paying position[—]about fifteen [dollars] per month, but George will have the pleasure of giving Dr. Kirby a bath. That seems to be the reason we demand his dismissal.

Our opening ceremony at the last meeting would of been a peach but every man in the house had a bad cold but Klaliff Johnson and it embarrasses him to sing alone.

That Kligrapp Fosner presented Bruce Dennis in behalf of this Klan the sum of fifty dollars to be given to the local Red Cross. Gov. Pierce was present at this occasion. Thus you see why Bruce gave us such a wonderful lot of space on the very front page. I predict that Bruce would like to be a Klansman but no one seems anxious to get his application, as no one wants to see any more political blunders sent from this county. This includes some prominent businessmen of Portland who told Senator Eberhard that if we sent Bruce down there again we would never get him back.

That our City Comm[issioners] are beginning to sit up and take notice that there are a few citizens in this community who think we should at least have a municipal judge with these requirements: brains, character, and honor among thieves. Just keep the little drops of water falling on the stone and before very long we shall have a new municipal judge. We have had about all of this pedigreed bunk handed us that our conscience will allow, and if we don't succeed in having him removed by these city comm[issioners] at the next election, we will have some new commissioners. That is the fundamental basis where we must obtain our hold.

We have corruption in our Police Dept. for this reason: that police officers of this town are underpaid and they accept the bribe in order that they may also obtain a livelihood in this struggle for existence. I believe in nothing cheap, not even the city health officer.

That the motion to collect the balance of provisional dues be laid on the table 'til it is forgotten, I hope.

Klansman Millering reporting on Cross Comm. Trespassing of J. E. Foley Land was incomplete as all the returns listing the dead were not in.

That the biscuits left over from the last feed were given to the Salvation Army. Some Klansman reported that Supt. Bollons declared that they were sold on the train and for scab prices.

That Klansman Fields's editorial on the strength of this Klan surprised many of the natives.

That Rev. [A. R.] Sitton of the Baptist Church of this city had the extreme pleasure last Friday evening of meeting at least fifteen Klansmen. The party started with Klansman Dr. Vehrs and the Rev. in front of Glass Drug Co. about five bells in the evening and continued until all Klansmen passing by had been duly introduced to him. He gave us the once-over, complemented us very highly, and told us that he would consider taking out a policy in our Co. at the earliest possible date.

That the sum of $37.38 was collected at the feed held on the 17th. The collection consisted mostly of pennies and I would suggest that we get a bank and start a relief fund for the needy, and every time a Klansman has a birthday make him put in a penny for each year he has lived. The bank would be placed in front of the E.C. station. This may pay our flower bill for the sick.

That Klansman Weeks and Kligrapp Fosner drove to Hot Lake Thursday and took Klansman Lapham some fruit and grape juice.

That Mr. Harding, assistant cashier of the U.S. National Bank, in a very pleasing and charming manner, gladly filled the request of your kligrapp when he asked that the bank furnish some check blanks with the Klan title and number. We now have those at hand and I think the bank officials are well aware of our prestige in this community.

That the Grievance Board had a meeting in Mr. Geo. T. Cochran's office on last Friday evening for the following purposes: to select two school directors, one clerk, one justice of the peace, one municipal judge, one city health officer, and appoint a comm. of fifteen Klansmen to approach our businessmen and get them on the Roll of Honor. The system of attack will be little drops of water falling on the stone[—]will make it wholly and acceptedly for this cause.

That a comm. be appointed to interview Klansmen Sawyer and Short and see if they would not change their views before the final edict of banishment was sent to them.

The announcement relative to the Klan Tailoring Co. was very much of a blunder and Klansmen, do not discontinue ordering from the Zweifel Tailoring Shop, for up to date we don't know of any American tailoring houses in the U.S.[—]they are all Jews. This will be remedied in time by the Klan Bureau of Adjustments.

The following bills were paid by the kligrapp this week:

to Klansman Ed Fields for Song Helper and dishes, $8.35
to Stilwell Meat Co., $17.35
to C. H. Tull, $1.99 for cross fixtures
to Lilly's Hardware for dynamite, $1.45
to Gar Holm, $23.69
to Red Cross Donation Fund, fifty dollars
fruit and grape juice for Klansman Lapham, $1.86
for stamps and registering mail, five dollars
Total: $108.69

Klansman Harry Williams, late captain of last war, gave short talk on American Legion and earnestly urged that all members who are eligible join at the earliest possible date.

The next Red Cross election will be held in October. Why should Jack Peare be secretary of that wonderful organization?

Don't forget to see Klansman Rhodes for application blanks for the Ladies of the Invisible Empire.

You may pay your charter dues beginning with tonight if you wish. Don't forget your robe orders. They are very essential things in our initiation work and only those having robes are permitted to wear them.

MARCH 27, 1923

The La Grande Klan continued to recruit from surrounding towns like Imbler and Summerville, the latter about fourteen miles northeast. Fourteen new knights included two farmers and two city firemen, as well as a carpenter, real-estate agent, electrical contractor, laborer, engineer, teamster, lumber worker, locomotive engineer, railroad foreman, and retiree.

The *Oregon Daily Journal* was a statewide daily newspaper published in Portland.

Kligrapp Fosner took the occasion of this meeting to draft another extemporaneous essay in which he reiterated the Invisible Empire's professed moral standards and aspirations.

Klansmen present: 109.

Opening song service complete with ceremony.

Klansmen authorized to show cards when giving password. . . .

Total number of applications read: Forty-four.

Total number of applications endorsed by Klansman H. Last: Twenty-one.

The names of the following were turned down by the Board of Klokans: Mr. Ira Kestler, Mr. Alonzo Dunn, and Mr. Harold R. Taal.

Discussion relative to this issue led to a motion that a short and precise reason be given for the rejection of any man. This motion was tabled for further discussion.

Our E.C. suggested that when giving the password please do not say it so that the man next to you can also hear.

Nat. ceremony was held in full. . . .

Klansman Winn's daughter was reported sick and flowers were ordered to her home.

Motion made and passed that robes be laundered and money be drawn on treasure to pay for same.

Motion made to adjourn at a very late hour.

The Office Cat on the Main Drag

That our night hawk, Klansman Mood Eckley, has been suffering from the effects of a broken ear drum due from the carelessness of Klansmen who insist on hollering the password instead of using the method taught in the ritual.

Did you know that you can get your robe by dropping in to see the tailor Rube Zweifel on your way home from work?

That the guiding hand of fate has led Klansman P. E. Wyrick away from the toils of business with the La Grande News Co. and you will at present find him working for the *Journal*. As Mr. Wyrick has informed me, this may not be permanent. We asked that anyone wanting a good man please get in touch with him or myself. We don't want an idle Klansman in town.

Did you ever stop and realize that most of this talk you pick up on the street is all bunk? Klansmen, you should live above the rabble of everyday clamor. Remember when you come to lodge that this is not an old maids convention. It don't take brains to promote these little personal issues. So let's think more deeply, act more in harmony, and sacrifice more for the cause we pursue and in the end we shall be the better for it.

That our new applications one thousand strong have arrived for distribution in this valley. Let's fill them all and order more.

That the charter dues are now due. Payable by quarter, six months, or for the whole year.

That your kligrapp now has the pedigree of every Klansman complete except for the fingerprints, so stay within the bounds of mercy.

That a comm. of fifteen Klansmen, mostly businessmen, are going to meet in the very near future and discuss the plan of attack which shall be directed against their fellow men who are also in business but have not their names written on the Roll of Honor.

Order your robes at Klansman Zweifel's tailoring shop. Remember, only those possessing same may have the privilege of wearing them in klonklave assembled.

That forty-four applications in one week shows a tendency toward progression that was never equalled since the history of this Klan. That Klansman Harry Last should of been at the last meeting to hear his name honored as never before.

That we have three very intelligent and just men on the Board of

Klokans. Now aren't you sorry for your unjust indiscriminations offered on their behalf at the last assembly?

That we wish to thank the musicians for their continued efforts in behalf of the nat. ceremony in which they play a most important part.

Popular sentiment has arrived to the conclusion that we have naturalization ceremony every two weeks instead of every week.

It is rumored that the *Western American* is rapidly becoming one of the most popular papers in town. Our continued support will make it a daily in time. We are told public opinion is molded by the press.

When you hear of a new Klansman coming to our village to reside, kindly notify the kligrapp so that he may be accorded a royal welcome to our midst and a hearty invitation to our klavern. Courtesy and fellowship are those golden possessions that when all things lie down to sleep, we dream of the joys the morrow shall bring.

APRIL 3, 1923

Organizational discipline and the maintenance of economic solidarity remained the primary topics of chapter concern during this period. *Chinks* was a derogatory reference to the Chinese. C. W. Bunting worked at the family's Maxwell auto dealership.

Note the frankness concerning rank-and-file difficulty in sustaining KKK moral precepts.

The visiting Tillamook Bay minister undoubtedly was Rev. J. T. Keating, who had addressed the klavern two months earlier.

Number of Klansmen present: Eighty-seven.

Opening song service held in full. . . .

Number of new applications read: Twenty-eight.

Motion made and passed that naturalization ceremony be held every two weeks.

Visitors in our klavern were as follows: Kleagle Farmer, E.C. Nelson, and Klaliff Spaulding of Boise, Idaho. . . .

The following announcements were made before this body:

That in the near future Klansman Rev. O. W. Jones would talk in the city of Island City, Oreg. on the merits of the Klan.

That Klansman Boyd of the Enterprise Klan had bought half interest in what is called the Rex Barber Shop.

That the city commissioners had called a meeting for the purpose of appointing a new municipal judge.

That Dr. Landis has resigned as railroad doctor and that Dr. Vehrs was sponsored to accept the position.

General discussion was held relative to a new school house being built on East Adams Ave. Action passed to Board of Directors.

Discussion of open air initiation ceremony to be held at some specified place between the following Klans: Walla Walla, Pendleton, Baker, Boise, and La Grande. Comm. appointed to function in this behalf as follows: Klansmen Tull, C. W. Bunting, and O. W. Jones.

That a form letter be written to men who are not practicing Klannishness. The contents of this letter to pass the judgment of this body.

Final announcement by E.C. that our regular ceremony of nat. would be held on the following Tuesday.

Meeting adjourned in short order.

Along the Main Drag

That but very few Klansmen have stopped at Zweifel's and ordered their robes. Kindly bear this in mind as they are absolutely essential to the full perfection of our order.

That this organization is not to clean up politics but to clean up America.

It is reported that all good K.C. carry a 32-automatic when they go out at night. Be careful, Klansmen.

That Klansman Gar Holm reports that the Klan grocery store is doing a better business than was expected but that there are still many Klansmen who are not giving him their support.

That a letter on the practice of Klannishness will go out to these half-baked Klansmen requesting that they observe their oath or come before this body and explain why it is impossible to do so. If you will be a man about it this body will give your case a reasonable consideration.

That the old gang who have always taken their meals at Herman's Lunch Counter are still continuing to do so. As a Klan we can't sponsor this act so kindly step to the next door and eat a real honest-to-goodness American meal [even] if it does cost a trifle more.

That we have a few Klansmen who even go as far as to go the bond [advance the bail] of bootleggers and Chinks. You are living in America, now, not in a foreign country.

That the kligrapp, who thinks he is a very important man, didn't get very far in promoting the issue of having a naturalization ceremony every Tuesday night instead of every two weeks as was the final verdict. Anyway, he wishes to thank the old loyal guards who stayed with the ship 'til she sank to the depths below. Every day there are many men who have their applications in this order stop me on the street and in the office and ask when the time will come when their names can be placed on the Roll of Honor along with the rest of the Americans. I hate to tell them it takes six weeks. Besides, I don't mind the extra work.

That the charter dues are . . . payable by quarter, half year, or by the year. Standing dues six dollars. Don't put it off.

That our exalted cyclops has been studying the Constitution and is now prepared to tell you how we are to deal with these different issues.

Klansmen, kindly remember if you are not personally acquainted with a man or are not very sure he is O.K., do not ask him to become a citizen of this Empire for you may have to disappoint him in the end.

Order your robes from Zweifel the tailor.

Were you present at the last meeting and heard the E.C. of the Boise Klan deliver the oration on the Delivery of the Robe? Well, the least to say it was a masterpiece, and in the very near future this Klan is going to appoint a Daniel Webster to repeat the oration for the benefit of those absent as well as for an inspiration to order your robe.

That the privilege the body granted to the kligrapp to order anything in the line of material for his work will be greatly appreciated, I assure you.

That Klansman Whissler has departed for Kelso, Washington, where he expects to find something in his line of work. May God's speed attend him in these efforts.

That Klansman Don Scott reports the restaurant business is surpassing all hopes. May the mercy of Him who endows us with all earthly blessings continue in his behalf.

That Judge Kitchen, who has been acting in the capacity of municipal judge, is tired of his job. It's just like Tanalic, it works both ways.

That Reverend of Tillamook, Ore., who is working in behalf of the *Western American* and the Ladies of the Invisible Empire, was a visitor in our city and made a wonderful inspiring talk before the esteemed body of ladies. He reports the *Western American* cannot keep up the great demand of Klansmen; just be a little patient if your paper don't reach you in time for I assure you that in the very near future things will be adjusted to the pleasure of all concerned.

That Klansman Rev. O. W. Jones, Klansman Frank Turner, Rhodes, and Kligrapp Fosner drove to Island City last Saturday for the purpose of renting a hall in which Klansman Jones has volunteered to speak on the merits of the Ku Klux Klan. I wish to say that we met with very good success and secured the Odd Fellow[s] Hall for the sum of five dollars. And on next Friday evening, April the 13th, at the hour of 8 P.M., we are going to have a real honest-to-goodness Klan meeting presided over by our 100 Percent Klan preacher, Rev. O. W. Jones. I'll tell the world we don't have to go outside for our talent in the progress of making Americans. Bills are now being printed, music is being arranged, and boys, let's fill that old hall so full that the citizens of Island City shall tell their grandchildren of the day when the Ku Klux Klan took possession of their village and brought to them the dawn of a nobler realization.

If any of you Klansmen ever get the wanderlust and desire to know the ways of the gypsies, you may get the details in full by having a personal interview with Klansman C. W. Bunting.

If you married Klansmen insist on going out with another man's wife be awful sure she doesn't belong to a Klansman. You may have an occasion to meet that gentleman in the klavern and I am sure it would be a very embarrassing position for each of you.

APRIL 10, 1923

Among the ten new initiates inducted at this klonklave was railroad foreman C. E. Happersett, a former commander of the local Eagles.

The klavern continued to be concerned about pharmacist Adolph Newlin. George Noble, another Klan target, was a twenty-one-year-old wholesale produce dealer. Union County census records for 1920 indicate that his parents had been born in Scotland.

E.C. McPherson, whose professional practice demanded frequent evenings, was one of the town dentists.

A subsequent segment of the minutes contained the correction that Klansman Parsons was not the Ford salesman at Perkins Motor Co.

The third page of the four-page supplement to the minutes for this date is missing from the collection.[23]

No. of Klansmen present: Ninety-one.

Visitors in our klavern were as follows: kligrapp and klaliff of the Baker

Klan, Klansman Butler of Elgin, and Klansmen Watson and son of the Pendleton Klan. . . .

Naturalization ceremony was held in full. . . .

After the close of this ceremony our E.C. gave the candidates a splendid lecture on Klannishness and then departed for home and Klaliff Johnson resumed the chair.

Discussions on the floor were as follows:

Open air nat. ceremony to be held alternately between the Baker and La Grande Klans on about the 25th of May. Robes for this occasion to be borrowed from the Pendleton Klan.

That another organization has a key to our locker and that Klansman Kessler volunteered to supply us with a new lock for same.

That this Klan, if at all possible, is going to give Adolph Newlin the limit.

That [it] is the duty of every Klansman to have a robe.

That our new officers for the coming year be appointed at least two weeks before the installation.

Motion made and passed: that a letter be written by Klansman Cochran to our grand dragon, Fred L. Gifford, relative to the Newlin case, asking him to advise this Klan as to what action we can take which shall eventually lead to his prosecution.

Announcements were as follows:

That Kligrapp L. D. Smith of the Baker Klan has been appointed deputy dragon of the Royal Riders of the Red Robe, having in his jurisdiction the following counties: Baker, Union, and Wallowa.

That O. W. Jones would speak at Island City on the merits of the Klan on Friday, April 13th, and all Klansmen and their families were requested to be at the Club Cigar Store at twenty minutes to eight, where cars would be waiting to take them to Island City.

For the encouragement of the Klan we had a number of short talks and the kligrapp read the business places that are right.

Meeting closed in short.

Current Events of the Past Week, April 10, 1923

This week has been a very eventful one in the history pertaining especially to our own little village.

First of all I wish to call your attention to Rev. O. W. Jones's speech at Island City on last Friday evening. The very least to say it was a

masterpiece and I think all who had the pleasure of hearing him will
bear me out in this statement. I especially wish to thank the many
Klansmen for their loyal support in attendance and for their cars used
in transportation. The meeting, as the phrase goes, was a most howling
success and the old hall has not seen such a crowd in many a day. At the
close of the meeting many of the natives asked for further information
regarding our organization and I know that our efforts centered there
shall not be in vain. I not only think that these speeches should be made
in all the surrounding towns, but I think Klansman Jones should receive a
compensation for services rendered.

We must continue wholeheartedly in the education and growth of our
splendid organization, and the way to accomplish that end is to so fully
believe that our cause is a just one that we also make others believe. Let us
continue in the approach of our citizens without fear or favor, remembering
that all Protestants owe their support to this organization, and that the
fulfillment of our many purposes are yet within their infancy.

Have you ordered your robe from Zweifel the tailor this week? If not,
don't fail to do so at the next opportunity.

That the election of officers will take place on the sixth day of May or
on the meeting night nearest to this date. Installation of officers will follow
in the prescribed manner according to our choice of the date.

Dues collected during the week: forty dollars.

That the letter written by Geo. T. Cochran to Fred L. Gifford relative
to Adolph Newlin case was very well formed and contained an appeal that
cannot help but arouse our grand dragon to immediate action, and in the
very near future we hope to be able to break up the old undercurrent that
has so far as we are concerned brought that man's release. If we combine
our efforts in this behalf we shall prove to this city that the Klan is
being instrumental in cleaning up this town and that we stand for the
full enforcement of the law, be he Catholic or Klansman, gentile, alien,
or Jew.

That the kligrapp has sent in an order for twenty more robes and is very
desirous to send in just as large an order this coming week.

That Klansman Miller, the dentist who has taken Dr. Ruckman's place,
was a visitor in our klavern and stated that he was very favorably impressed
with the harmony accorded in our meetings. We extend a hearty welcome
to this new dentist as the Klansmen in this village are working a hardship
on our exalted cyclops, for there is seldom an evening that he does not
work and many a night he burns the midnight oil.

That we have a Klansman from the Portland Klan by the name of Murphy. I wonder where he was born?

That supplies amounting to the sum of $45.75 were ordered from Atlanta last week.

That we should have our by-laws drawn up at the earliest possible date. The kligrapp has some forms that will be very helpful in their construction and adoption. . . .

If within our power and to the glory of all concerned, this Klan No. 14 of La Grande, Oregon must not rest until they have seen the bars closed on two of the worst violators the city has had for many days, and they are Adolph Newlin, the hop merchant, and Geo. Noble, king of bootleggers.

I wish to state at this time that any Klansman who is contemplating buying a Ford car, be sure that you purchase same through Klansman Parsons of the Perkins Motor Co., as that is his only means of livelihood as connected with that company.

That the members of the Elgin Klan assembled in the Christian Church of that city and presented that worthy pastor a donation in behalf of the Klan. Our greetings to Elgin.

That Klansman Winn thanked this body for the splendid floral offering presented during the illness of his daughter.

That the La Grande Klan since being chartered has nat. twelve men, the balance going to Kleagle Carter.

That the kligrapp paid five dollars in cash for the rent of the Odd Fellows Hall at Island City, Ore. Trusting this meets with the approval of all concerned. . . .

APRIL 17, 1923

There is no discussion of the fact that a Klansman had become an employee of the much maligned Herman's Lunch Counter, whose proprietor, Herman Roesch, was a German American and Roman Catholic.

The George Noble case continued to interest the La Grande Klan. Noble was found guilty of liquor possession, fined three hundred dollars, and sentenced to ten days in jail on April 16.

Municipal Court Judge R. J. Kitchen's alleged "change of heart" may have been tied to an earlier pronouncement that "drunkenness has got to be stopped, especially at the dances." The judge may have been seeking to neutralize Klan opposition.

Klansman Dexter McIlroy was the deputy sheriff.

The reference to the "big town" no doubt is to Portland.

The remainder of the supplement to the minutes for this date is missing. Whether this gap in documentation is a result of the lost segment's containing a conversation with Governor Pierce is impossible to ascertain.[24]

... Klansmen present: Seventy.

Opening ceremony held in full.

No. of applications read: Fifteen. . . .

Visitors in our klavern were as follows: Kleagle Carter; Klansman Evans of Baker; Klansman Boyd, formerly of Enterprise and now part owner of the Rex Barber Shop of this city; Klansman Cox of the Roseburg Klan, now employed at Herman's Lunch Counter; and Klansman R. R. Carey of the Walla Walla Klan, who will be transferred to this Klan in the very near future. . . .

Discussion relative to the Noble case was quite out of harmony and Klansmen Fields and Phieffer were immediately dispatched to the police office to learn the truth. They reported on returning that Mr. Noble was sitting quietly in his cell reading a book and seemingly not enjoying the company of his fellow companions, they being wops and coons. . . .

Klansmen Bunting, Gilbert, and Johnson were appointed on the comm. to draw up the by-laws for this Klan.

Motion made and passed that Klansman Rev. O. W. Jones be given the sum of twenty-eight dollars for which to purchase a license for his car. This is a little token of our appreciation for the speech he made at Island City, Ore.

Our E.C. then told us that Judge Kitchen had suffered a change of heart. He went so far as to ask him if he thought his petition would be turned down should he turn it into this Klan. The sentiment, I think, is quite in the affirmative.

That the actions of Klansman Phy be turned over to the Grievance Committee.

Discussion relative to the hotel at Reith, Ore. led to the suggestion that the kligrapp send a letter to the Pendleton Klan assuring them of our support in helping them to clean up that joint.

That the Foley Hotel is called a mad house by all traveling men.

Klansman Dexter McIlroy's speech brought forth the evidence that the officers were doing their part but the district attorney is the man who is lax and that is the man to clean up.

Motion made and passed that the members of the Grievance Board appoint a comm. to talk to all magistrates of the city and county relative to the full enforcement of our laws.

Discussion relative to the Daggett family brought forth the donation of $25.30 by the Klansmen present for her immediate relief. Motion made that our E.C. present this in person and tell her who it is from and where she could spend it and be right.

Motion made and passed that the Klan buy two books of dance tickets sent from Astoria, Oregon, amounting to the sum of twenty dollars, and that if we draw the lucky number that wins the car, we can reimburse our treasury by the sale of same. Any Klansman desiring one of these tickets may obtain same from kligrapp free of charge.

Klansman Williams then announced that on next Friday evening the Endeavor people of the city would give a feed at the YMCA for the moderate sum of fifty cents and requested that all Klansmen attend this banquet.

Klansman Gilbert announced that he had a day's work on the wood pile for some Klansman that followed that particular line of work.

Our E.C. then suggested that the kligrapp write to the Baker Klan and find out the cost of laundering the robes and if they can be laundered intact.

For further information to all Klansmen I wish to state that your robe can be transferred by the authority of the E.C. . . .

Along the Main Drag

That the last meeting held Tuesday evening brought forth many issues of local importance, and I sincerely wish that more Klansmen would of been present to hear the discussions.

That Rev. O. W. Jones wishes to thank this body for their appreciation in behalf of his speech at Island City, Oregon.

That only three robe orders have been turned in during the past week. This is not very commendable for this organization considering its strength.

Klansman Gar Holm reports that the newly made Klansmen are giving him their entire support but that the original Klansmen are still catering to the Pope and following the line of least resistance.

I wish to call your attention at this time to the fact that if we continue giving from the abundance of our hearts that some day when we want to put over some big issues we are going to find the cupboard bare. So let's practice just a little more economy, giving in the spirit of appreciation and not in abundance.

Klansman W. A. Richardson, proprietor of the La Grande News Co., was a visitor in the big town the past week and he returned with more literature and dope than we have had in some time. Immediately upon arriving in the big village he set for the *Western American* H.D.Q. and read the riot act to those officials who promised us that in the future we could get our papers without the varied complication[s] that have seemingly been our lot in the past. From there he made his way to the jewelry store that makes all kinds of Klan pins and emblems and was duly appointed the local agent for same. He then held a personal interview with Klansman Gov. Walter Pierce who informed. . . .

APRIL 24, 1923

Hugh McCall, whose application had been held up since February, was the Union County treasurer and former manager of a bank in nearby Cove.

Membership in the Utah-based Church of Jesus Christ of Latter-Day Saints was controversial for potential Klan recruits since the Mormons were not considered Protestant Christians and the church hierarchy had named the KKK in a denunciation of "secret societies." The issue was an important one because 30 percent of the religiously affiliated residents of Union County identified themselves as Mormons, a higher figure than for any single denomination.

"E.C." Fields refers to the initials in the Klansman's name; he did not assume the post of exalted cyclops.

The klavern maintained great interest in school board politics and district director, James Russell, who had initially supported the Klan by voting against the reinstatement of Catholic teacher Evelyn Newlin.[25]

. . . Klansmen present: 160.

Visitors present: F. C. Hart of Baker and Joe Burock of Baker

Meeting opened by the singing of our Klan song.

Number of new applications read: Fourteen.

The applications of the two previous meetings were reread and those read for the third time were turned over to the Board of Klokans for the final acceptance or rejection.

The following applications which have been held up for some time pending further investigation were read before the body and the following action taken:

W. M. Keefer held for further investigation, Hugh McCall passed,

Thomas O. Barnwell of Telocaset rejected, Harry Sandoz rejected, and Earl Kesler rejected. The men rejected have been duly notified of same.

Naturalization ceremony was held in full and twenty-eight men were made Knights of the Invisible Empire.

Next in discussion on the floor came the question as to whether men of the Mormon faith were eligible to be Klansmen. This argument brought forth a motion that the kligrapp write to our grand dragon and obtain a proper correction.

Our E.C. then informed us that he had delivered the donation given by this body to Mrs. Daggett and that she wished to thank the Klan from the abundance of her heart. The result of this worthy donation brought forth the application of a man we have been working on for some time.

The treasurer's report left us with a balance of $239.37.

Motion made and passed that E. C. Fields bear the responsibility of having the robes cleaned for the sum of fifty cents each, money to be drawn from the treasury to pay for same. . . .

Next in discussion came the School Board and their progression and Klansman Eberhard imparted this information in full. His talk brought forth the fact that the other side had won J. A. Russell over and that the Board would have another election in the near future and reelect Mrs. Newlin. Following this announcement a motion was made and passed that our E.C. appoint a comm. to wait on Mr. Russell and convince him that he could not possibly gain anything by going contrary to his own convictions.

Meeting closed in short at a very late hour.

MAY 1, 1923

The La Grande klavern focused on chapter business on this date. Except for its persistent anti-Catholicism the organization appeared to be a conventional fraternal order.

. . . No. of Klansmen present: Ninety-three. . . .

No. of new applications read: Eight. . . .

The comm. who performed the operation on Mr. Russell regarding the reelection of Mrs. Newlin were all absent and the report was laid over until the following meeting.

Motion made and passed that the kligrapp's salary be raised from twenty-five dollars to fifty dollars a month.

Motion made and passed [that] the kligrapp rent an office and furnish same according to his own judgment.

Recommendations were made as follows: that the Klan keep the safety deposit box at the U.S. Bank and that all valuable papers be kept in Klansman Ben Decious's safe.

Klansman C. W. Bunting, chairman of the By-Laws Comm., presented same at the last klonklave and they were read and passed before that respective body.

Klansmen appointed on comm. to nominate officers are as follows: Klansman Cochran, chairman; Klansman Rev. O. W. Jones; and Klansman Harry Williams.

Motion made and passed that Klansman Earl Silvis's hospital bill amounting to the sum of sixty dollars be paid out of the treasury.

Motion made and passed that one thousand cards which give the issue of the Klan relative to the Roman Empire be printed and given to all Klansmen to use as they see fit.

In regard to the donation that the Salvation Army ask this Klan to give them, it was suggested that Capt. Buchanan be asked to place one of the iron kettles in our klavern, thus giving all Klansmen the privilege of donating to the fund as they feel able to give.

There were no Klansmen reported sick or in need of financial asst.

Motion made and passed that the kligrapp write a letter to Atlanta asking for permission to hold our open air nat. ceremony, explaining the details in full and asking that they wire the answer upon receipt of letter.

Announcement was then made that our regular nat. ceremony would be held on the next meeting night, Tuesday, May 8th.

Meetings from this date until further notice shall be called at 8 P.M. instead of 7:30 P.M.

Meeting closed in short form.

MAY 8, 1923

Since Governor Walter Pierce was an Island City native and an honorary Klansman who had received Klan political support, klavern leaders worked for patronage appointments to the new state administration. Pierce appointed La Grande Klansman Ed Reynolds to the State Fair Board in March. The local Klan also promoted the prospects of Robert Hugh Baldock in the state Highway Department and made a special effort to recruit other bureau employees as well.

Note the standards klavern leaders employed when vetoing eight recruits. The rejects included retired dentist Dr. R. J. Ruckman, as well as a retail merchant, soldier, train conductor, railroad brakeman, and Union Pacific employee.

Among the nominees for the coming year's offices was Douglas J. Kline, a railroad clerk who had applied for Klan membership earlier in the year, and insurance agent Lyman W. Weeks.

. . . No. of Klansmen present: Eighty-nine.

Opening ceremony held with song service.

Klansman Osbourn, klokard of the Pendleton Klan, was a visitor in our klavern and he put on the work of that office during the nat. ceremony.

A special vote was taken on the applications of W. C. Crews and J. N. Bishop of the State Highway Dept. and they were duly requested to report for nat. along with the other class.

Klansman Ray Fleeman of Lewiston, Idaho, who took only the oath in that respective city, was given the work along with the other candidates. Klansman Fleeman is employed as a clerk in the Foley Hotel. Klansmen, drop in and make this Klansman welcome to our midst.

No. of new applications read: Six. . . .

Total No. of applications on hand in the kligrapp's office: Eighty-six.

The following men were rejected by the Board of Klokans and by a vote of the klonklave assembled: Howard Grove, part Indian; Roy Clapp, for bankruptcy too many times; William Snell, for living with a woman not officially his wife; Dr. R. J. Ruckman, for selfish motives; Morris Chinlund, bad reputation; Avery Harrison, for being involved in unlawful proceedings regarding an estate; Alonzo Dunn, character and affiliations questioned; Frank Childers, too fond of moonshine. These men were duly notified in a most pleasing manner for we bear no malice with the request that at the expiration of one year, should they so desire, they may re-petition for citizenship in this order. The man who was part Indian was not requested to re-petition for membership in this order.

Klansman Harry Williams, sub. as chairman of nominating, read the following names nominated by the comm. to be the officers of Klan. No. 14, Realm of Oregon, for the coming year:

Exalted Cyclops, Rev. O. W. Jones
Klaliff, W. K. Gilbert

Klokard, Alfred J. Johnson, now acting as klaliff

Klansman Dallas Green was nominated to retain his office as kludd of
the Klan.

Kligrapp H. R. Fosner to retain his office.

Klabee, Dr. J. L. McPherson, our exalted cyclops.

Kladd, Klansman C. H. Tull

Klarogo, Klansman Douglas Kline

Klexter, Klansman Gar Holm

Klokan Chief, L. W. Weeks

Klokan, Dexter McIlroy

Klokan, C. W. Bunting

Our E.C. then informed us that according to an announcement made at
the meeting held previous, the election would take place at the next regular
meeting of this Klan. This gives all Klansmen plenty of time during the
week to nominate any man for office that they so desire. The ballots with
the names of the nominees are at hand, leaving a space for other men who
may be nominated from the floor or turned in to the chairman of the
committee.

A motion was then made and passed that the report of the Nominating
Comm. be accepted.

Naturalization ceremony was held in full and twenty-five loyal citizens
took the oath of allegiance and are now Klansmen among us. Welcome to
our city.

Klansman E. C. Fields then requested that all Klansmen write their
names in their helmets and thus avoid getting them mixed up.

Announcement was then made to the effect that Klansman Helvey was
badly in need of an empty five-room house and the E.C. requested that
any Klansman knowing of same report to either him or Klansman Helvey.
Klansmen, bring your griefs before this body and let us help you with your
many conflicting troubles. That is Klannishness[—]helping each other[—]
so don't be bashful if you have got something on your chest that is causing
a wrinkle on your brow. Tell it to us and we will try and help you iron out
the high spots.

Our E.C. then announced that the old officers would give a feed in
honor of the newly elected officers, Klansmen all included, to eat and
pay homage to the brave warriors who so nobly consented to bear the
responsibilities of the coming year.

A motion was then made and passed that the check amt. to the sum of sixty dollars which was drawn to pay the hospital bill of Klansman Silvis be taken to him early the next morning.

Motion made and passed that a comm. of three men be appointed to provide a way to create a sinking fund for this Klan that will be used to defray the expenses of Klansmen who are sick or in need of financial assistance. This comm. is as follows: Klansmen Byers, Woodell, and K. Williams. Included in this motion was the suggestion that the kligrapp write to H.D.Q. at Portland relative to the Klan Komfort Fund. . . .

Treasurer's report left us with a balance of $388.91

After hearing a splendid report on promoting Klansman Baldock to the position of State Highway Engineer this Klan went on record as heartedly favoring this plan to the extent that we begin an active campaign in behalf of Klansman Baldock. Letters are to be sent to the governor and State Highway Comm[issioner] and to all the larger Klans in the state of Oregon. Klansmen, don't forget this. Let's make it a personal issue and see that we have a 100 percent American at the head of this very important position. . . .

MAY 15, 1923

As applications continued to mount, the La Grande chapter attempted to sustain organizational admission standards. The rejected Harold Taal was a grocery clerk. C. E. Short, the subject of perpetual banishment from the order and an alleged ally of local Catholics in a rumored candidacy for the city school board, was the manager of the J. C. Penney store.

The reports of a financial arrangement in Atlanta related to the disbursement of compensation to Klan founder Col. William Joseph Simmons following the appointment of Hiram Wesley Evans as imperial wizard.

Klansmen promoted the Pendleton street parade and festival of the Dokkies, because the organization was the fun order of the Knights of Pythias, a fraternal organization the KKK acknowledged as compatible with its interests.[26]

. . . No. of Klansmen present: 123.

Opening ceremony held by singing of "America"

No. of new applications read: Seven.

Klansman Geo. Cochran then gave the report of the Grievance Board relative to the application of Harold Taal. A vote was then taken by the klonklave assembled and he was turned down by four [dissenting] votes and the application tabled for another period of time.

Minutes of last meeting read and approved.

Our E.C. then announced that we would now have the election of officers. There were no other nominees besides those named by the Nom[inating] Comm. and Klansman Williams made a motion that the exalted cyclops have the kligrapp declare [a] unanimous ballot, which was done in regular order and the men thus nominated were duly elected to office.

Visitors in our klavern are as follows:

E. Cyclops Caul of Baker; kligrapp, klokard of Baker; Klansman J. E. Turpin of Bend, Ore.; Klansman J. F. Hutchinson of Union; Klansman Andrews of Imbler; Klansman Evans of Baker; and Klansman Campbell of the Roseburg Klan, who is now employed at the Union Trail Garage. . . .

Motion made and passed that Klansman C. E. Short and Klansman W. G. Sawyer be banished forever from the Knights of the K.K.K.

The comm. who waited on Mr. Russell relative to him casting an affirmative vote that would reelect Mrs. Newlin reported that Mr. Russell told them that he would endeavor to keep away from the school meetings and I don't think he lied for he is now in Sumpter and I think he intends to stay there for a while.

An announcement was then made to the effect that the Catholics were going to put C. E. Short up for one of our school directors at the next election. We are hoping that he will be short.

Another announcement was then made to the effect that Klansman Clyde Webb had accepted the holy bonds of matrimony and departed on the evening train for the land of peace and plenty.

The school election this year will be held on the eighteenth day of June from the hours of 1 P.M. 'til 8 P.M. Qualifications to vote at this election are as follows: you must be capable of being a legal voter, having resided in the state six months previous to the election and in the county at least thirty days. Klansman Cochran has promised to have the petitions of the men we will back at hand in the very near future and wherever possible to elect a 100 percent man, we are going to do.

Klansman C. S. Shultz then gave a report on the committee who has been getting all the dope relative to the possibilities of building a new school house down on East Adams Ave. and things are looking brighter this year than ever before.

Klansman E. C. Fields then gave a very spirited talk in behalf of the Holm Grocery Store, urging that all Klansmen begin a most rigid practice of Klannishness, thus eliminating the possibility of this store having to make another assignment.

A communication from Gifford read to the effect that the recent disbursements at Atlanta are now settled to the pleasure of all concerned and that from now on harmony would reign supreme at H.D.Q.

It was then announced that the Dokkies would have a grand blowout in the city of Pendleton on May the 18th.

After the feed the old dishpan was passed around and we realized the sum of $21.64, which will go to help pay for same.

A motion was then made and passed that a cross be burnt on the hill next Saturday evening and volunteers were called for to do the job. It was then suggested that after this it would be a good plan for the E.C. to appoint a silent man giving him power to act at any time he may see fit to place a cross upon the hill.

A motion was then made and passed that a housing comm. be appointed to supply room for our rapidly growing Klan.

The comm. from Baker and La Grande reporting on the open air nat. ceremony stated that the ceremony would take place on the 25th of July at 8 P.M. All Klansmen are urged to have a robe for this occasion. They also stated that a certain number of naturalized Klansmen would be the candidates, thus eliminating the chance of any exposure on the part of candidates as we first planned.

Our E.C. then suggested that we endeavor to make a special drive for members during the next two months.

Motion made and passed that Rev. Jones make a speech on the merits of the Klan at Imbler, Ore. about three weeks from tonight.

Klansman Lindsay then announced that the Klan Orchestra would back us up when we stage our grand open air ceremony.

Klansman Williams then announced that Mr. Paign, who runs the restaurant at Imbler, Ore., was a 100 percent man.

Motion made to adjourn at a very late hour.

MAY 22, 1923

The campaign in behalf of Robert Baldock appeared to be bringing results. Later in the year, Governor Pierce appointed Baldock as district engineer for the state Highway Commission. In 1932 he moved on to the post of Oregon chief highway engineer. The section of Interstate 5 running between Portland and Salem subsequently became known as the "Baldock Freeway."[27]

. . . No. of Klansmen present: Sixty-three.

The application of W. F. Cain was voted on and passed before the assembly and he was naturalized with those notified to appear.

The application of Rev. [E. J.] Gillestrap was held over owing to the fact that he was not recorded as being a resident of this province for a year previous to the date the application was presented.

Owing to the fact that Mr. Keinle of the E. O. Music Co. is intending to leave in the very near future, his application was accepted on the night of presentment and he was called to appear for naturalization.

Motion made and passed that the quota amounting to the sum of $2.50 for the Old Oregon Trail Pageant be paid through the regular channels.

One communication was read from Walter Pierce regarding the appointment of Mr. Baldock for State Highway Engineer and all conditions look very favorably toward that end.

An announcement from Baker read to the effect that the Fiethian Furniture Co., which is 100 percent, would ship furniture to any Klansman and pay the freight on same.

Next came Hessler's report on the Housing Comm. composed of the following men: Melville, Green, Westenhaver, Richardson, and Hessler.

After this report, which was given in detail together with a set of plans showing the changes to be made, a motion was made and passed that the Klan accept the lease and complete the plans as presented by the Building Committee.

Naturalization ceremony was held in full and eighteen men became Knights of the Invisible Empire.

Mr. Cochran then announced that the Board of Directors would hold a meeting tomorrow afternoon in his office for the purpose of lining up the men we are going to back up in the school election.

Discussion was then held relative to the trip to Baker and all Klansmen with cars and those without were requested to meet at the Club Cigar Store at about 6:30 P.M.

Motion made and passed that the Housing Comm. arrange to have a dance at our new hall at the time of the grand opening.

Motion made and passed that we hold another nat. ceremony next Tuesday night for the benefit of some candidates who are going to leave.

Klansman Bennett from the Walla Walla Klan was a visitor in our klavern and made a very nice talk. . . .

The treasurer's report left us with a balance of approximately $815.83 now on hand in the treasure.

Meeting closed in short form at a very late hour.

MAY 29, 1923

Five members were inducted into the secret order at this meeting, including Eugene minister E. J. Gillestrap, as well as a railroad fireman, locomotive engineer, creamery proprietor, and auto mechanic. As an expanding Klan confidently made plans for a larger meeting hall, klavern leaders continued to focus on the order's special relationship with Governor Walter Pierce and on its endorsement of two Klansmen for places on the city school board.

No. of Klansmen present: Seventy-five.

Opening ceremony held in full by singing one verse of "America"

Visitors in our klavern are as follows: Klansman McFarland of Yakima, Wash. Prov. Klan, Klansman McDonald of [T]he Dalles Prov. Klan, Klansman Cox of the Walla Walla Klan.

No. of new applications read: Eleven. . . .

Total No. of applications now on hand in kligrapp's office: Ninety-nine.

Naturalization ceremony was held in full. . . .

. . . A motion was then made and passed that warrants be drawn on the treas. as the work of construction progressed on the Rex Hall but not to exceed the sum of $540, the estimate[d] cost.

A motion was then made and passed that a Finance Committee be appointed to examine all bills coming in or going out of this Klan. This comm. will be appointed by the E.C. some time during the week. . . .

Klansman Cochran then submitted in full detail the report of the Nom[inating] Comm. appointed to nominate two school directors who we are going to back in the school election to be held June 18, 1923. The men nominated are as follows: Klansman L. W. Weeks and Klansman R. P. Landis.

A motion was then made and passed that the report of the Nominating Committee be accepted and that L. W. Weeks and Dr. R. P. Landis will be our candidates for directors on the School Board.

One communication from Fred L. Gifford, grand dragon, Realm of Oregon, read to the effect that he was on his way to Washington, D.C.

to attend a meeting of the grand dragons held for the purpose of outlining the national plans and program of the Knights of the Ku Klux Klan for the coming year. Immediately upon his return he will call a convention of the delegates elected by their respective Klans, at which time he will present the national program of the Imperial Palace and elect the Realm officers to form the State Klorero. Klansman Cochran was then duly appointed to be our representative at that meeting.

A motion was then made and passed that a comm. be appointed to get out and petition for names in behalf of our nominees for school directors, namely L. W. Weeks and Dr. R. P. Landis. The comm. appointed are as follows: C. W. Bunting, W. K. Gilbert, and G. H. Glass.

A motion was then made and passed that the Baker Klan be notified that our opening dance announced for next Saturday night would be postponed until a later date.

An announcement was then made to the effect that our governor would be at his farm the first of the coming week, and the kligrapp was duly instructed to invite him to attend our next regular meeting, at which time we would have a feed and invite the Baker and Pendleton Klans respectively.

A motion was then made and passed that after this date the fee of ten dollars must accompany the application when presented to this Klan.

Also, a motion was made and passed that applicants who have been passed by this Klan be notified only twice to appear for nat. The notices are to give the future dates when these men can be nat., thus eliminating the work in the kligrapp's office.

The kligrapp was then requested by the exalted cyclops to notify as many Klans as he deems necessary to the effect that Klansman W. H. Stockwell of this Klan was not a member in good standing, owing to the fact that he took advantage of his title for personal gain, thus breaking the oath as prescribed in the constitution of this order.

A motion was then made and passed that all Klansmen must show their cards both at the outer door and to the night hawk who takes the password in klonklave assembled.

A motion was then made and passed that all correspondence of any importance or of personal nature going from the kligrapp's office first be read in klonklave assembled and passed by that body. . . .

General discussion was then held relative to Dr. Landis and his dismissal from the O.W. as their company doctor, but owing to the lateness of the hour the matter was laid over to the next meeting, at which time some final action would be taken. . . .

JUNE 5, 1923

The documentation of dentist E. O. Willson as a visiting Klansman from Elgin is significant in light of the legal difficulties he subsequently would experience.

A bland reference to Atlanta's investigation of Oregon Grand Dragon Gifford's Klan Komfort Fund indicates controversy over the program.

Dr. Landis's dismissal as railroad physician touched a nerve among lodge brothers who believed that Union Pacific's Catholic managers discriminated against Protestant employees. So did the dismissal of a Klansman from a La Grande department store. The Klan pictured economic solidarity and networking as one of its prime functions and continually portrayed Roman Catholics as the economic adversary.

Patronage played an important role in the implementation of Klannishness. Note the case of La Grande's William B. Peare, a three-term member of the State Board of Optometry. Peare was the son of Union County Republican Committee Chair Jack Peare, an Irish Catholic. The klavern supported Peare's replacement by George S. Birnie, a La Grande jeweler and optometrist whose store carried the *Western American*. Birnie was ineligible for Klan membership because he was Canadian-born.

Klansman and political insider George Cochran also kept the chapter informed about the patronage opportunities arising from Governor Pierce's administration in Salem. Pierce had signed a compromise graduated income tax law in February. Under legislation that took effect in May 1923, he sanctioned creation of the state Tax Supervisory and Conservation Commission. The governor now had the power to select three officials from each county to set tax levies. Significantly, Pierce entered the La Grande klavern for his second visit just after discussion turned to gubernatorial appointments. The governor had arrived by train late the previous evening.[28]

Klansmen present: 110.

Visitors from the following Klans were present at our klonklave: Klansm[e]n Knight, E. O. Willson, Breadshears, and Klansman Grey, Elgin Klan; Klansman Cunliffe of Baker; and Klansman Curney of Pendleton. . . .

The committee investigating the Klan Komfort account reported that it was being tested as to validity by the officials in Atlanta.

Dr. R. P. Landis then gave a full account of why he was dismissed from being the local railroad physician, the cause being very unjust, and as we naturally expected, there was a Catholic in the woodpile. . . .

Klansman Hessler then reported that we would have a dance in our new hall next Saturday night and it was suggested that Baker and Pendleton be invited to attend the gala occasion.

Klansman Bunting then reported that Klansman Brandt had been dismissed from the N. K. West store on account of his affiliations with our organization.

Klansman Cochran then made a very earnest appeal in behalf of our candidates for school directors and urged every man to do his utmost to put them over.

It was then reported that Little Willie Peare, who at present is state examiner on the Board of Optometry, stands a good chance of losing this position in favor of our friend, G. S. Birnie.

Chief among the topics of discussion was the Tax Commission and the men to be appointed on that board. This law went into effect on the twenty-fourth day of May and it is one of the most important bills put through our last legislature, as it gives three men in each county the sole power to ascertain the amount of tax money to be spent for our various facilities. Fur further information relative to this bill I will recommend you to Klansman Cochran.

Just as the kligrapp had finished reading a letter from our Gov. that it would be impossible for him to attend our meeting, the door opened and in he walked. That was the hour of great rejoicing.

It was then suggested that the kligrapp notify the Enterprise, Wallowa, and Lostine Klans that O. W. Jones would be glad to make a speech on the merits of the Klan whenever they could make the necessary arrangements. Motion made and passed that we send the Boise exalted cyclops a special invitation to attend the open air ceremony and deliver the speech entitled "The Delivery of the Robe."

Klansman Williams, chairman, then gave a complete report of the House Committee which was accepted by the klonklave assembled.

Klansman Cochran has volunteered to make an investigation of lodge fixtures while in Portland and report same to the House Comm.

Motion made and passed that an invitation be sent to our grand dragon to attend our open air initiation ceremony.

Motion made and passed that the House Comm. be instructed to arrange for some place whereby people can come and engage our hall.

Meeting closed at a very late hour.

JUNE 12, 1923

Lodge business matters often played a large role in the recorded proceedings of the La Grande klavern. Yet like most Klans of the 1920s, the chapter placed great importance on social issues, such as management of the public schools. Consequently, the upcoming school board election continued to hold vital interest.

Meeting opened by singing Klan song.

Klansmen present: Seventy-four. . . .

Klansman Williams of the House Comm. made a report in full and requested the following: that the Klan give its approval or rejection of secondhand stove purchased for the sum of fifty dollars and that the House Comm. be allowed the sum of one thousand dollars with which to furnish our hall.

A motion was made and passed that the bill for the stove be allowed and that the sum of one thousand dollars be raised by issuing 6 percent bearing notes of interest, the minimum sum being ten dollars, and the notes extending for a period of not more than two years, and that they be paid off in numerical rotation.

A motion was made and passed that the House Comm. be given authority to spend this one thousand dollars for purchase of lodge fixtures and repairs.

Klansman Hessler of the Dance Comm. reported a net profit from the dance given Sat., June 10 of $7.40.

Nat. ceremony was held in full and twelve men became Knights of the Invisible Empire.

Motion made and passed that we continue to call this hall the Rex.

General discussion of the evening was the election of our school direc[tor]. Motion made and passed that separate tickets be printed for our candidates, giving the reason why they should be elected and these be placed under every door in town on Sunday, June 17. The committee appointed to frame these cards are as follows: Klansmen Williams, Eberhard, and Westenhaver.

Motion made and passed that the kligrapp be authorized to mail every

Klansman in the district an election notice which shall be returned to the kligrapp immediately after he has voted.

Meeting adjourned at the hour of 12 P.M.

JUNE 19, 1923

Minutes for this date are preceded by the written response of Boise's exalted cyclops to La Grande's invitation to participate in the July open-air naturalization.

The June 18 school board election brought a solid victory for La Grande knights. As turnout exceeded that of previous school contests by 50 percent, Klan candidates Landis and Weeks gathered a combined 3–1 plurality over their rivals. The two joined former state senator Colon Eberhard to form a KKK majority on the five-person board.

Klan leaders made plans to cancel their July 3 meeting so that members could attend President Warren G. Harding's dedication of the Oregon Trail at Meacham, a town at the crest of the Blue Mountains halfway between La Grande and Pendleton. The event marked the eightieth anniversary of white settlement in the region.

Klavern petitions for the appointment of James E. Reynolds to the Union County Tax Supervisory and Conservation Commission resulted in success when Governor Pierce named the distinguished Klansman county tax supervisor in July and chair of the tax commission in August. But three months after statewide commissioners attended their first meeting in September, the Oregon Supreme Court ruled that the law that had created the bodies was unconstitutional.

North Powder, the target of Klan organizing, is twenty-four miles southeast of La Grande.

It is unclear whether the installment of "The Main Drag" mentioned by the kligrapp was not included in the collection of minutes or was subsequently lost.[29]

Number of Klansmen present: 112.

Opening ceremony held by singing one verse of "America."

Klansman Graham of Baker Klan No. 13 was a visitor in our klavern. . . .

No. of new applications read: Four. . . .

Our E.C. then appointed the following Klansmen to meet with the new school board and present to them the desires of this Klan: Klansmen Bunting, Cochran, and Leffel. . . .

We were then informed by our E.C. that the new officers would be duly installed the first klonklave held in the month of July.

Discussion was then held relative to having the Ladies of the Invisible Empire hold their meetings on the same night as ours. Following this discussion a motion was made to the effect that the small hall be kept vacant on the night that this Klan meets.

A motion was then made and passed that we continue to have our dances every Saturday night unless otherwise directed by klonklave assembled or until such a time as it is rented or leased to some responsible party.

Owing to the fact that Tuesday, July third, is the date set for the beginning of the Old Oregon Trail Pageant, there will be no meeting of this Klan but the following Tuesday we will assemble in our regular order.

Klansman Ed Reynolds of La Grande, Ore. and Klansman H. H. Huron of Imbler, Oregon are the men recommended by the committee and pledged by this Klan for representatives on the Tax Commission.

A motion was then made and passed that Klansmen Gilbert, Leffel, and Bunting circulate a petition in behalf of Klansman Reynolds for the appointment of Tax. Comm[i]s[sione]r and that a likewise petition in behalf of H. H. Huron be circulated in the city of Imbler.

A motion was then made and passed that the kligrapp send in the names of the two Klansmen recommended together with the petitions to our governor, Walter M. Pierce, for his approval or disapproval.

Klansman Graham, who resides in North Powder, gave a short talk in which he stated that both the Baker and the La Grande Klans were neglecting the city of North Powder and recommended that we get busy and get some more Klansmen from that place.

After some discussion regarding our New Game Comm[ission] and how they lined up we had a short and spirited speech from our newly elected school director, Mr. L. W. Weeks.

A motion was then made and passed that the outgoing officers be permitted to draw on the treasure for the purpose of giving a feed to all Klansmen and their newly elected brothers. This feed will take place on the tenth of July.

After this discussion Dr. R. P. Landis, our other elected director, appeared on the scene and in a very pleasing manner he told us of his great appreciation in behalf of the La Grande Klan No. 14.

After the reading of "The Main Drag," the E.C. suggested that the board hold a meeting in the early part of the week to discuss some very important issues.

Motion made to adjourn at the hour of 11 P.M.

JUNE 26, 1923

This relatively brief meeting dealt with organizational matters and a report on the new school board.

> Officers present: 100%
> Klansmen present: 103. . . .
> Number of new applications read: Five. . . .
> The application of M. G. Berry, read in the klavern April 4, 1923, is still held in the kligrapp's office for further investigation. The application of Warren H. Primm has been turned down by the Board of Klokans.
> Total number of applications on hand in kligrapp's office: Ninety-four.
> After the reading of the applications Klansman J. E. Reynolds gave a report of the last school director's meeting and gave the reasons for the recommendations of paying certain of our teachers higher salary than was paid previous.
> Our E.C. then appointed the two members of this Klan who reside in North Powder to locate a place in that town where we can give a lecture on the merits of the Ku Klux Klan. . . .
> Nat. ceremony was held in full and twelve Klansmen were made Knights of the Invisible Empire. . . .
> Motion made and passed that we have no more initiation ceremonies until July 25, 1923. . . .
> Meeting closed in short form at the hour of 11:15.

JULY 10, 1923

Klansmen held no meeting on July 3 so that members could attend President Warren Harding's dedication of the Old Oregon Trail Pageant in nearby Meacham, a celebration that occurred one month before Harding's death by heart attack. The *Sunday Oregonian* stated that KKK placards appeared at the Meacham event and that knights distributed free coffee beneath one. Yet another article contained criticism of Governor Pierce for allegedly attempting to overshadow the state's distinguished visitor. Pierce had "insisted on introducing

everyone to the president," asserted the *Oregonian*, until the crowd had demanded he "'shut up' and 'sit down.'" The news story reported that Harding
privately had confided that Pierce's introductions were designed to elevate the
governor's own political standing. An *Oregonian* editorial subsequently chastised state Democrats for expecting politicians like Pierce to "change life long
habit on the instant."

Criticism of Pierce provided La Grande Kligrapp Harold Fosner with the opportunity to convey the secret order's support of the governor (see the frontispiece). Typed on official klavern stationery on July 11, 1923, Fosner's letter
blamed Pierce's bad press on partisan opponents—Oregon Republican National
Committeeman Ralph E. Williams, who had defeated a Klan-endorsed candidate for his post in 1922, and state Republican Chair Walter L. Tooze, Jr., the
chief opponent of the governor's tax program. Fosner boasted that the La
Grande Klan recently had elected Knights Dr. R. P. Landis and L. W. Weeks as
city school commissioners. But the purpose of the letter was to ask the governor
to support La Grande Klansmen Ed Reynolds and H. H. Huron as the klavern's
nominees for the new tax commission. Pierce responded to Fosner with a note
on July 13 acknowledging that he was "glad to know that my real friends still
believe in me."[30]

The July 10 Klan meeting reflected the klavern's interest in patronage and
local politics. Newly elected exalted cyclops O. W. Jones was the delegate to the
Portland klorero, or convention of the Oregon Realm, called by Fred Gifford
after the state Klan leader's return from a May meeting of grand dragons in
Washington, D.C.

Before falling out of favor with the Pendleton Klan, Republican James H.
Gwinn had received organizational support for an unsuccessful attempt to unseat Representative Nicholas Sinnott in the 1922 primary.

Both the Society of the Sisters of the Holy Names of Jesus and Mary in
Oregon and Hill Military Academy filed suit in U.S. District Court in June
1923 to seek an injunction restraining enforcement of the Oregon school bill,
scheduled to go into effect in 1926.

The reference to Klan adversary Fred Meyers seems to relate to traffic violations.[31]

Opening ceremony held by singing one verse of "America."
Number of Klansmen present: Ninety-seven. . . .
Number of new applications read: Eight.
Our E.C. then announced that we could get the Old Baptist Church at

North Powder, Ore., where we plan to have Klansman Jones speak in the very near future.

Klansman Cochran, chairman of the Grievance Comm., reported that that body had rendered a new decision in the case of Avery Harrison, who was turned down by this order some time ago, and that they desired to have his application reinstated in good faith and go through the regular channel prescribed in our constitution. . . .

Klansman Cochran then suggested that we circulate petitions in behalf of Klansman Ed Reynolds and Klansman Huron, whom we desire to see appointed on the Tax Board to be appointed by our governor in the very near future, and the kligrapp promised to get busy at this on the following day. Klansman Cochran also stated that the comm. working in connection with the school board recommended Klansman Harry Williams first choice for school clerk and Klansman Albert second choice.

Following this report Klansman O. W. Jones, our delegate to the [klorero] meeting, gave a report in full regarding the issues of that meeting.

Mr. Bob St. Claire, kligrapp of the Pendleton Klan and grand titan of Province No. 6, Realm of Oregon, who came to install our new officers, conducted this ceremony in a very pleasing manner and our newly elected officers take their worthy stations from this date.

A motion was then made and passed that the robe belonging to our past exalted cyclops, Dr. J. L. McPherson, be purchased by the Klan, who will retain possession of same for all future e. cyclops[es].

A communication from the Pendleton Klan read to the effect after this date please be advised that the following Klansmen have been suspended until charges against them had been investigated: Klansman J. H. Gwinn, Klansman C. H. Conroy, and Klansman D. B. Snider.

Comm[unication] from the grand dragon gave this Klan the authority to nat. all Klansmen reported to him who had lived in this jurisdiction for less than the period of one year.

A local comm. from Klansmen Decious and Slutz, proprietors of the New Sommer Grille, read to the effect that they were now duly opened for business and that they would be glad to meet their fellow Klansmen at that place of business. Their motto is we strive to please.

After the reading of these communications we held a general discussion relative to the president of Hill Military Academy, who has gone to court to test the validity of our school bill. It was suggested that the kligrapp keep in touch with the progress of this issue.

Following this we closed our meeting as directed in our ritual and entered the dining room there to partake of a most delightful and cooling repast.

We also discussed the fact that Mr. Fred Meyers had been pinched twelve times and up to date had not had to pay any fine whatsoever. A comm. was then appointed to investigate these rumors and ascertain why this worthy gentleman should go free when our past E.C. was forced to decorate the mahogany.

JULY 17, 1923

La Grande Klansmen continued to show their frustration in dealing with Catholic banker Frederick Meyers.

The "rape" case discussed in the klavern may have concerned former La Grande Police Chief Roy Flexer, who was arrested in Portland five days before the meeting for transporting a woman across state lines for immoral purposes, a violation of the federal Mann Act. Flexer claimed that after resigning his La Grande post in August 1922, he left his wife and children to accompany a married woman with whom he was infatuated on auto trips across the country. The one-time law enforcement official received a fifteen-month sentence from a federal court in October 1923.

The meeting also brought discussion of an automobile crash in nearby Union in which a fifteen-year-old girl was killed when a drunken driver lost control of the Dodge roadster in which she was riding. The *La Grande Evening Observer* portrayed a community "plunged into deep gloom over the sudden death" of the young victim. A twenty-one-year-old man was charged with manslaughter and driving while intoxicated and received a one-year prison sentence after prosecution by Deputy District Attorneys and Klansmen Colon Eberhard and George Cochran. In December 1924, however, the Union County district attorney dismissed all charges against the defendant because he had not received a speedy trial.

Further discussion concerned the growing enmity between *Western American* editor Lem Dever and Governor Pierce over Klan-related patronage.[32]

Opening ceremony held in full.

Number of Klansmen present: Sixty-eight. . . .

The Comm. reporting on the charges referred against Fred Meyers announced that the facts presented some time ago were very erroneous.

A motion was then made and passed that each member be mailed a complete outline of just what to do and where to go on the night we are to hold the big open air nat. ceremony.

Suggestions were made as follows: that the kligrapp be instructed to write for the new password and that Klansman O. S. Humphreys have complete charge of the Fiery Cross Committee for next Wednesday night.

Discussion in our klavern was held relative to two cases recently committed: one rape case and one case of a man driving a car while under the influence of liquor which resulted in the death of an innocent party.

The klavern in general also took a rap at the *Western American* for its various decrees against our governor, and a motion was made and passed that the kligrapp be instructed to write a letter to the editor embodying the sentiments of this Klan relative to his many editorials which have not met with our approval.

Closing ceremony held in full.

JULY 24, 1923

As the klavern prepared for the next evening's open-air naturalization ceremony, this brief meeting dealt with financial matters.

Opening ceremony held in full.
Klansmen present: Seventy-four. . . .
A motion was made and passed that a committee of one be appointed to collect in all the $10 pledges that were subscribed to the building fund, Mr. Roy Currey being appointed to act on this committee. . . .

JULY 31, 1923

The *La Grande Evening Observer* reported that several thousand spectators watched some 325 white-robed and masked Klansmen parade through the city's business district on July 25. Led by the municipal band and robed horsemen carrying the American flag and a lit cross, the evening procession moved on to a filled grandstand at the county fairground where Klan leaders lectured on patriotism and citizenship. The ceremony climaxed with the apparent initiation of seventy-five new members, although the following minutes indicate the real number. Klan festivities coincided with the annual reunion of the Union County pioneers earlier in the day.

The minutes for this date were handwritten instead of typed as a substitute filled in for Kligrapp Fosner.[33]

> Opening ceremony held in full.
> Number of Klansmen present: Seventy-one. . . .
> Four new applications for membership were read. . . .
> Was moved and passed that we hold no more naturalization ceremonies until the first meeting in September.
> Eighteen Klansmen who were admitted into the order on July 25th were given the password and secret signs of the klavern. . . .

AUGUST 7, 1923

The *La Grande Evening Observer* reported that five hundred Klansmen participated in the much-anticipated parade organized by the Baker klavern.

La Grande delegates to the KKK province convention were railroad accountant and Klokard Alfred J. Johnson, city school board member and former railroad physician Dr. R. P. Landis, Deputy Sheriff and Klokan Dexter McIlroy, and insurance salesman Claude L. Beery. The provincial assembly followed a national conference of Klan leaders in Asheville, North Carolina.

As Kligrapp Fosner prepared to give up his duties as chapter secretary, auto salesman C. H. Tull acted in his place.[34]

> . . . Klansmen present: Seventy.
> Klansman John Allen was reported sick at his home and Klansman
> L. C. Henderson was reported confined at the local hospital.
> An announcement was made of the open air nat. ceremony to be held in Baker Wednesday night, August 15th, and Klansmen Holm, Brandt, and Silvis were appointed on a comm. to secure conveyance for all to go to Baker.
> Our exalted cyclops then announced that the first province convention No. 6 would convene in this hall at 1 P.M., August 8th.
> Motion made and passed that the kligrapp send out notices to all the Klansmen relative to the open air ceremony in Baker, Oregon.
> Delegates appointed to attend the province convention from this Klan are as follows: Klansmen Johnson, Landis, McIlroy, and Beery.
> Motion made and passed that Kligrapp Fosner's resignation be tabled until a later date.

Moved and passed that the kligrapp move his office from the Roach Building to the Rex Hall and after the fifteenth of this month, your kligrapp will occupy one of the rooms in this hall.

Moved and seconded that we adjourn.

AUGUST 14, 1923

"The Office Cat" was a local male-oriented gossip and humor column that frequently appeared in the *La Grande Evening Observer*. Kligrapp Fosner, who resumed his duties at this date, had included a supplement called "The Office Cat on the Main Drag" in the March 27 minutes. Yet the reference in this segment is not clear.

Since 1919 the La Grande city water system had experienced frequent shortages and had gone through a particularly bad summer in 1922. Klan interest in the subject reflected the particular concerns of Dr. Landis but also demonstrated the secret order's commitment to civic affairs.

Although the Klan expressed worries about the survival of the local Red Cross and YMCA, it was compelled to acknowledge that its adversaries played important roles in the management of both organizations. Bruce Dennis and Jack Peare served as officials of the Red Cross, while Dennis, former Klansman C. E. Short, and Frederick Meyers sat with Klansman George Cochran on the Y's board of directors.[35]

. . . Four Klansmen nat. at our open air ceremony were given the secret work.

Number of new applications reads: Three. . . .

Our exalted cyclops then requested that the kligrapp write to the Boise Klan asking for recommendations for the local manager of the Woolworth store who has his application in this Klan.

After the reading of "The Office Cat" Klansman Harry Williams, chairman of the House Comm., gave a very good report relative to its rental, asking that the members who had failed to pay their notes please do so at the earliest possible moment, as we need the funds to complete the hall, making it in condition to rent.

It is now rumored that City Manager Hayes will tender his resignation in the very near future.

After a lengthy discussion of the conditions of our local water system a comm. of three men were appointed to attend the meeting held for this purpose in the City Hall, Wednesday, Aug. 15.

The following motions were made and the comm. to be appointed at the next meeting:

That a 100% executive be appointed for our local Red Cross.

That we investigate the various tax budgets when submitted by the Tax Commission.

That we take an active interest in the progress of the local YMCA relative to its future in this community.

Meeting closed in short form at an early hour.

AUGUST 21, 1923

Matters of Klannishness and economic solidarity in confronting the Catholic community arose several times at this meeting. Klansman Noyes owned a local barber shop. Note the growing dispute with *Western American* editor Lem Dever over Governor Pierce's appointments. Fosner's reference to "Klansman" Birnie was figurative since the La Grande jeweler was Canadian-born and ineligible for KKK membership.

Meeting opened in regular order with fifty-two Klansmen present. . . .

Discussion for the good of the order are as follows:

That when you are in need of wood don't forget Klansman W. H. Berry who lives on Greenwood St.

That we would like to see Klansman Bill Wilson, the tailor, have his clothes delivered by a Protestant boy instead of a red neck.

That we make it a point to find out why Klansman Ben Noyes has given up part of his shop to a big K.C.

That it would be much more in harmony if Klansman Decious didn't have a Catholic cook working in his restaurant.

That if our present officers would see that their subs. are here during their absence it would promote the good cause.

That we write the esteemed editor of the *Western American*, calling his attention to the fact that Walter Pierce done a worthy deed when he relieved Wm. Peare of his title and gave it to Klansman Birnie.

That we renew our energy in behalf of getting some more good material in our organization.

Motion made and passed that this order extend to Klansmen Holm and Fields a vote of thanks for taking care of the robes at the open air ceremony held in Baker, Aug. 15.

Motion made and passed that the Grievance Board give a decision on the following questions and that they make a report back to this organization:

Chinese cooks employed at the Foley Hotel.

Catholic cook at the Sommer Grille.

Catholic delivery boy at Wilson Tailor Shop.

Meeting closed in short form at an early hour.

AUGUST 28, 1923

Klavern business on this date addressed the local and statewide political influence of the KKK and the chapter's financial relationship to state and national offices. The *Imperial Night-Hawk* reported in mid-August that a greater proportion of fees and taxes would be returned to local chapters and that robe charges would be reduced from $6.50 to five dollars. The newspaper placed national KKK assets at more than nine hundred thousand dollars.

A klectokon was the Klan initiation fee.[36]

Meeting opened in regular order by singing opening song.

Number of Klansmen present: Forty-eight. . . .

Motion made and passed that we have a feed at our next regular meeting and that a notice to attend the next meeting be published in the *La Grande Evening Observer*.

Committee appointed to work in behalf of electing a new Red Cross executive is as follows: Chairman C. R. Eberhard, L. W. Weeks, Dallas Green, James Rosembaum, and Albert Curry.

Committee appointed to investigate the various tax budgets are as follows: Chairman Klansman Alfred Johnson, Geo. T. Cochran, C. K. McCormick, Cass Humphreys. Also Hugh Huron, Dr. Landis, C. W. Bunting, and L. W. Weeks.

Committee appointed to investigate the future of our local YMCA are as follows: Chairman Jess Andrews, Roy Currey, and C. W. Bunting.

Motion made and passed that Klansman J. E. Reynolds be our representative at the meeting to be held in Portland August 30th for the purpose of selecting a suitable candidate for United States senator.

Bulletin Number Five published from the grand dragon's office contained some very important facts:

That the state of Oregon has paid in full its imperial tax.

That the state of Alabama is going to have a school bill copied after the famous Oregon bill.

That we can now order all our supplies from the grand dragon's office.

That the finances of the Klan is full and overflowing.

That for the good of all Klansmen concerned it is suggested that we devote a certain amount of our time in klavern assembled for study of the by-laws and constitution.

That our past exalted cyclops[es] may now have conferred upon them the honorary title of Klan Giants.

That in the very near future we may retain in our local treasure $7.50 klectokon instead of five.

That robes and supplies will be reduced and imperial taxes cut in half. Let us pray.

That the Knights of the Ku Klux Klan is the strongest organization in the world today.

Klansman Walter Price and Klansman Humes, who were naturalized at the Baker ceremony, were given the sacred work in our klavern.

On the seventh day of September the governor will declare a holiday to celebrate the signing of the Constitution, and on the night of the eighteenth our exalted cyclops plans to have some entertainment of a patriotic nature. . . .

Number of men ordered to report for naturalization: Eighty-six.

Total number of applications on hand: Ninety-two.

September 4, 1923

J. E. Reynolds was La Grande's representative to a statewide Klan caucus held in Portland on August 30. The convention of delegates from all thirty-six Oregon counties unanimously endorsed Grand Dragon Gifford for the Republican nomination for the U.S. Senate seat of Oregon Republican Charles L. McNary. Despite similar support from the Portland klavern and the *Western American,* Gifford declined to run, citing the Klan's "unfinished business." Potential KKK involvement in the Senate campaign became a major source of speculation over the next several months.

The reference to trouble in Pennsylvania involved an armed clash on August 25 between Klansmen and working-class Catholics in Carnegie, an industrial suburb of Pittsburgh. When ten thousand Klansmen gathered on a hillside for initiation ceremonies and paraded into town, violence broke out and Klansman Thomas Abbott was shot to death. The next week, a second confrontation was narrowly averted in the nearby town of Scottdale.

John Rogers, whose membership application was finally processed at this meeting, was the proprietor of a taxi stand. Sixteen men were inducted into the secret order on this date.

These are the last minutes submitted by Harold Fosner.[37]

. . . Klansmen present: Seventy-eight. . . .

As the Klansmen entered the klavern the seal was stamped on their cards. When the night hawk took up the new password he found many lacking in this knowledge and they were called before the E.C., who gave them the necessary credentials whereby they may enter the klavern. . . .

The application of Mr. Worthington, local mang. of the Woolworth store, was voted on and passed by the klonklave assembled and he was naturalized along with the other class. . . .

Our representative, Klansman J. E. Reynolds, who attended the meeting in Portland called for the purpose of selecting qualified men for all offices, gave a full report of same. He desired to call our attention especially to the fact that under no circumstances would Gifford become a candidate for any political office. The kligrapp has on hand a full report of this meeting and any Klansman may obtain same upon request.

Communications contained the following information:

That our imperial wizard, H. W. Evans, will be unable to visit Oregon during the month of September owing to the trouble in Pennsylvania and his arrival will be announced at a later date.

That the price of robes beginning September first will be five dollars.

That Gov. Pierce has failed to register 100% in the observation of the editor of the *Western American*.

That the names of the candidates for offices selected by the Knights of the Ku Klux Klan will be held secret from the public until just a few days before the election.

After the reading of the correspondence Klansmen Lindsay and Sellers began playing a march and the following aliens entered the klavern in search of the waters of life: . . .

. . . Following a report of expenditures by J. E. Reynolds, who was our representative in Portland, a motion was made and passed that this money be refunded him from this Klan. A bill for this amount has been sent to our grand dragon and this money will be refunded to us in the near future.

The application of Mr. John Rogers that has been held up for some time was voted on and accepted by the klonklave assembled.

Klansman Tull then took the floor and told us that the Enterprise Klan was all but dead and that they requested this Klan come to their city any night and put on a ceremony and restore the spirit of our noble order. After much discussion Klansman Eberhard won the argument and a committee of the following men—Eberhard, Tull, and Fosner—were appointed to complete the program.

Our exalted cyclops then dismissed the klavern in short form and we retired to the lunchroom and were served with a most delightful repast.

SEPTEMBER 11, 1923

The klavern's response to Red Cross pleas came in the wake of a major Japanese earthquake on September 1 in which hundreds of cities and towns were destroyed. Initial reports put the death toll at two hundred thousand in Tokyo and Yokohama alone. Relief efforts were endorsed by an editorial in the *Western American*.

Although rumors suggested that Grand Dragon Gifford was using the state KKK to encourage a recall drive against Governor Pierce, Oregon's Klan leader publicly denied the order's participation. As the deadline for signatures on the recall petition approached, the effort fell twelve thousand names short.

The La Grande klavern continued to support the governor and denounce *Western American* criticism. Yet the chapter cooperated with Gifford by agreeing to send a representative to a meeting of the Good Government League, a debating society that the Oregon grand dragon had converted into a Klan caucus that endorsed political candidates. The purpose of the Portland meeting was to lay the groundwork for involvement in the U.S. Senate campaign.

The Pendleton Round-up is a rodeo held each September.

Readers may detect a note of coolness in the klavern's response to appeals for aid to the widow of the knight slain in the Carnegie riots. The *Imperial Night-Hawk* subsequently recorded the La Grande chapter's contribution and listed donations from Klans in the Oregon towns of Sherwood, Toledo, and Rainier.[38]

. . . Klansmen present: Forty-two.

Klansman Clark and a representative of the *Western American* was a visitor in our klavern.

Klansman John Stricker was reported still sick at Hot Lake and it was requested that all Klansmen when out that way be sure to drop in and leave a word of good cheer. It was further requested that some flowers be sent him.

Klansman Silvis requested information concerning Mr. C. C. F. Lloyd, a local barber, and upon hearing no reactions from the klonklave assembled, was requested to bring in his application.

After reading a communication from Mrs. D. M. Pague, local secretary of the Red Cross, appealing to this organization for a contribution to the Japanese relief fund, a motion was made and passed that we donate the sum of $25 to this worthy cause.

The treasurer's report left us with a balance on hand in the bank, $1,847.80. . . .

A telegram was read from the Publicity Dept. of the Klan at Atlanta and contained an appeal for funds to be given Mrs. Abbott, wife of the Klansman murdered in Penn. just recently. A motion was then made and passed that this Klan donate the sum of ten dollars in her behalf, and make an appeal to our grand dragon asking that a national fund be created to meet these emergencies.

Klansman Reynolds then submitted a resolution resolving that the Klan has the utmost confidence in the Pierce administration, and that we deplore continued and inflammatory criticism of his official acts by those who should be defending him. Upon motion, this resolution was adopted by this Klan and a copy of same was ordered sent to our governor, grand dragon, and editor of the *Western American*, also retaining a copy on Klan files.

Klansman Clark then gave a report of his mission to our city, stating that he was soliciting advertisement in behalf of the *Western American*, which is going to publish a birthday number on the same week the Round-up is to be held. He cited a number of worthy phrases in behalf its editor but popular sentiment of the klonklave assembled gave him some very sharp rebukes.

A motion was then made and passed that Klansman J. E. Reynolds be our official rep. at Good Gov't League political meetings and that we trust him to use his own judgment relative to the decisions he will have to make.

September 18, 1923

These are the first minutes compiled by Vade R. King, a railroad office worker. Among the dozen new initiates was the county treasurer, Hugh McCall.

Meeting opened with regular ceremony.
Klansmen present: Forty-five.

Officers present: Seven. . . .

Announcement made that Sister Mary Angel, ex-nun, was to lecture at the Christian Church on Thursday afternoon at 2:30 for women only and in the evening at 7:30 for everybody. All are urged to attend. . . .

Due to the fact that he wished to attend school this winter Kligrapp H. R. Fosner tendered his resignation after a brief talk. Moved and seconded that Fosner's resignation be accepted and that he be given a vote of thanks for all that he has done for this Klan.

Moved and seconded that vacancy be filled by nomination from the floor and following nominations were made for kligrapp's office: E. E. Silvis and V. R. King. Ballot was taken and King elected.

Rev. Jones's talk on the Constitution of the U.S. was excellent and assuredly made better citizens out of all of us.

Owing to small number of officers meeting was closed in short form.

SEPTEMBER 25, 1923

As a purity crusader in the community, the YMCA won strong Klan backing; however, the La Grande Y faced yearly operating losses and an overdue mortgage on its building.

U. G. Couch, with whom a Klan committee consulted over appointment of a justice of the peace, was the county judge.[39]

Meeting opened by regular ceremony.

Klansmen present: Fifty.

Owing to absence of kligrapp, minutes of previous meeting were not read but will be read at following meeting.

Motion made and seconded that a resolution be made and forwarded to Mr. Cochran of condolence on account of the death of his brother. Committee appointed to do this were Klansmen Bunting, Smith, and Rhodes.

Communication from C. D. Bailey, kligrapp of the Enterprise Klan, regarding open air initiation which is to be held at Enterprise on Oct. 6, 1923. Letter was answered by Colon R. Eberhard, who will report on same at the next meeting.

No committee reports but in connection with YMCA situation Rev. Jones reported that he had a conversation with Mr. Dillon, who has control of the YMCA in the state of Oregon, stating that there was some possibility that the state organization might take over the local YMCA for operation. However, nothing has yet been definitely decided.

Discussion came up regarding appointment of justice of peace and a committee of five were appointed to consult with Judge Couch in this regard and same will be reported upon later. Committee consisted of Klansmen R. H. Baldock, Jim Hutchinson, C. W. Bunting, J. K. Fitzgerald, and Geo. T. Cochran, chairman.

Question of heating of hall came up but as none of House Committee were present no action was taken.

Meeting was closed in short form at about 10:15.

Claude Beery elected night hawk by ballot.

OCTOBER 2, 1923

The reluctance of members to meet organizational financial demands appeared to be a recurring theme at this point in the La Grande Klan's history.

Meeting opened with regular ceremony.

Number of Klansmen present: Sixty-five. . . .

Visitors in our klavern were Klansman Hamilton of Portland Klan #1, Klansman Lukes of The Dalles, and Klansman Matthews from Richmond.

Reported that Klansman Courtney was at the hospital here in town and that Klansman Striker was again in the hospital at Hot Lake. . . .

The House Committee reported that they were unable to do anything further until they had more money to work with. Motion made and seconded that an assessment of $1 be levied on each member to finish putting the hall in shape to rent. Motion also made and seconded that the rental for the large hall be made $4 per night and the small hall be $3. Motion did not carry.

Reported that Enterprise Klan wants to hold their open air ceremony on Saturday, Oct. 6th. Klansmen will assemble at the Club Cigar Store and transportation will be provided. Clyde Bunting appointed for this purpose.

Meeting was closed in short form at a very late hour.

OCTOBER 9, 1923

Among prospects mentioned for KKK membership at this meeting were a dentist, furniture-company proprietor, railroad worker, clothing-store operator, truck driver, electrician, sign painter, photographer, blacksmith, mill foreman, millworker, locomotive engineer, and grocery clerk. The last, Holm's Grocery employee George B. Richardson, was the only one of the group ultimately naturalized into the secret order.

The city's water crisis once again became an issue in klavern discussions. A delegation of three Klansmen had attended a meeting about the matter at city hall in August. Upon the recommendation of the Union County Chamber of Commerce, city commissioners decided to seek the help of a geologist to determine if an artesian well should be dug to augment La Grande's surface-water supply. Discussion continued through early October when the *La Grande Evening Observer* reported that most members of the Chamber preferred a deep well to a gravity-flow system. The newspaper cited Dr. Landis's observation that the artesian alternative would not require chlorination.

The Klan opposed Catholic Hugh E. Brady for justice of the peace, an office voted upon by the Union County Court, presided over by Judge U. G. Couch.

Klavern leaders continued to show interest in civic affairs by monitoring local government and school budgeting.

The Good Government League's meeting in Portland in September had failed to deliver an endorsement for the Republican nomination for U.S. senator. Grand Dragon Gifford declined to run for the office, perhaps fearing the risk of political defeat.[40]

Meeting opened at 8 P.M. by Geo. T. Cochran with only three officers present. Substitute officers were appointed and opening ceremony held in full.

Klansmen present: Forty-one. . . .

Motion was made that we forward Klansman Combs a letter of condolence due to the death of his wife. . . .

Dr. Landis reported that the water question for La Grande was as yet undecided but that we were due for some kind of a water system in the very near future. It is thought that an artesian well will be best as the water obtained from this source is the nearest to pure water that can be had while any surface water obtainable is more or less polluted with germs, bugs, and various other substances which make it undesirable for drinking water. The cost of an artesian system is very small compared to a gravity system, the latter costing probably around one million dollars and probably ten thousand dollars a year to maintain. Therefore, it is up to us to put forth our best efforts to get the artesian system.

Report of the Justice of Peace Committee stated that Hutchi[n]son
was against Brady but that Judge Couch, who cast the deciding vote, had
previously decided that he would vote for Brady and could not be talked
out of it. Judge Couch is, however, a Protestant and will no doubt some of
these days see the light.

Klansman Reynolds reported that the city, county, and school budgets
were to be investigated on Oct. 17 and that he would like to see a
committee of men there from this organization to assist in seeing that
everything was right. The following men were appointed on the Budget
Committee in addition to the ones previously named: Klansmen L. W.
Weeks, Hugh Huron, Dr. Landis, and C. W. Bunting.

The House Committee held a meeting previous to our klonklave and in
reporting stated that the hall was practically rented for three dates in the
very near future, and that the three front rooms would in all probability be
rented for apartments, if possible to Klansmen, and if not, to some outsider
to be vouched for by a Klansman. The rent of the three rooms to be $25
per month. The rental of the hall and other rooms will be taken care of by
John Allen, at the Club Cigar Store, or any of his employees.

Bill for $2.80 for the *Evening Observer* was read and ordered paid.

Klansman Reynolds reported that the meeting of the Oregon Good
Government League which he attended was a very stormy one but that
they really accomplished a few things at that.

Klansman Geo. T. Cochran gave his appreciation of the letter of
condolence forwarded to him by this Klan.

OCTOBER 16, 1923

Elected in June 1923 as grand master of the Oregon Masons, Klansman George
Cochran was selected as a delegate to the dedication of the George Washington
Masonic National Memorial in Alexandria, Virginia, the following fall. Presi-
dent Calvin Coolidge laid the cornerstone for the two-hundred-foot granite
structure and tower midway between Washington, D.C., and the first presi-
dent's Mt. Vernon estate. The close relationship between the KKK and the
Masons was reflected in the klavern announcement of Cochran's trip to the
East.

Klansmen maintained an interest in Italy because of a bitter dispute between U.S.-based Methodists and the Catholic Church. The controversy centered on Methodist plans to build a temple and university on a hill in Rome

overlooking the Vatican. In the spring of 1923, Catholic officials publicly condemned the project as offensive to the traditions and sentiments of the Eternal City and asked the government of Benito Mussolini to prevent its completion.

The *Rail Splitter*, in which La Grande Klan leaders showed interest at this meeting, was an anti-Catholic newspaper published by William L. Clark in Milan, Illinois.

Although Grand Dragon Gifford declined to seek the Republican nomination for the Senate seat held by Charles McNary, the La Grande klavern prepared for the 1924 primaries. The precinct list of Klansmen and their political affiliations may have been part of a statewide information sheet on three thousand knights that Rev. Stanton Lapham subsequently offered Governor Pierce.[41]

> Meeting opened with full ceremony.
>
> Klansmen present: Forty-five. . . .
>
> Motion was made and passed that we have a Sick Committee appointed. This committee consisted of the following men: R. E. Byers, chairman, and Klansmen Clyde Bunting and V. R. King. Any case of sickness or financial distress should be reported to one or more of this committee at once.
>
> It was announced that the Klan at Elgin wish to have a public indoor meeting of some sort in the near future but no arrangements have as yet been made.
>
> Klansman Cochran stated that in talking with a Klansman from the East he was informed of the following: that in the state of Indiana there were naturalized during the month of May fourteen thousand Klansmen, in June seventeen thousand, and in July twenty-two thousand; and that they were going to completely control the next election in both Indiana and Ohio. Also that the Indiana Klan had acquired the title to the Valpar[a]iso University, the entire faculty of which are Klansmen. Klansman Cochran is going to Washington, D.C. to help dedicate the memorial monument to Geo. Washington, to be built on the site originally chosen by the committee on which to build our capitol buildings.
>
> Motion made that the kligrapp correspond with the Baker Klan in regard to the Methodist minister who lectured there, also showing pictures of their work in Italy, and if possible get him to come to our klavern for the same purpose.

Motion made and passed that we procure some propaganda from *Rail Splitter* at once. Klansman Dallas Green was appointed to work with the kligrapp in doing this.

Klansman R. W. St. Claire from Pendleton was a visitor in our klavern and stated that he was very glad to be with us and see us doing so nicely.

Motion was made and passed that a committee of five men be appointed to get a map of the precincts of Union County, together with a list of members and their politics, for the election to be held next May. Also to enlist the Elgin Klan in this.

Motion made and passed that a committee of three be appointed to investigate the condition of our hall and with the OK of the proper city officials, same to be announced in the paper.

No further business being brought up, meeting was closed at a late hour.

OCTOBER 23, 1923

The K of P Hall, the site of a Klan social event in nearby Elgin, was the headquarters of the Knights of Pythias fraternal order.

Kladd candidate R. H. Helvey worked for the railroad. His participation in the secret order was indicative of the large number of recruits among Union Pacific employees.

Note the casual announcement of a forthcoming cross burning.

Minutes for this date provide the first glimpse of Klan concern with alleged incidents of drunken behavior in the city's African-American district on the near-north side.

. . . Visitors in our klavern were Klansman Redmond from Portland, Klansmen Klinghamer, Merith, and Blanchard from Elgin.

The resignation of Klansman C. H. Tull as kladd was read and accepted.

Klansman Klinghamer of Elgin stated that they wished to have their speech at Elgin on Monday, Sept. 12 at the Opera House and afterward there will be a feed at the K of P Hall.

It was announced that there were forty-seven Klansmen initiated at Boise, Idaho last Monday.

Nominations for kladd were Nolan Skiff, Jr. and Robert Helvey. Count of ballots gave Klansman Helvey forty-eight and Skiff eight.

There will be a cross up on the hill Saturday night.

Motion made and carried that we start a complaint book, entering specific instances only of complaints against various persons.

Motion made and carried that a committee be appointed to take up the matter of Negroes on the North Side with the city officials. On this committee are Klansmen J. K. Fitzgerald, Wm. Fitzgerald, Ed Fields, R. A. Helvey, M. Elledge, Charlie Weagle, J. D. Plank, W. H. Berry, Tom Flemming, and Klansman Stiles as chairman. . . .

Meeting adjourned at the hour of 10:30.

October 30, 1923

Signs of organizational fatigue surface on this date: both the chair of the House Committee, who also served as the city school clerk, and Exalted Cyclops Jones, a Christian Church minister, asked to resign their offices.

The Gideon Society, membership in which the Klan expressed interest, distributed Bibles for public use.

Visiting Rev. Lapham was the Baptist minister whose initiation fee had been paid by the klavern in 1922.

Meeting opened with regular ceremony.

Klansmen present: Forty. . . .

Harry Williams, chairman of the House Committee, reported that the committee work took up more time than he could spare and due to this fact would like to be relieved of his duties. Same being done by the exalted cyclops. No one has as yet been appointed in his place.

The following men were appointed on the Election Committee: Klansmen A. J. Johnson, W. K. Gilbert, R. E. Byers, C. K. McCormick, and C. R. Eberhard, chairman.

Final arrangements have now been made concerning the lecture at Elgin. Klansmen wishing transportation will be at the Club Cigar Store not later than seven o'clock.

Motion made and passed that we apply for membership in the Gideon Society.

Klansman Rev. Lapham was rather a visitor in our klavern and gave us a talk in which he instilled more ideas and ideals into our hearts than we have had for a long time, and was surely appreciated by all.

Motion made and passed that we communicate with Grand Dragon Gifford and obtain permission to use our robes at Elgin next Mon.

The mayor of Elgin, who was a visitor in our klavern, reports that Elgin is a very law-abiding community.

Meeting closed in short form at the hour of 10:15.

NOVEMBER 6, 1923

This meeting demonstrated how racial issues intersected with the Klan's focus on civic affairs.

Meeting opened with regular ceremony.

Klansmen present: Forty-seven. . . .

The committee appointed to investigate the Negro situation on the North Side reported that as yet nothing had been done but that the following committee would draw up the necessary papers as soon as possible: Klansman J. K. Fitzgerald, Art Weagle, C. W. Bunting, and Klansman Pearl Stiles, chairman.

Motion made and passed that we have a Municipal Affairs Committee to investigate as much as possible all city affairs. The following men were appointed on this committee: Klansman Geo. T. Cochran, chairman, L. W. Weeks, C. W. Bunting, and J. K. Fitzgerald.

A motion was made, seconded, and duly passed that we go on record as approving of the deep well water system as suggested by Dr. R. P. Landis for this city.

Motion was made and passed that we postpone our initiation next Tuesday and notify all Klansmen that we are going to have a discussion of municipal affairs which are vitally important. . . .

NOVEMBER 13, 1923

Note the huge turnout for discussion of controversies over La Grande's water supply, the paving of city streets, and public behavior on the North Side.

Meeting opened with regular ceremony.

Klansmen present: 110.

As this was a special meeting the regular order of business was not followed and Rev. O. W. Jones at this time turned the chair over to W. K. Gilbert.

The water question was the first to come before the meeting and was thoroughly outlined by Dr. R. P. Landis, who has, by the way, assisted by Klansman Fitzgerald, been doing most of the work on this water situation. It was shown that the Mill Creek proposition, while supplying pure water and plenty of it, would cost between $465,000 and $500,000. Mr. Durant, a reputable well driller from Walla Walla, has guaranteed to drill a 1000-ft. well for $15,000, with everything included, and if successful the total cost of this system, that is about four wells, a pump, and a reservoir, would only be approximately $100,000 or a saving of nearly $400,000.

The paving situation was next taken up and was pretty well cleared up by Klansman Knight, who is the paving inspector for the city. He reported that all of the paving, with the exception of that on Penn Ave., was good and that the paving on Penn Ave. would have to be either done over or repaired in such a way that it would be satisfactory to all concerned.

There was no definite report on the Negro situation but it is expected that something will develop in the very near future.

It was announced by the E.C. that we were to have the Methodist minister with his movie in our klavern on next meeting night.

Motion was made and passed that one week from today we have a turkey feed in this hall. Committee appointed to look after this were Klansmen W. K. Gilbert, J. R. Rhodes, and Klansman Ed Fields.

Meeting adjourned at 11:15

NOVEMBER 20, 1923

Having created a special committee to draw up a petition protesting the "Negro situation" north of downtown, the klavern focused on presenting the document to city authorities. La Grande Klansmen also prepared for their pre-Thanksgiving turkey "feed." The evening's meeting produced a warm appraisal of the lecture on alleged harassment of Protestants in Catholic Italy by Baker's Methodist minister. "Casey's" was a slang term for the "K.C.s," or members of the Knights of Columbus.

Meeting opened with regular ceremony.

Klansmen present: on time, forty-five, and there were twenty-eight late arrivals

Committee on Negro situation reported that they had drawn up a petition and had a large number of signatures attached and that this petition would be presented to the city commissioners on Wed. evening, Nov. 21. It was requested that as many of the Klansmen as possible be present to back up the petitions.

The Eats Committee for the feed to be held next Tuesday reported that practically all arrangements had been made and that it was necessary that each Klansman bring with him the following: knife, fork, spoon, cup, saucer, and plate, and that same was to be forgotten and left here in the hall.

Klansman E. J. Phillips was reported to be very sick at his home on X Ave. Same was reported to the Sick Committee.

The illustrated lecture to which we were treated was surely interesting as well as educational and only goes to show that we are not the only ones that are on the warpath with the Casey's.

A motion was made and passed that the application of all eligible men be passed by the Board for initiation at our next meeting.

Meeting adjourned at 10:30

NOVEMBER 27, 1923

Two days before Thanksgiving, the La Grande Klan's "turkey feed" accounted for the biggest indoor gathering in the klavern's history. The secret order also celebrated a central role in the distribution of what the *La Grande Evening Observer* called "one of the largest petitions" ever presented to a governing body in the city. Of nearly two hundred signatures presented to the city commission on November 21, at least twenty-one can be identified as La Grande Klansmen.

The citizen's petition demanded that city authorities take "stringent steps . . . to 'clean up' alleged immoral and undesirable conditions existing in what is known as La Grande's colored town." Klansman Moose Elledge told the commission that the district was "a nuisance" lying halfway between the north and south sides of the city near the business area. Elledge charged that inebriated black men in the vicinity repeatedly had accosted or insulted "white women and children." The wife of Klansman and laborer J. D. Plank pointed out that "the decent colored feminine element" was among those victimized by drunken and disorderly blacks and Hispanics. When Klansman Ed Fields insisted that Dee Rogers, an African-American man named as a repeat offender, be immediately arrested, city police complied. Authorities apprehended fifty La Grande inhabitants and convicted forty-three on liquor-related charges during November 1923.

New initiates at this meeting included a railroad pipe fitter, mechanic, American Express employee, and railroad car inspector.[42]

Meeting opened with regular ceremony.
Klansmen present: about 225. . . .

Visiting Klansmen were from Pendleton, Baker, Elgin, and various other places.

The chairman of the committee appointed to investigate the Negro situation on the North Side was not present but it was reported by others who were present that the meeting with the City Commission was very successful. . . .

Rev. O. W. Jones again brought up the subject of the series of three lectures to be given by Rev. Lapham. It was moved and seconded that this matter be referred to the Board of Klokans, same to be reported by them on the following Tuesday.

Our E.C., O. W. Jones, is to give a Thanksgiving address at the Methodist Church on Thanksgiving morning and all Klansmen are urged to attend.

A motion was made and passed that a joint committee with the Elgin Klan be appointed to take up and investigate any matters which might be of interest to both Klans. This committee to be appointed on next meeting night. . . .

Rev. Lapham gave us a message of instructions to Klansmen which surely was worthwhile.

The meeting was followed by the big turkey feed which held the attention of all until it was over. The collection to cover the cost of the feed amounted to $71.12.

Klansman Geo. Cochran gave us a short review of his trip to Washington, D.C., stating among other things that all of the Klans he came in contact with were wide awake and doing things.

All Klansmen reported home at a very late hour.

DECEMBER 4, 1923

This meeting was presided over by dry-goods merchant and klaliff, W. K. Gilbert. The impending resignation of Klansman Hugh McCall from his county treasurer's post was a blow to La Grande klavern leaders. McCall had formally been inducted into the Klan less than three months earlier.

Once again, the secret order found itself frustrated by Union County Republican Chair Jack Peare.

Klansman Ray Cook's arrest on a Prohibition charge further embarrassed the Invisible Empire. Financial difficulties in maintaining Rex Hall, moreover, appeared to offer bleak prospects.

Due to absence of nearly all officers meeting was opened in short form. . . .
Klansmen present: Forty-three. . . .

It was announced Hugh McCall will resign as county treasurer and that
the party to be appointed in his place is a Protestant but adheres to Jack
Peare's footsteps very closely. However, nothing can be done about this
until next election.

The Grievance Committee reports that Ray Cook has been arrested and
fined for violation of our liquor laws. Motion was made that he be notified
to appear and give reason why he should not be banished.

The fact was brought out that the family of Ed Phillips was financially
unable to take care of themselves and a motion was made that $50 be
withdrawn from the treasury for the immediate relief of this family, and
that same be replaced by circulation of petition calling for a small donation
from each Klansman. Anything taken in over the $50 to be turned over to
them for their use.

Rube Zweifel is also sick in the hospital, having undergone an operation
for appendicitis.

The chairman of the House Committee reports that if something is not
done to obtain some revenue from our hall in the very near future . . . it
will be necessary to circulate a petition to keep us from going broke. Every
Klansman will take this to heart and try to think of some way in which
we may at least break even on our hall.

Meeting adjourned in short order at a late hour.

December 11, 1923

Klan efforts to aid the local Red Cross appeared to fall short. Nevertheless, a
large turnout of knights came to hear Grand Dragon Gifford push the congressional candidacy of La Grande Klansman George Cochran. The prominent
eastern Oregon attorney had been elected grand master of Oregon's Scottish
Rite Masons in June and state leader of the Knights Templar, another Masonic
order, in October. Gifford now sought to groom Cochran to take on Representative Nicholas Sinnott, a Catholic, in the 1924 Republican primary. "I
am here to call upon members of the Ku Klux Klan to get better acquainted
with La Grande and eastern Oregon and to urge the nomination of George T.
Cochran," Gifford told the *La Grande Evening Observer*. The grand dragon
combined support of Cochran with a plea for Klansmen nationwide to settle in
Oregon, a theme consistent with the goal of state economic development that
the *Western American* had been promoting for a year.

Gifford continued to push the Klan-dominated Good Government League, which announced in early December that it intended to make an endorsement for the Republican nomination for the U.S. Senate. Oregon state legislator Kaspar K. Kubli, front-runner for League backing, soon inaugurated his campaign.

La Grande Klan leaders predicted passage of a state bill to tax church property. State representative D. C. Lewis, an anti-Catholic Portland attorney supported by the Klan in the 1922 elections, had introduced such a measure in February 1923, but the measure failed by a 35–24 margin.

The reference to the "Newlin Drug Case" suggests that La Grande Klansmen still had not given up on one of their most bitter adversaries.

Chief of Police Clint Haynes, whom the Klan wished to support, had cooperated with petitioners at the protest meeting at city hall.[43]

Meeting opened with full ceremony.

Klansmen present: 105. . . .

An announcement was made that the local Red Cross organization had passed out of existence.

Grand Dragon F. L. Gifford was a visitor in our klavern. He told us that our next job was to put Sinnott out as congressman and to put Klansman Geo. Cochran in instead. This is going to be a hard piece of work as Sinnott has a very strong backing from both sides and it will be necessary for everyone to hit the ball from now on. Klansman Gifford suggested that every Klansman donate $1 to the Oregon Good Government League of which we are all members, to finance the campaign which we and not Geo. Cochran are going to carry on. It is absolutely [important] that we defeat Sinnott in order to have three congressmen who are white men. A bill is going to be initiated in the very near future providing for the taxation of all church property, and as the Catholics have about $55 million in church property in this state, they in all probability will be pretty busy with that for a while.

Motion was made that the kligrapp correspond with Grand Dragon Gifford in connection with the Newlin Drug Case.

The joint committee with Elgin is composed of the following men: Klansmen McIlroy, Gilbert, and Johnson. A meeting of this committee is to be held in the Elgin klavern on next Monday eve.

Motion made and passed that this organization forward a letter to Chief of Police Clint Haynes, assuring him and the rest of the force that we are supporting them all of the time.

Klansman H. H. Little of Cove is very desirous of obtaining someone to lecture at that point and the following committee were appointed to investigate and arrange: Klansmen McPherson, Chris Mayes, and Happersett.

The next regular meeting of the Klan will be a special meeting of the Oregon Good Government League.

Meeting adjourned at a late hour.

DECEMBER 18, 1923

This Klan meeting was overshadowed by the convening of Gifford's Good Government League.

Meeting opened with regular ceremony.

Klansmen present: Thirty-five. . . .

Committee appointed to investigate the possibility of having a lecture at Cove reported that nothing definite had as yet been done but that the meeting would more than likely be held on the second Wednesday in January.

Motion was made and carried that our meetings for the next two weeks be held on Wednesday instead of Tuesday due to Christmas and New Year's falling on those dates.

The joint committee with Elgin reported that they had held a meeting in the Elgin klavern but stated that nothing definite had been done.

Meeting adjourned at about 9 P.M. to permit a meeting of Oregon Good Government League.

DECEMBER 26, 1923

These are the last typewritten minutes in the La Grande collection.

The Klan sought to retain Rev. V. K. "Bearcat" Allison, the former pastor of the Christian Church of Lebanon, a town in the central Willamette Valley. Allison had a reputation as the most powerful and popular anti-Catholic lecturer in the state.

A railroad fireman and another Union Pacific employee were two of the three men initiated on this date.[44]

Meeting opened with full ceremony.

Klansmen present: Fifty-eight. . . .

Two new applications read for the first time.

Motion made and carried that the kligrapp correspond with various Klans to see if Bert Vanderpool can be located.

Motion made and passed that kligrapp correspond with Grand Dragon Gifford in regard to having Rev. Allison to come here and lecture as soon as possible. . . .

Moved and seconded that the Klan pay the bill for light switch supposedly broken by the Royal Neighbors.

Meeting adjourned at 10:30

APRIL 1, 1924

The La Grande minutes skip three entire months before the following scrawled and terse entry. The meeting was called to order by W. K. Gilbert, serving as kligrapp. There is no record of an exalted cyclops presiding.

Klansman George Cochran had announced his candidacy for the Republican nomination for the U.S. House after a February 20 torchlight parade through the heart of La Grande. The event attracted fifteen carloads of supporters from Pendleton and twenty from Baker. Klavern officers Alfred Johnson and W. K. Gilbert served as president and secretary, respectively, of Cochran's political organization. The candidate also received public backing from Baker Klan leader C. T. Godwin, Portland's Rev. Allison, and La Grande physician and Klansman R. P. Landis. The *La Grande Evening Observer* noted that "a large element throughout the district is understood to be firm supporters," a coded reference to Klan allies. Cochran embraced the national KKK program of "selective restrictive immigration."[45]

No. present: Forty-five.

Reading of minutes.

Reports of committees.

Discussion of Cochran problems.

Matter of Mrs. Embrey and night police. Motion made for committee carried.

Klansmen from Elgin.

APRIL 8, 1924

These cursory notes suggest that the Good Government League had become more important than the local Klan.

60 Klansmen present, Klaliff Johnson Acting E.C.

Minutes read, approved.

Bills read, applications.

Johnson bawls out the "talkin'."

Meeting adjourned at an early hour to make way for meeting of Good Gov. Club.

April 15, 1924

This set of minutes appears on the same page as those for the previous week.

The "Kloran," requested by klavern leaders, was the Klan ritual book used to conduct meetings and initiations.

Once incumbent senator Charles McNary announced his candidacy in April, the race for the Republican nomination for the seat intensified. Rival candidate Kaspar Kubli toured central and eastern Oregon and spoke to a large gathering at The Dalles on April 23. Endorsed by Lem Dever, Kubli had strong backing among Klansmen outside Portland. He incorporated national KKK policies by focusing on immigration restriction, a national compulsory school amendment, and creation of a federal department of education. Kubli also en-dorsed farm relief and abolition of tax-exempt securities.[46]

50 present.

Send for two sets Kloran. . . .

Reading of clipping as regards removal of flag from American soldiers.

Initiation ceremony: Wright, Utley, Ohl.

Motion lost.

Closed short for Kubli.

April 22, 1924

This is the last set of minutes to have survived the La Grande Ku Klux Klan. It appears on the same sheet of paper as the minutes for April 1.

The handwritten notes appear to describe Dr. E. P. Mossman, a La Grande dentist, as presiding over this final recorded meeting.

Opened at 8:00. Mossman in chair. Seventy present.

Reg[ular] opening ceremony.

Reading of minutes—approved.

Motion made that $21.45 be drawn from general fund and charity fund and bills of Mrs. Embrey help be paid. Carried.

Nominating Comm.: Ralph Byers, Eugene Millering. Terry Happersett, Fitzgerald. To report on or before May 6th.

E.C. resigned. Motion to accept resignation passed.

Motion made that nomination for E.C. be postponed until next meeting.

Klansmen Happersett and Byers appointed B[oar]d of Klokans.

Meeting closed for Good Gov. League in short order.

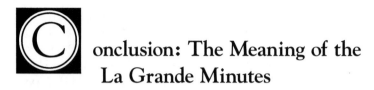

onclusion: The Meaning of the La Grande Minutes

THE RESIGNATION OF Exalted Cyclops O. W. Jones provided only one indication of the deteriorating fortunes of the La Grande Ku Klux Klan. As klavern leaders dropped from prominence, the chapter faced a series of demoralizing developments. Just as the financially plagued Union County Red Cross dissolved after Klan efforts to revive it in December 1923, the state YMCA director convened an emergency meeting at city hall to avoid a sheriff's sale of the headquarters of the La Grande Y. Local business leader August Stange paid off the outstanding debt and offered the organization's board an option to repurchase the facilities. Yet when the Y failed to come up with the funds to save the building, the facility closed in April 1924.[1]

The Invisible Empire suffered another disappointment when La Grande's city manager sought to address local water shortages by recommending a gravity-flow system instead of the artesian wells advanced by Klan physician R. P. Landis. When both alternatives were placed on a single three-hundred-thousand-dollar city bond issue in May 1924, voters defeated the measure by a 3–1 margin. Klansman Landis managed to win a spot on the La Grande City Commission the following November. Yet the secret order failed to advance Knight George Cochran past Representative Nicholas Sinnott in the May Republican congressional primary. With strong KKK backing, Cochran publicly had predicted victory. Despite a 4–3 plurality in Union County, however, the Klan activist took less than 40 percent of the overall vote. In November Baker Klansman and Democrat James Harvey Graham again lost the general election to Catholic incumbent Sinnott.[2]

While Cochran and Graham struggled at the polls, state senator and *La Grande Evening Observer* publisher Bruce Dennis faced no opposition in the 1924 Republican primary. Dennis went on easily to defeat a Democrat opponent in November. The senator's broad appeal should not have been surprising. Although a Republican, the outspoken Klan adversary stood behind Walter Pierce, who thanked him "for the magnificent support that you have given this administration." Dennis sold the La Grande newspaper in 1925, resigned his senate seat, and moved to Portland the following year; he later relocated to California to do public relations for Safeway.[3] Yet the departure of Bruce Dennis was too late for local Klansmen to appreciate.

The decline of the La Grande KKK appeared to coincide with the sensational prosecution of Dr. Ellis O. Willson, an Elgin dentist and active Klan participant. In February 1924, a Union County Grand Jury indicted Willson on charges of raping his clerical assistant and of committing manslaughter by performing an abortion on her. Although the Circuit Court dismissed the rape charge, overflowing crowds attended the ensuing trial. The testimony of Dr. Landis, a La Grande Klansman and school commissioner, figured heavily in the dentist's conviction. Willson received a three-year prison sentence and moved to Portland while awaiting appeal. After the Oregon Supreme Court ordered a new trial, a second jury again convicted the defendant in June 1925. The following December, the court reversed the second conviction on technical rules of evidence, some of which related to Dr. Landis's failure to conduct a full pregnancy examination.[4]

The demise of the La Grande Invisible Empire remains hidden in the sparse minutes of April 1924. No evidence of local Klan activity has surfaced for the following period, although former Knight Carl Eugene Millering claimed that the organization lasted until about 1927. Harold Fosner, who conveyed great enthusiasm as klavern chronicler, eventually moved to Texas and married. When he returned to Oregon in 1951, Fosner settled in the coastal community of Seal Rock, where he worked for the Waldport Water District. He later became a self-employed brush cutter and died in a Newport foster home in 1986. Klavern leader George Cochran, in contrast, maintained his law partnership with Colon Eberhard and his specialty in agricultural water rights. Cochran died at the age of eighty-seven in 1965. The De Molay youth chapter of the La Grande Masons is named for him. Klansman Eberhard also remained in La Grande, losing a bid to return to the state senate in 1926 but prevailing two years later. Eberhard, who served on the city school board until 1936, was named master of the La Grande Masonic Lodge in 1930.[5]

While the La Grande Klan faced diminished prospects, the Oregon KKK fared little better. Atlanta's *Imperial Night-Hawk* boasted of the Portland klavern's mass inductions and rallies during the first half of 1924. Yet the state organization experienced political frustration, internal division, and its own share of scandal. In March 1924, the U.S. District Court for Oregon ruled the Klan-supported state school bill unconstitutional and granted an injunction against its enforcement. When attorneys for the state appealed the decision, the U.S. Supreme Court upheld the district panel, ruling in *Pierce v. Society of Sisters* (1925) that Oregon could not compel parents to send children to public schools as long as private institutions met required standards.[6]

The Oregon Klan's tenuous relationship with Governor Walter Pierce provided further grounds for disunity within the secret order. Patronage constituted a particularly troubling issue that often placed the Democratic chief executive in conflict with his own party. "To my mind the appointment of a few men to office is a minor matter," Pierce wrote to *Oregon Journal* editor and supporter B. F. Irvine during his first year in office. But the governor acknowledged in a subsequent letter to A. C. Hampton, superintendent of La Grande public schools, that "certain people would like to dictate every appointment." Pierce especially resented Klan pressure to replace Dr. Robert E. Lee Steiner as superintendent of Oregon State Hospital. The governor's memoirs later included the charge that KKK leaders demanded to name the secretary of the Oregon State Board of Control as a means of collecting commissions from wholesalers doing business at the state capital. Finally, Pierce objected to Klan efforts to replace state Prohibition Director George L. Cleaver, a dry Imbler banker and longtime public-power ally.[7]

Western American editor Lem Dever conducted a bitter crusade against Cleaver, whom he accused of appeasing Portland bootleggers. By the summer of 1923, Dever was directing his anger toward Pierce for betrayal of alleged patronage promises to the Invisible Empire. Control of appointments undoubtedly played a role in covert Klan support of a gubernatorial recall drive that garnered eighty-four thousand signatures by the end of the year. The Pierce administration escaped only when promoters failed to agree upon a date for placing the measure on the ballot. As a result, the movement fizzled and a Pierce recall election never materialized.[8]

Klan disunity over the Pierce relationship reflected deeper fissures within the Oregon secret order. Grand Dragon Fred Gifford promoted bitter controversy with arbitrary policies and endorsements. During the 1924 Republican senatorial primary campaign, Gifford appeared to offer Klan support to both Oregon House Speaker Kaspar K. Kubli and Portland Mayor George Baker. But despite Kubli's strength outside Portland, Gifford told members of the Invisible Empire to refrain from supporting a primary challenge to incumbent Senator Charles L. McNary, the third candidate. The grand dragon's machinations also brought criticism from the Oregon Federation of Patriotic Societies, a consortium of fraternal orders that objected to Klan endorsement tickets that competed with their own. When the federation won a court injunction against Gifford in May 1924, the grand dragon avoided the judgment by distributing similar endorsement tickets printed by the Good Government League.[9]

Gifford and the Oregon Klan were no strangers to controversy. As early as November 1922, Portland journalist Ben Titus had published a three-part exposé in the *Portland Telegram* entitled "I Was a Klansman." Titus attacked the secret order's anti-Catholicism and claimed that Gifford had offered liquor to new initiates in the Portland klavern. Other critics spread allegations that the grand dragon's wife was Catholic and that two daughters attended St. Mary's Academy, a Catholic secondary school in Portland. Gifford also faced discord over attempts to merge the Ladies of the Invisible Empire with Women of the Ku Klux Klan, a national order officially recognized by Atlanta in June 1923.[10]

Allegations of Gifford's arbitrary rule and interference with local chapters led to the secession of the Pendleton Klan in August 1923 and continuing assaults on the grand dragon's leadership. When Gifford suspended Luther Powell in a power play in November, the former Klan organizer responded by demanding the grand dragon's resignation to "purify" the Klan. Some insurgent knights joined Powell in a new group called Allied Protestant Americans. Meanwhile, Lem Dever resigned as editor of the *Western American*. By November 1924, the *Oregonian* was quoting Dever's charge that the Klan was a "national menace."[11]

After faring poorly in the 1924 Republican primaries, the Oregon Klan went underground during the fall's general election. Gifford left the Invisible Empire in 1925, just as some ex-Klansmen formed a new political organization called Independence Hall of Oregon. The next year brought creation of the Improved Order of Klansmen, an autonomous state Klan whose leaders came from outside Portland. By 1926, C. T. Godwin, grand dragon of the remnants of the Oregon Ku Klux Klan, was proclaiming that the secret order no longer dictated the electoral choice of its members. The focus of the Invisible Empire, observed the *Oregon Voter*, was exclusively on support for the public schools and law enforcement.[12]

Although Oregon Klans in Tillamook, Cottage Grove, and other towns survived until the late 1920s, the state KKK never recovered from patronage disputes, internal conflicts, and persistent charges of graft, corruption, and scandal. A reputation for divisiveness also made it extremely difficult in Oregon to revive the secret order. When former Grand Dragon Fred Gifford attempted to resurrect the state organization in 1937, his efforts met with widespread indifference or ridicule.[13]

Scandal, controversy, and divisiveness also contributed to the waning of the "second" Klan's national reputation. In December 1923, *Imperial Night-Hawk* editor Philip Fox received a life prison term for the murder of William S. Coburn, a national KKK official and attorney. Although Imperial Wizard Hiram Wesley Evans dismissed the incident as a "personal affair" not involving organization business, the scandal detracted from the Invisible Empire's image as a pillar of social morality and law enforcement. Worse yet was the 1925 murder conviction and life sentence of Indiana Grand Dragon David C. Stephenson, whose abduction and rape of a secretary had prompted her suicide. When the Klan-supported governor refused to pardon Stephenson, the former knight produced evidence that sent several Indiana politicians to prison on corruption charges and sealed the end of the secret order's status as a mass movement.[14]

Demoralized, divided, and shorn of its major issue by passage of immigration-restriction legislation in 1924 and 1927, the Ku Klux Klan reverted to its southern roots in the Depression Era of the 1930s. Although leaders attempted an abortive alliance with the fascist German-American Bund, the Klan's notoriety stemmed from a renewed commitment to vigilante violence. During this period, knights in the Piedmont textile-manufacturing area resorted to antiunion terrorism. Meanwhile, Klansmen in Georgia and Alabama instigated vicious harassment campaigns against communists and all advocates of black equality. Tax difficulties with the federal government during World War II and the public's negative response to racial extremism led to the formal disbanding of the KKK in 1944. Yet an Atlanta Klan resurfaced after the war. Following the Supreme Court's endorsement of racial integration in the public schools in 1954, the southern Klans took on a new life. By 1959 a revitalized Atlanta-based Invisible Empire claimed fifteen thousand members.[15]

Reacting to the Civil Rights movement of the late 1950s and early 1960s, the resurgent Klan turned to the bombing of black churches and to assaults on racial-equality activists. As Klan strength approached fifty thousand by the mid-1960s, southern terror campaigns resulted in the murder of at least twelve rights organizers. Fiery crosses, which 1920s knights claimed as symbols of purity and dedication, once again served as preludes to terror and assassination. Under increasing pressure from northern African Americans and liberal allies, Washington directed the Federal Bureau of Investigation to infiltrate the secret order and mount charges against violent offenders. As a result, overall Klan membership dropped to around fifteen hundred by the early 1970s.[16]

Just as the influence of the "third" Klan appeared to be waning in the mid-1970s, new organizers, such as Alabama's Bill Wilkinson, sought to revive the secret order as a white-supremacist mass movement. Peaking at around ten thousand members by 1982, the Invisible Empire returned once again to its roots in violence. In 1979 a group of Greensboro, North Carolina, Klansmen and Nazis killed five members of the Communist Workers Party participating in an anti-Klan demonstration. Four years later, two officers of Robert Shelton's United Klans of America were convicted for the lynching of an African-American Alabama teenager. A seven-million-dollar civil damage suit required the organization to surrender all assets in 1987. Meanwhile, Louisiana activist David Duke formed the Knights of the Ku Klux Klan and appealed for support among urbane whites of the middle class.[17]

With fewer than six thousand followers in the late 1980s, the "fourth" Klan fell within two categories. The first, consisting of southerners in the Invisible Knights of the Ku Klux Klan and remnants of the United Klans of America, sought a return to racial segregation. The second involved Klansmen affiliated with Duke's more radical knights. Accepting Catholics but advocating the nationwide expulsion or extermination of nonwhites and racial minorities, these hard-core KKK loyalists blamed Jews for conspiring to destroy the white race and rule the world. They sought to create a nationalistic and militaristic white republic devoted to free enterprise and the restoration of "Christian" values and practices.[18]

Although Klan groups helped to disseminate such views, new organizations usurped the Invisible Empire. The Posse Comitatus, founded in Portland in 1969, spread across the West by combining antigovernment conspiracy themes with anti-Semitism and racial supremacy. Richard Butler's Idaho-based Aryan Nation advanced a racially oriented "Christian identity" philosophy in which white Nordics are God's chosen people. The Order, a neo-Nazi terrorist group based in the western mountain states, declared war on the U.S. government in 1984. The White Aryan Resistance, founded by former California KKK Grand Dragon Tom Metzger, recruited hundreds of young neo-Nazi "skinheads" in Portland and other West Coast cities in the mid-1980s. White-supremacy ideologies spread further when David Duke left KKK ranks and ran for president of the United States in 1988 as a candidate of the Populist Party. In the 1990s, ex-Klansmen were among those to join the militia movement, active in the Midwest and interior West, which armed followers for ultimate confrontation with a collectivist and culturally decadent "new world order."[19]

The Ku Klux Klan's repeated association with white supremacy, rural nativism, and vigilantism has influenced the manner in which historians have dealt with the "second" Klan of the 1920s. Richard Hofstadter's *Age of Reform* linked the post–World War I Invisible Empire to the "shabbiness of the evangelical mind" and to small towns inhabited by "relatively unprosperous and uncultivated native white Protestants." As late as 1988, David Bennett's *Party of Fear* described the 1920s KKK as fostering a "repressive" and "right-wing subculture" of "outsiders and losers" that comprised "traditional nativism's last stand." Nancy MacLean's *Behind the Mask of Chivalry* viewed the secret order of postwar Georgia as a reactive movement of "middling" white males seeking to recover racial privilege, reclaim control over rebellious wives and children, and reassert a place in a changing economic order. For MacLean, "reactionary" and bigoted populists in the Klan of the 1920s made up the first nationwide, sustained, and self-consciously ideological vigilante movement.[20]

Do the La Grande Minutes support such approaches, or do they sustain the emphasis that "revisionist" scholars have placed on Klan involvement in 1920s' purity reform and citizen empowerment? Did the Klan embody the efforts of privileged elites to hold on to racial, ethnic, and gendered power or the attempts of beleaguered middle-class citizens to keep pace with social change? Do the Oregon documents depict the post–World War I Invisible Empire as irrevocably "racist" and hopelessly "reactionary" or as the "first loud shout of modern-day conservative populism?"[21]

Certainly racism and nativism permeated the recorded discourse of La Grande knights. Klavern minutes include references to "Niggar Soup," "coons," "Japs," "Chinks," "wops," "Irish stew," "red neck" Catholics, and "old black crows" (nuns), to cite a few.[22] The offhanded coarseness of such language raises disturbing questions. How does one evaluate a movement that espoused Christian ethics and democratic values only to contradict the notions of goodwill and fair play inherent to both? Could Klansmen celebrate the virtues of individual character and accomplishment and continue to judge others by family, ethnic, and racial background? Could a social crusade dedicated to community cohesion continue to polarize the local citizenry on the most arbitrary and narrow-minded criteria of social origins? Could the Invisible Empire's ritualistic deference to national unity and constitutional procedure be reconciled with its obsessions with secrecy and ethnocultural "solidarity"?

Like the Moral Majority and Christian Coalition of the 1980s and 1990s, the Jazz Age Ku Klux Klan of La Grande appeared as a "valuecentric" movement expressing "vague discontent" toward modern society.[23] Yet in their effort to elevate middle-class social mores as the criteria of political and social relationships, 1920s Klansmen neglected to see that traditional values often were embodied in the ethnic and racial cultures they thoughtlessly denigrated. Proud of their commitment to social reform, La Grande knights failed to realize that they had embraced an organizational identity and set of symbols that terrorized the groups they disparaged.

As post–World War I enactment of strict immigration quotas demonstrated, however, racism and nativism were by no means unique to the Invisible Empire. Indeed, anti-Klan activists frequently shared racial prejudices with members of the secret order. Since knights of the 1920s reacted mainly to the abstract stereotypes of ethnics and racial minorities, moreover, much of their racial abuse was verbal not substantive. Although lack of documentation does not rule out the possibility of violent activity, the La Grande Minutes do not include any hint of physical coercion or vigilantism. Even the hostile *La Grande Evening Observer* published no accounts of such behavior by Union County Klansmen. Nationwide, revisionist scholarship minimizes Klan-related violence in the 1920s. In the racially explosive South, for example, lynchings declined dramatically after 1922. The region's leading historian of vigilante executions has concluded that decreasing Klan violence in the 1920s was rarely directed against Jews, Catholics, or African Americans but targeted "whites accused of sexual indiscretions, bootlegging, divorce, and other perceived moral failings."[24]

Rather than being a remnant of marginalized extremism, the "white Protestant nationalism" of the 1920s Ku Klux Klan expressed mainstream perspectives. Such views were rooted in a historic belief that the people of the New World had been "chosen" for a special destiny in which their "free" social values would prevail. Emboldened by an enterprising middle-class ethic, white Protestants were to be liberated from "European" tyrannies, such as monarchy, titled aristocracy, or state religions. The priesthood of the Roman Catholic Church played a symbolic role in such thinking because it represented the clerical monopoly of knowledge that allegedly condemned ordinary people to illiteracy, ignorance, and superstition. Klan nativism also tapped common roots when it embraced the tendency of independent merchants to view minority tradespeople as members of dangerously cohesive blocs who adhered to shoddy business practices.[25]

The mainstream sensibilities of the 1920s Klan obviously resonated with many of La Grande's townspeople, officeholders, and clergy. Evidence of this surfaced when Kligrapp Fosner and school commissioner Eberhard reported that most American Legionnaires in the city and statewide Elks were members of the Invisible Empire. The popularity of the secret order seemed evident when local knights held an open-air, Saturday night ceremony, complete with burning crosses on a nearby hillside, to mark the receipt of the La Grande klavern's formal charter on St. Patrick's Day, 1923. The following July, KKK adversary Bruce Dennis reported in the *La Grande Evening Observer* that 325 uniformed

Union County Klansmen conducted a nighttime parade before thousands of spectators through La Grande's business district to the county fairground.[26]

Coming to terms with the Invisible Empire's pervasive appeal and influence requires a careful reading of Klan documents like the La Grande Minutes. Although the secret order undoubtedly offered social and economic advantages based on race and ethnicity, it is important to see beyond the racial and ethnic themes of Klan discourse. The La Grande documents suggest that the KKK of the 1920s provided important attractions of fraternity and moral reform. They demonstrate that law enforcement and purity activities were not designed to mask privilege and harass cultural minorities, although they occasionally had that effect. Instead, the La Grande Minutes reveal that the social crusades of the Invisible Empire helped to legitimize a movement serving community interests, even when such efforts failed to achieve their goals.

After consideration of the La Grande records, one must place this important Oregon Klan within the model advanced by recent Klan revisionists—that of a popular crusade of mainstream citizens seeking to strengthen traditional values and practices in the freewheeling era following World War I. Striving to enhance the life of their families, community, and nation, La Grande Klansmen mirrored what historian Shawn Lay has described as "the hopes, fears, and guiding values of much of the American public in the 1920s."[27] The La Grande records, a product of the majority culture of ordinary people, provide scholars with the challenge of exploring Middle America without dependence on unthinking predispositions, stale formulations, and unwarranted stereotypes.

Although it is tempting to judge Jazz Age Klansmen by the standards of later generations, the story provided by the minutes is a complex one—a chronicle of both compassion and complicity in cruelty, of positive social accomplishment and arbitrary and dysfunctional divisiveness. Seeing themselves as victims of social forces, La Grande knights lashed out against those with even less power than they held. The saga of this Klan of the 1920s presents historians with the opportunity to place the imperfect actors of the past in their full social and human context. For such a task, no better resource can be found than the once-secret and profoundly suggestive minutes of the Ku Klux Klan of La Grande, Oregon.

Notes and Index

otes

INTRODUCTION: SETTING THE CONTEXT

    1. See "Prominent Attorney Dies Here," *La Grande Observer* (January 29, 1968): 1; Willard K. Carey to David A. Horowitz, June 6, 15, 1994, Author's Files.

    2. Leonard J. Moore, *Citizen Klansmen: The Ku Klux Klan in Indiana, 1921–1928* (Chapel Hill: University of North Carolina Press, 1991), xii.

    3. Conventional Klan historiography includes John Moffatt Mecklin, *The Ku Klux Klan: A Study of the American Mind* (New York: Russell and Russell, 1924); Richard Hofstadter, *The Age of Reform: From Bryan to F.D.R.* (New York: Alfred A. Knopf, 1955), 288–301; Wyn Craig Wade, *The Fiery Cross: The Ku Klux Klan in America*, rev. ed. (New York: Oxford University Press, 1998); David H. Bennett, *The Party of Fear: From Nativist Movements to the New Right in American History* (Chapel Hill: University of North Carolina Press, 1988), 1–14, 199–237; and Nancy MacLean, *Behind the Mask of Chivalry: The Making of the Second Ku Klux Klan* (New York: Oxford University Press, 1994). Revisionist scholarship includes portions of David M. Chalmers, *Hooded Americanism: The History of the Ku Klux Klan*, rev. ed. (New York: Franklin Watts, 1981); as well as Charles C. Alexander, *The Ku Klux Klan in the Southwest* (Lexington: University of Kentucky Press, 1966); Kenneth T. Jackson, *The Ku Klux Klan in the City, 1915–1930* (New York: Oxford University Press, 1967); Robert A. Goldberg, *Hooded Empire: The Ku Klux Klan in Colorado* (Urbana: University of Illinois Press, 1981); Larry R. Gerlach, *Blazing Crosses in Zion: The Ku Klux Klan in Utah* (Logan: Utah State University Press, 1982); Shawn Lay, *War, Revolution, and the Ku Klux Klan: A Study of Intolerance in a Border City* (El Paso: Texas Western Press, 1985); Lay, *Hooded Knights on the Niagara: The Ku Klux Klan in Buffalo, New York* (New York: New York University Press, 1995); William D. Jenkins, *The Ku Klux Klan in Ohio's Mahoning Valley* (Kent, Ohio: Kent State University Press, 1990); Moore, *Citizen Klansmen*; and Kathleen M. Blee, *Women of the Klan: Racism and Gender in the 1920s* (Berkeley: University of California Press, 1991). For revisionist case studies on the western KKK, see Shawn Lay, ed., *The Invisible Empire in the West: Toward a New Historical Appraisal of the Ku Klux Klan of the 1920s* (Urbana: University of Illinois Press, 1992). Summaries of revisionist scholarship can be found in Leonard J. Moore, "Historical Interpretations of the 1920s Klan: The Traditional View and the Populist Revision," *Journal of Social History* 24 (winter 1990): 341–57, also published as "Historical Interpretations of the 1920s Klan:

The Traditional View and Recent Revisions," in Shawn Lay, ed., *The Invisible Empire in the West: Toward a New Historical Appraisal of the Ku Klux Klan of the 1920s* (Urbana: University of Illinois Press, 1992), 17–38. See also Leonard J. Moore, "Good Old-Fashioned New Social History and the Twentieth-Century American Right," *Reviews in American History* 24 (December 1996): 559–63; Michael Kazin, "The Grass-Roots Right: New Histories of U.S. Conservatism in the Twentieth Century," *American Historical Review* 97 (February 1992): 140–45; and Lay, *Hooded Knights*, 177–91. The findings of recent Klan case studies are synthesized in Robert A. Goldberg, "Invisible Empire: The Knights of the Ku Klux Klan," in *Grassroots Resistance: Social Movements in Twentieth Century America* (Belmont, Calif.: Wadsworth, 1991), 79–82, 87–89; Stanley Coben, *Rebellion against Victorianism: The Impetus for Cultural Change in 1920s America* (New York: Oxford University Press, 1991), 136–39; Lynn Dumenil, *The Modern Temper: American Culture and Society in the 1920s* (New York: Hill and Wang, 1995), 235–45; and David A. Horowitz, *Beyond Left and Right: Insurgency and the Establishment* (Urbana: University of Illinois Press, 1997), 82–89.

4. For the origins of the Ku Klux Klan, see Shawn Lay, "Introduction: The Second Invisible Empire," in Shawn Lay, ed., *The Invisible Empire in the West: Toward a New Historical Appraisal of the Ku Klux Klan of the 1920s* (Urbana: University of Illinois Press, 1992), 1–2; Chalmers, *Hooded Americanism*, 8–21. For speculation on the organization's name, see Goldberg, "Invisible Empire," 65; "The Definition of Klannishness," *Imperial Night-Hawk* 1 (March 5, 1924): 1.

5. For the genesis of the second Klan, see Lay, "Introduction," 4–5; Chalmers, *Hooded Americanism*, 22–30.

6. See Nancy MacLean, "The Leo Frank Case Reconsidered: Gender and Sexual Politics in the Making of Reactionary Populism," *Journal of American History* 78 (December 1991): 917–48; Lay, "Introduction," 6; Horowitz, *Beyond Left and Right*, 82–83. A useful description of Klan terms and officer designations can be found in the glossary in Goldberg, *Hooded Empire*.

7. See Lay, "Introduction," 7–8; Chalmers, *Hooded Americanism*, 31–38; Jackson, *Ku Klux Klan*, 15, Table 1.

8. See David A. Horowitz, "The Klansman as Outsider: Ethnocultural Solidarity and Antielitism in the Oregon Ku Klux Klan of the 1920s," *Pacific Northwest Quarterly* 80 (January 1989): 19, and *Beyond Left and Right*, 83–85; Chalmers, *Hooded Americanism*, 113–14; Lay, "Introduction," 9.

9. See Hiram Wesley Evans, "The Klan's Fight for Americanism," *North American Review* 223 (March 1926): 33–63, and *The Public School Problem in America: Outlining Fully the Policies and the Program of the Knights of the Ku Klux Klan toward the Public School System* (Atlanta: Knights of the Ku Klux Klan, 1924); "The Klan of Tomorrow," *Imperial Night-Hawk* 2 (October 15, 1924): 1–3. For Klan imagery and core values, see "The Seven Symbols of the Klan," *Imperial Night-Hawk* 1 (December 26, 1923): 6–7; Horowitz, *Beyond Left and Right*, 85–86.

10. See Horowitz, *Beyond Left and Right*, 85–88; Coben, *Rebellion against Victorian-*

ism, 136–39; "Lynching Decreases as the Klan Grows," *Imperial Night-Hawk* 1 (July 25, 1923): 8; "The Klan's Attitude toward Whipping," *Imperial Night-Hawk* 1 (September 12, 1923): 1.

11. See Horowitz, *Beyond Left and Right*, 83; Chalmers, *Hooded Americanism*, 39, 43–46, 201.

12. See Chalmers, *Hooded Americanism*, 50–54, 202–12, 281–88.

13. See Lawrence J. Saalfeld, *Forces of Prejudice: The Ku Klux Klan in Oregon, 1920–1925* (Portland: Archdiocesan Historical Commission, 1984), 2–3; Eckard V. Toy, "The Ku Klux Klan in Oregon," in G. Thomas Edwards and Carlos A. Schwantes, eds., *Experiences in a Promised Land: Essays in Pacific Northwest History* (Seattle: University of Washington Press, 1986), 270–71; C. Easton Rothwell, "The Ku Klux Klan in the State of Oregon" (bachelor's thesis, Reed College, 1924), 117. For a contemporary view of KKK organizing in Oregon, see Waldo Roberts, "Ku Kluxing in Oregon," *Outlook* 130 (March 14, 1923): 490–91. Father Saalfeld's book was a reworking of his 1950 M. A. thesis for the Catholic University of America. Many of his findings appeared in Chalmers, *Hooded Americanism*, 85–91, and in Jackson, *Ku Klux Klan*, 196–214.

14. See Eckard V. Toy, "Robe and Gown: The Ku Klux Klan in Eugene, Oregon, during the 1920s," in Shawn Lay, ed., *The Invisible Empire in the West: Toward a New Historical Appraisal of the Ku Klux Klan of the 1920s* (Urbana: University of Illinois Press, 1992), 154–55, and "Ku Klux Klan in Oregon," in Edwards and Schwantes, eds., *Experiences in a Promised Land*, 272–73; Saalfeld, *Forces of Prejudice*, 3.

15. See Toy, "Ku Klux Klan in Oregon," in Edwards and Schwantes, eds., *Experiences in a Promised Land*, 273; Chalmers, *Hooded Americanism*, 87–88; Rothwell, "Ku Klux Klan," 135–36; Saalfeld, *Forces of Prejudice*, 2–3, 26, 29, 30, 47, 52–53.

16. See Toy, "Ku Klux Klan in Oregon," in Edwards and Schwantes, eds., *Experiences in a Promised Land*, 271, and "Robe and Gown," 154; Saalfeld, *Forces of Prejudice*, 3, 7–8, 10–13; Horowitz, "Klansman as Outsider," 19, and "Social Morality and Personal Revitalization: Oregon's Ku Klux Klan in the 1920s," *Oregon Historical Quarterly* 90 (winter 1989): 369–71.

17. See Toy, "Ku Klux Klan in Oregon," in Edwards and Schwantes, eds., *Experiences in a Promised Land*, 272, 274, 276; Saalfeld, *Forces of Prejudice*, 5. For one dramatic rally, see "Gathering of Klan at Dallas," *Oregon Statesman* (April 16, 1924): 1.

18. Saalfeld, *Forces of Prejudice*, 20; "Klansmen Honor Fred L. Gifford," *Oregonian* (March 4, 1923): 8.

19. Horowitz, "Social Morality," 372–74; Toy, "Ku Klux Klan in Oregon," in Edwards and Schwantes, eds., *Experiences in a Promised Land*, 277; Proclamation of Governor Benjamin Olcott, May 13, 1922, Oregon State Archives, Salem; "Denounces Masked Mobs," *La Grande Evening Observer* (May 13, 1922): 1, 6. For a contemporary view of Medford incidents, see Harry N. Crain, "Three Assaults of Kluxey," *Salem Capital-Journal* (October 31, 1922): 1, 5. For historical perspectives, see "Knights of the Ku Klux Klan in Southern Oregon," *Table Rock Sentinel* 3 (September 1983): 12–19, (October 1983): 13–20, and (November 1983): 3–15; as well as Jeff LaLande,

"Beneath the Hooded Robe: Newspapermen, Local Politics, and the Ku Klux Klan in Jackson County, Oregon, 1921–1923," *Pacific Northwest Quarterly* 83 (April 1992): 42–52.

20. See Toy, "Ku Klux Klan in Oregon," in Edwards and Schwantes, eds., *Experiences in a Promised Land*, 277–79.

21. See Toy, "Ku Klux Klan in Oregon," in Edwards and Schwantes, eds., *Experiences in a Promised Land*, 279–82; Saalfeld, *Forces of Prejudice*, 38–39; Horowitz, "Klansman as Outsider," 16–19.

22. The origins of the La Grande klavern are described in Minutes, May 11, 1922, and March 13, 1923, Ku Klux Klan, La Grande, Or. Chapter, Records, 1922–1923, Oregon Historical Society (OHS), Mss. 2604. For La Grande's development, see *Oregon and Washington State Gazetteer and Business Directory, 1921–1922* (Seattle: R. L. Polk, 1921), 242; *Polk's Union and Wallowa Counties Directory* (Portland: R. L. Polk, 1917), 9; F. E. Brinkman, comp., *La Grande City Directory* (La Grande, 1921), 7; Earl C. Reynolds, "La Grande, Oregon: The Industrial Capital of Eastern Oregon," *Union Pacific Magazine* 4 (December 1925): 5, 31; Dietrich Deumling, "The Roles of the Railroad on the Development of the Grande Ronde Valley" (master's thesis, Northern Arizona University, 1972), 83; "La Grande's Schools Are in the Lead," *La Grande Evening Observer* (September 8, 1923): 5.

23. See Reynolds, "La Grande, Oregon," 31; Brinkman, comp., *La Grande City Directory*, 5; Barbara Ruth Bailey, *Main Street, Northeastern Oregon: The Founding and Development of Small Towns* (Portland: Oregon Historical Society, 1982), 27, 87; *An Illustrated History of Union and Wallowa Counties* (n.p.: Western Historical Publishing, 1902), 221; Bernal D. Hug, *History of Union County, Oregon* (La Grande: Union County Historical Society, 1961), 100, 129–30, 135–37, 194–96.

24. Reynolds, "La Grande, Oregon," 31.

25. See John F. Stover, *American Railroads* (Chicago: University of Chicago Press, 1961), 210; Nelson Trottman, *History of the Union Pacific: A Financial and Economic Survey* (New York: Ronald Press, 1923), 385; Robert H. Zieger, *Republicans and Labor, 1919–1929* (Lexington: University of Kentucky Press, 1969), 109, 117–19, 132–33, 138; "Local Men Respond to Strike Call," *La Grande Evening Observer* (July 1, 1922): 4. For the contradictions of moral tradition and economic progress, see Horowitz, "The 'Cross of Culture': La Grande, Oregon, in the 1920s," *Oregon Historical Quarterly* 93 (summer 1992): 147–67.

26. See Lee C. Johnson, "History of Union County," *La Grande Evening Observer* (May 14, 1949): 4; Union County Vertical File Folder, OHS; Frank M. Jasper, "The Chinese in Union County" (unpublished ms., Union County Historical Society, 1960), 4, 8, 10–15.

27. Table 7, Population—Oregon, Department of Commerce, Bureau of the Census, *Fourteenth Census of the United States, Taken in the Year 1920, Population*, 3:837; "Opium Taken from Dope Joint Here," *La Grande Evening Observer* (August 19, 1922): 1; "Dope Raid Successfully Pulled by City Police," *La Grande Evening Observer*

(April 10, 1923): 1; "Len Chong, 75, Gets $250 Fine in Court on 'Nuisance Charge,'" *La Grande Evening Observer* (November 3, 1923): 1; "Orientals Must Await Action of U.S. Grand Jury on Opium Charge," *La Grande Evening Observer* (November 8, 1923): 1; Editorial, "Dope in La Grande," *La Grande Evening Observer* (March 21, 1924): 4.

28. Table 11, Population—Oregon, *Fourteenth Census*, 3:844; "Federal Men Aid Officers in Big Raid," *La Grande Evening Observer* (December 23, 1922): 1, 8; "Dee Rogers Is Found Guilty," *La Grande Evening Observer* (April 21, 1923): 1; "Pearl Fagin Found Guilty Bootlegging," *La Grande Evening Observer* (August 20, 1923): 1, 5.

29. Table 11, Population—Oregon, *Fourteenth Census*, 3:844; Table 32, Number of Members in Selected Denominations in Each State by Counties, 1926, Bureau of the Census, *Religious Bodies, 1926*, 1:664–65; "Many Arrests Made by Police; Blotter Is Busy," *La Grande Evening Observer* (April 14, 1923): 1; "Eleven Men Arrested during Past Three Days," *La Grande Evening Observer* (December 19, 1922): 1; "Round up Staged by Officers," *La Grande Evening Observer* (October 9, 1923): 1, 7.

30. Kitchen quoted in "Drunks Will Be Dealt With," *La Grande Evening Observer* (January 3, 1923): 1; "Whiskey Is Poured Out," *La Grande Evening Observer* (July 17, 1923): 1; "Two Men Slain in Baker," *La Grande Evening Observer* (October 10, 1923): 1, 4. For city and county Prohibition arrests, see "Eleven Men Arrested during Past Three Days," *La Grande Evening Observer* (December 19, 1922): 1; "County Records Show a Crime Increase," *La Grande Evening Observer* (January 5, 1923): 1; "Arrests by Police in Year Many," *La Grande Evening Observer* (January 5, 1924): 2.

31. See "Former Chief under Arrest," *La Grande Evening Observer* (July 12, 1923): 1; "Roy Flexer Is Sentenced to Prison Term," *La Grande Evening Observer* (October 20, 1923): 1; "Sold Booze to Children," *La Grande Evening Observer* (September 6, 1922): 1; "Lid Is Clamping down on Frequenting of Pool and Card Rooms by Minors," *La Grande Evening Observer* (December 14, 1922): 1.

32. Municipal Ordinance #850, Series 1907, April 9, 1917, Records of the City of La Grande; "Lid Clamped on Gambling," *La Grande Evening Observer* (January 1, 1923): 1; "Drive to Clean up La Grande Is in Progress," *La Grande Evening Observer* (December 23, 1922): 1.

33. Minutes, May 11, 1922, and March 13, 1923, Ku Klux Klan, La Grande, Or. Chapter, Records, 1922–1923, Oregon Historical Society, Mss. 2604.

34. See "Dr. E. A. Fosner Dies at Sherwood, Wash.," *Enterprise Chieftain* (October 2, 1941): 2; Washington County (1920), *Fourteenth Census*, 30:426; File on Harold Raymond Fosner, National Personnel Records Center, National Archives.

35. Willard K. Carey to David A. Horowitz, June 6, 15, 1994, Author's Files; Donor card for Willard K. Carey, March 17, 1980, Records of Oregon Historical Society.

36. R. Thomas Gooding to David A. Horowitz, April 4, 1994, John T. Evans to David A. Horowitz, January 1, 1990, and June 14, 1994, Author's Files. See also R. Thomas Gooding to David A. Horowitz, November 22, 1988, Author's Files.

37. R. Thomas Gooding to David A. Horowitz, n.d. (attached to David A. Horowitz to R. Thomas Gooding, June 10, 1994), John T. Evans to David A. Horowitz, Janu-

ary 1, 1990, and John T. Evans to R. Thomas Gooding, June 5, 1994, Author's Files; Jay Griffiths, "La Grande Group in Early '20s Non-Violent," *Observer* (November 29, 1985): 2, "Looking Back: LG Klan Member Reminisces," *Observer* (November 30, 1985): 2, and "Klan Used Fraternal Language, Shrouded in Secrecy," *Observer* (November 30, 1985): 2. In 1988 Gooding sent me the copy of the minutes returned to him by McLaughlin's widow. See R. Thomas Gooding to David A. Horowitz, November 22, 1988, April 4, 1994, and n.d. (attached to David A. Horowitz to R. Thomas Gooding, June 10, 1994), Author's Files.

38. "Carl Eugene Millering," *Observer* (April 12, 1990): 2; Arthur H. Bone, ed., *Oregon Cattleman/Governor, Congressman: Memoirs and Times of Walter M. Pierce* (Portland: Oregon Historical Society, 1981), 210. Millering is mentioned as a "very active" Klan participant in Minutes, March 13, 1923, 6, Ku Klux Klan, La Grande, Or. Chapter, Records, 1922–1923, Oregon Historical Society, Mss. 2604. The entry for April 22, 1924, the last segment of the La Grande klavern documents, lists Millering as a member of the Nominating Committee.

39. See Bone, ed., *Oregon Cattleman/Governor*, 210; "Celebrated the Charter Arrival," *La Grande Evening Observer* (March 19, 1923): 8; Harry N. Crain, "Ku Klux Active at La Grande," *Salem Capital-Journal* (October 19, 1922): 1–2. For La Grande Klan and local railroad industry, see David A. Horowitz, "Order, Solidarity, Vigilance: The Ku Klux Klan in La Grande, Oregon," in Shawn Lay, ed., *The Invisible Empire in the West: Toward a New Historical Appraisal of the Ku Klux Klan of the 1920s* (Urbana: University of Illinois Press, 1992), 194–96.

40. See Goldberg, *Hooded Empire*, 183–86. An occupational analysis of La Grande Klansmen can be found in Horowitz, "Order, Solidarity," 194–95.

41. Rumors of Pierce's initiation were reported by Rothwell, "Ku Klux Klan," 131. Pierce's appearances at the La Grande klavern were described in "The Bitter and the Sweet," supplement to Minutes, November 21, 1922, 1, 3, and Minutes, June 5, 1923, 1, Ku Klux Klan, La Grande, Or. Chapter, Records, 1922–1923, Oregon Historical Society, Mss. 2604. For Kligrapp Fosner's correspondence with Pierce, see Harold R. Fosner to Walter M. Pierce, July 11, 1923, The Walter Pierce Papers, Coll. 68, Department of Special Collections, University of Oregon Libraries; Bone, ed., *Oregon Cattleman/Governor*, 209–10. See also Lem A. Dever to Walter M. Pierce, July 27, 1923, Miscellaneous File, The Walter Pierce Papers, Coll. 68, Department of Special Collections, University of Oregon Libraries.

THE MINUTES

1. See "Dr. Sawyer Talks on Ku Klux Klan," *La Grande Evening Observer* (May 16, 1922): 6. For Sawyer's rhetoric and background, see R. H. Sawyer, *The Truth about the Invisible Empire of the KKK* (Portland: Knights of the Ku Klux Klan, 1922); Lawrence J. Saalfeld, *Forces of Prejudice: The Ku Klux Klan in Oregon, 1920–1925* (Portland: Archdiocesan Historical Commission, 1984), 19–20, 45–46.

2. See "Service Today for Minister," *Oregonian* (April 10, 1940): 8.

3. For Klan political activities, see "Ku Klux Fights Sinnott," *Oregon Voter* 29 (April 15, 1922): 81; "Olcott Is Gaining," *La Grande Evening Observer* (May 20, 1922): 1.

4. For Dever and the Klan's involvement in the Oregon Public Defense League and the 1922 primary, see Saalfeld, *Forces of Prejudice*, 31–34, 54–55; see also Lem A. Dever, *Confessions of an Imperial Klansman*, 2d ed. (Portland: Lem A. Dever, 1925).

5. For community support for the 1922 railroad strike, see the following *La Grande Evening Observer* articles: "Local Men Respond to Strike Call" (July 1, 1922): 1, 4; "No Strikers Return to Work" (July 3, 1922): 1; "Brotherhoods Meet with Shop Strikers" (July 6, 1922): 1; "Large Crowd Is Attracted" (July 12, 1922): 1; "Strike's End Is Forecast by Men Here" (July 14, 1922): 1; "Large Crowd at Rex Dance" (July 20, 1922): 1; "Benefit Old Tyme Dance for the Strikers" (July 25, 1922): 5; "Points Gun at Picket; Is Arrested" (July 10, 1922): 1; "Gun Pointing Drew a Heavy Fine in Court" (July 11, 1922): 1, 4; "Glenn Forwood Sues O.W. Co. for $100,000" (December 12, 1922): 1; Editorial, "Tribute to Order and Respect" (August 1, 1922): 4. For Klan involvement in strike, see Harry N. Crain, "Ku Klux Active at La Grande," *Salem Capital-Journal* (October 19, 1922): 1–2. For Klan support for Pierce, see Saalfeld, *Forces of Prejudice*, 34–35.

6. For Sister Lucretia, see Saalfeld, *Forces of Prejudice*, 22, 25.

7. For Pierce, the school bill, and Klan political support, see Saalfeld, *Forces of Prejudice*, 35–36; Arthur H. Bone, ed., *Oregon Cattleman/Governor, Congressman: Memoirs and Times of Walter M. Pierce* (Portland: Oregon Historical Society, 1981), 159–68. For KKK response to Olcott, see "Fiery Cross Burns during the Meeting," *La Grande Evening Observer* (October 19, 1922): 1. The Humphreys candidacy is described in "May Yet File for City Commission," *La Grande Evening Observer* (October 5, 1922): 1; "C. M. Humphreys Files Petition for Candidacy," *La Grande Evening Observer* (October 9, 1922): 1. For Sinnott, see "Body Will Be Taken to Dalles," *Dalles Chronicle* (July 27, 1929): 1. For Cochran, see listing in *Eminent Judges and Lawyers of the Northwest, 1843–1955* (Palo Alto: C. W. Taylor, Jr., 1954), 337. Gifford's Klan Komfort Fund was one of several financial projects that sowed dissent in state KKK. See Saalfeld, *Forces of Prejudice*, 56–57.

8. Results of the city commission election appear in "Black and Williams Are Elected," *La Grande Evening Observer* (November 8, 1922): 1; while the contests for justice of the peace and state senator are in "Taylor Winner over Eberhard in Close Race," *La Grande Evening Observer* (November 9, 1922): 1; "Eberhard Is 363 Ahead in This County," *La Grande Evening Observer* (November 11, 1922): 1. Sinnott's congressional race, the school bill results, and the Pierce victory are described in "School Bill Is Slightly in the Lead," *La Grande Evening Observer* (November 9, 1922): 1; "Official Majority of Pierce 34,237," *Oregonian* (November 24, 1922): 14. See also Bone, ed., *Oregon Cattleman/Governor*, 178–79. For occupational and ethnic backgrounds of Frederick L. Meyers, Chester Newlin, and John H. Peare, see listings under their names

in U.S. Census Records for Union County, Oregon, 1920, Multnomah County Public Library, Portland, Ore. The Dennis editorial appeared as "And out of the Chaos Came ——," *La Grande Evening Observer* (May 20, 1922): 4. Crain's exposé can be found in "Ku Klux Active at La Grande," *Salem Capital-Journal* (October 19, 1922): 1–2.

9. For background on Powell and Estes, see David A. Horowitz, "The Klansman as Outsider: Ethnocultural Solidarity and Antielitism in the Oregon Ku Klux Klan of the 1920s," *Pacific Northwest Quarterly* 80 (January 1989): 13, 16; George Estes, *The Old Cedar School* (Troutdale, Ore., 1922).

10. The Roesch family background can be found in "Pioneer Builder Julius Roesch Fatally Stricken at Age 98," *La Grande Evening Observer* (April 22, 1960): 1; "Marcus Louis Roesch," *La Grande Observer* (April 27, 1976): 2. For the tax issue under Pierce, see Bone, ed., *Oregon Cattleman/Governor*, 217–20.

11. For auto salesmen and fraternal orders, see Duncan Aikman, *The Home Town Mind* (New York: Minton and Balch, 1926), 116.

12. For the Gifford controversy in the Oregon Klan, see Saalfeld, *Forces of Prejudice*, 56. National KKK infighting is described in David M. Chalmers, *Hooded Americanism: The History of the Ku Klux Klan*, rev. ed. (New York: Franklin Watts, 1981), 100–106.

13. For background on Dr. James R. Johnson, see Saalfeld, *Forces of Prejudice*, 8, 13, 20–24.

14. Legal records for the Newlin case include *City of La Grande v. Adolph Newlin*, April 21, 1915, September 14, 1917, September 17, 1918, Records of the City of La Grande; *City of La Grande v. Adolph Newlin*, November 10, 1917, Records of Circuit Court of the State of Oregon for Union County. See also *Ray W. Logan v. The La Grande Pharmacy . . . and Adolph Newlin*, October 25, 1917, Union County Circuit Court Records. Newspaper accounts include "In Police Court," *La Grande Evening Observer* (April 22, 1922): 1; "Two Girls Fined," *La Grande Evening Observer* (April 23, 1915): 1; "A. Newlin Is Found Not Guilty by Jury," *La Grande Evening Observer* (November 10, 1917): 1; "Newlin Found Not Guilty by Jury," *La Grande Evening Observer* (November 12, 1917): 1; "L. C. Edwards Buys La Grande Pharmacy," *La Grande Evening Observer* (October 18, 1917): 1.

15. For the La Grande National Bank celebration, see "Old Business Institution Host to Many," *La Grande Evening Observer* (March 23, 1923): 1, 5. For Klan support for City Manager Kratz, see "Kinzie Strong for Mr. Kratz," *La Grande Evening Observer* (November 2, 1922): 5. Kratz's departure is covered in "O. A. Kratz Tenders His Resignation," *La Grande Evening Observer* (December 21, 1922): 1; "Mr. Stearns Selected as Manager," *La Grande Evening Observer* (December 28, 1922): 1. For activities of Klansman Ed Fields, see Crain, "Ku Klux Active," 1–2.

16. The origins of the term *Hooverized* can be found in David Burner, *Herbert Hoover: A Public Life* (New York: Alfred A. Knopf, 1979), 102. See advertisement, "Yes Sir—The Second Coming a Reality," *La Grande Evening Observer* (May 26, 1922): 6.

17. For the LOTIES controversy and the anti-Gifford revolt,, see Saalfeld, *Forces of Prejudice*, 46, 56. Klan patronage disagreements with Pierce and obstacles to the gover-

nor's tax and administrative proposals are described in Bone., ed., *Oregon Cattleman/ Governor*, 185–87, 195–97, 220–21, 255–58. For the Tillamook branding, see "Two Brand Woman in Home, She Says," *Oregonian* (January 14, 1923): 10; "Woman Says Klan Did Not Brand Her," *Oregonian* (January 17, 1923): 6; "Branding Story Greatly Magnified," *Tillamook Headlight* (January 19, 1923): 1; "Branding Charge Fails," *Oregonian* (February 10, 1923): 1; Eckard V. Toy, "The Ku Klux Klan in Tillamook, Oregon," *Pacific Northwest Quarterly* 53 (April 1962): 67. Klan support for Senator Mayfield and the Mer Rouge incident are described in Chalmers, *Hooded Americanism*, 43–48, 61–64. Klan support for national school legislation is outlined in Horowitz, "Klansman as Outsider," 15; Hiram Wesley Evans, *The Public School Problem in America: Outlining Fully the Policies and the Program of the Knights of the Ku Klux Klan toward the Public School System* (Atlanta: Knights of the Ku Klux Klan, 1924). For background on Father O'Connor, see William S. Stone, *The Cross in the Middle of Nowhere: A History of the Catholic Church in Eastern Oregon* (Bend, Ore.: W. S. Stone, 1993), 104. Carl Johnson is listed as an anti–school bill activist in Saalfeld, *Forces of Prejudice*, 80; Saalfeld also surveys state proposals to tax sectarian institutions. For liquor offenses by La Grande Klansmen, see "Five Moonshiners Caught," *La Grande Evening Observer* (June 17, 1922): 1; "Brown Admits Guilt Tuesday," *La Grande Evening Observer* (December 12, 1923): 1; "2 Convicted; 2 Freed by Court," *La Grande Evening Observer* (December 15, 1923): 1–2; "Police Officers Active during Month of Jan.," *La Grande Evening Observer* (January 30, 1923): 1.

18. For the Garb Bill, see Bone, ed., *Oregon Cattleman/Governor*, 188–90; Saalfeld, *Forces of Prejudice*, 38–40. For Eberhard, see "Death Claims Former Solon," *Oregonian* (January 30, 1968): 13; "Prominent Attorney Dies Here," *La Grande Observer* (January 29, 1968): 1.

19. For the Royal Riders of the Red Robe and Gifford's financial schemes, see Saalfeld, *Forces of Prejudice*, 44–45.

20. See "The Twelfth Chapter of Romans as a Klansman's Law of Life," *Imperial Night-Hawk* 1 (March 5, 1924): 2–3, 7. For local newspaper coverage of the Medford cases, see "Night Rider Trial Comes to an End," *La Grande Evening Observer* (March 15, 1923): 1. Historical assessments include "Knights of the Ku Klux Klan in Southern Oregon," *Table Rock Sentinel* 3 (September 1983): 12–19, (October 1983): 13–20, (November 1983): 3–15. See also Jeff LaLande, "Beneath the Hooded Robe: Newspapermen, Local Politics, and the Ku Klux Klan in Jackson County, Oregon, 1921–1923," *Pacific Northwest Quarterly* 83 (April 1992): 42–52. For KKK calendar and other terms, see glossary in Patsy Sims, *The Klan* (New York: Stein and Day, 1978), 335–38.

21. For the St. Patrick's Day cross burning, see "Celebrated the Charter Arrival," *La Grande Evening Observer* (March 19, 1923): 8. Former city manager Kratz's problems in Astoria are described in "Setters Denies Goblin Ordered Kratz Attack," *Astoria Evening Budget* (March 16, 1923): 1; "O. A. Kratz Fires His Broadsides," *Astoria Evening Budget* (March 17, 1923): 1, 5; "Portland Klan Calls Brothers to Back Mayor," *Astoria*

Evening Budget (March 20, 1923): 1; "Klan Stand in City Row Is Live Issue to Members," *Astoria Evening Budget* (March 22, 1923): 1. For Rev. O'Hara's campaign against the school bill, see Saalfeld, *Forces of Prejudice,* 63, 80–82.

22. For newspaper coverage of the Klan charter and cross burning, see "Celebrated the Charter Arrival," *La Grande Evening Observer* (March 19, 1923): 8. The Red Cross gift is described in "Red Cross Gets Klan Donation," *La Grande Evening Observer* (March 23, 1923): 1.

23. For family background of George Noble, see U.S. Census Records for Union County, Oregon, 1920, Multnomah County Public Library, Portland, Ore.

24. The Noble arrest is treated in "George Noble Not Appealing Case," *La Grande Evening Observer* (April 16, 1923): 1. Judge Kitchen's pronouncement appears in "Drunks Will Be Dealt With," *La Grande Evening Observer* (January 3, 1923): 1.

25. For the Klan's relationship with the Mormons, see Larry R. Gerlach, *Blazing Crosses in Zion: The Ku Klux Klan in Utah* (Logan: Utah State University Press, 1982), "A Battle of Empires: The Klan in Salt Lake City," in Shawn Lay, ed., *The Invisible Empire in the West: Toward a New Historical Appraisal of the Ku Klux Klan of the 1920s* (Urbana: University of Illinois Press, 1992), 121–52, esp. 133. Denominational figures for Union County residents can be found in religious census records compiled by the U.S. Government; see Table 63, Number of Members in Selected Denominations in Each State, by Counties: 1916, Bureau of the Census, *Religious Bodies, 1916,* 1:302–3, and Table 32, Members in Selected Denominations, by Counties: 1926, Bureau of the Census, *Religious Bodies, 1926,* 1:664–65.

26. For the power struggle between Simmons and Evans, see Chalmers, *Hooded Americanism,* 100–107. For Knights of Pythias festival, see "'Dokkies' Have First Claim on Pendleton," *East Oregonian* (May 18, 1923): 1.

27. See "Service Career Long," *Oregonian* (February 21, 1932): 4; "Ex-Highway Official Baldock Dies at 79," *Oregonian* (September 14, 1968): 8.

28. The Peare-Birnie controversy is outlined in "Says Politics Responsible for Removal," *La Grande Evening Observer* (August 17, 1923): 1; "G. S. Birnie Is Appointed," *La Grande Evening Observer* (August 18, 1923): 1. See listings for the two in U.S. Census Records for Union County, Oregon, 1920, Multnomah County Public Library, Portland, Ore. For Pierce's signing and implementation of the income-tax measure, see Bone, ed., *Oregon Cattleman/Governor,* 212–26.

29. For the school board election, see "Landis and Weeks Win by Big Majority," *La Grande Evening Observer* (June 19, 1923): 1. The Old Oregon Trail Pageant was previewed in "Highway Now Lined with Celebrants," *La Grande Evening Observer* (July 2, 1923): 1. For Reynolds's appointment to the county tax commission, see "Supervisors Are Selected," *La Grande Evening Observer* (July 27, 1923): 1, 5; "J. E. Reynolds Is Chairman of Tax Board," *La Grande Evening Observer* (August 13, 1923): 1. The tax commission's short history is detailed in Bone, ed., *Oregon Cattleman/Governor,* 225–26, 448, n. 71.

30. For descriptions of the Harding visit and the Old Oregon Trail Pageant, see

"Main Event with Pageant Opens Today," *La Grande Evening Observer* (July 3, 1923): 1; "President Addresses Oregonians," *La Grande Evening Observer* (July 4, 1923): 1; "Oregon Spirit Grips Harding," *Oregonian* (July 4, 1923): 1–2; "Day in Sun, Then Thud for Pierce," *Sunday Oregonian* (July 8, 1923): sec. 1: 1, 10; "Harding's Visit Uncovers Politics," *Sunday Oregonian* (July 8, 1923): sec. 1: 10; Editorial, "Whoa!" *Oregonian* (July 11, 1923): 10. The governor was defended in Editorial, "Pierce and the President," *Oregon Daily Journal* (July 10, 1923): 10. For the Old Oregon Trail Association's rejection of Pierce criticism, see Secretary-Treasurer A. W. Nelson to Walter M. Pierce, July 9, 1923, The Walter Pierce Papers, Coll. 68, Department of Special Collections, University of Oregon Libraries. The political activities of Williams and Tooze are described in Bone, ed., *Oregon Cattleman/Governor*, 153, 164, 173. For Fosner's letter and Pierce's response, see Harold R. Fosner to Walter M. Pierce, July 11, 1923, and Walter M. Pierce to Harold R. Fosner, July 13, 1923, The Walter Pierce Papers, Coll. 68, Department of Special Collections, University of Oregon Libraries.

31. For legal action to contest the school bill, see Saalfeld, *Forces of Prejudice*, 90–91.

32. The ex-police chief's legal problems are described in "Former Chief under Arrest," *La Grande Evening Observer* (July 12, 1923): 1; "Roy Flexer Is Sentenced to Prison Term," *La Grande Evening Observer* (October 20, 1923): 1. For the Union auto accident, see "15-Year-Old Girl Killed in Smashup," *La Grande Evening Observer* (July 11, 1923): 1, 5. Legal records include Union County Grand Jury Indictments, *State of Oregon v. Sid Turner*, October 5, 1923; Union County Circuit Court, *State of Oregon v. Sid Turner*, October 26, 1923; Motion to Dismiss Indictment, *State of Oregon v. Sid Turner*, December 31, 1924, Records of the Circuit Court of the State of Oregon for Union County. For the Dever-Pierce dispute, see Lem A. Dever to Walter M. Pierce, January 18, 1923, and July 27, 1923, Walter M. Pierce to Lem A. Dever, January 20, 1923, Lem A. Dever to Ward Irvine, July 2, 1923; all in The Walter Pierce Papers, Coll. 68, Department of Special Collections, University of Oregon Libraries. See also "Governor Pierce Surely Will 'Can' This Awful Boob," *Western American* (October 19, 1923): 8; Bone, ed., *Oregon Cattleman/Governor*, 196–98, 202.

33. For coverage of Klan festivities, see "Klan to Stage Big Ceremonial," *La Grande Evening Observer* (July 23, 1923): 8; "Instruct Public Is the Klan Aim," *La Grande Evening Observer* (July 24, 1923): 5; "Knights of Ku Klux Klan Held Open Air Initiation," *La Grande Evening Observer* (July 26, 1923): 1. See also "Pioneers of County Meet in Reunion," *La Grande Evening Observer* (July 26, 1923): 1.

34. See "Baker K.K.K. Stage Parade," *La Grande Evening Observer* (August 16, 1923): 1. For the North Carolina meeting, see "Grand Dragons and Great Titans Will Hold National Conference at Asheville in July," *Imperial Night-Hawk* 1 (July 4, 1923): 3.

35. The La Grande city water crisis is addressed in "City Water Supply Discussed," *La Grande Evening Observer* (August 16, 1923): 1, 5; "Water Situation Explained," *La Grande Evening Observer* (August 30, 1923): 1, 4. For Klan foes in the Red Cross, see "Red Cross Gets Klan Donation," *La Grande Evening Observer* (March 23, 1923): 1;

"Many Orders to Assist Red Cross Roll," *La Grande Evening Observer* (November 6, 1923): 1. For the YMCA, see "'Y' Directors Are Elected," *La Grande Evening Observer* (February 27, 1923): 1.

36. See "New Economies Affect Every Klansman," *Imperial Night-Hawk* 1 (August 15, 1923): 5, 7.

37. For Klan involvement in the Senate campaign, see "Klan Asks Gifford to Run for Senate," *Oregonian* (August 31, 1923): 8; "Klan Paper Toots Mr. Gifford's Horn," *Oregonian* (September 1, 1923): 7; "Gifford Declines to Run for Senate," *Oregonian* (September 2, 1923): 10; "Klan Lays Plans to Enter Politics," *Oregonian* (September 9, 1923): 20. See "The People Want Gifford," *Western American* (September 7, 1923): 4. The Carnegie riot is described in Chalmers, *Hooded Americanism*, 283–39.

38. For details on the Japanese earthquake, see "Tokio, Yokohama and Other Japanese Cities Destroyed by Earthquake," *Oregonian* (September 2, 1923): 1. See Editorial, "Our Nation's Sympathy for Japan," *Western American* (September 7, 1923): 4. Gifford's relationship to the Pierce recall drive is discussed in Bone, ed., *Oregon Cattleman/Governor*, 198, 203–4, 207–8. For the Good Government League meeting, see "Klan Fails to Find Senate Candidate," *Oregonian* (September 14, 1923): 18. Lem Dever claimed that he nominated Gifford to be the Klan's Senate candidate to steer the order away from support for Portland Mayor George L. Baker. See Dever, *Confessions of an Imperial Klansman*, 36–37. The La Grande klavern's donation to the widow of the Carnegie Klansman was recorded in "Thomas R. Abbott Trust Fund Now Amounts to $11,579.14," *Imperial Night-Hawk* 1 (November 11, 1923): 6.

39. See "Dillon Tries to Resurrect the YMCA," *La Grande Evening Observer* (October 9, 1923): 1, 7; "Support for Y Opening to Be Sought," *La Grande Evening Observer* (November 7, 1923):1.

40. For the La Grande water crisis, see "Several Will Talk on Water Problem Here," *La Grande Evening Observer* (September 9, 1923): 3; "Gravity Plan Support Not Very Strong," *La Grande Evening Observer* (October 10, 1923): 1, 5. The Good Government League's meeting is described in "Klan Fails to Find Senate Candidate," *Oregonian* (September 14, 1923): 18. For Gifford's unwillingness to risk a Senate campaign, see Saalfeld, *Forces of Prejudice*, 41.

41. For Cochran's selection as leader of Oregon Masons, see "G. T. Cochran Grand Master," *La Grande Evening Observer* (June 15, 1923): 1. The Washington Memorial was described in "Masons of America Will Raise Memorial Tower to Washington," *New York Times* (October 14, 1923): sec. 9: 11; "Coolidge Helps Lay Washington Stone," *New York Times* (November 2, 1923): 12. For the religious controversy in Italy, see "Methodists in Rome," *New York Times* (May 13, 1923): sec. 9: 5; "Methodists in Italy," *New York Times* (June 10, 1923): sec. 8: 5; "Dr. Tipple Quits College in Rome," *New York Times* (November 21, 1923): 6. The Klan political list is mentioned in Bone, ed., *Oregon Cattleman/Governor*, 208.

42. See "Alleged Immoral Conditions Now in La Grande's Colored Town Aired by Citizens before City Commission," *La Grande Evening Observer* (November 22, 1923):

1, 5; "Petition One of Largest," *La Grande Evening Observer* (November 22, 1923): 1. Antivice activity was reported in "50 Persons Are Arrested during November Month," *La Grande Evening Observer* (December 4, 1923): 1.

43. The plight of the Red Cross was depicted in "Legion Will Superintend Actual Work," *La Grande Evening Observer* (December 4, 1923): 1. For Cochran's Masonic credentials, see "G. T. Cochran Grand Master," *La Grande Evening Observer* (June 15, 1923): 1; "Templars Elect George Cochran," *La Grande Evening Observer* (October 13, 1923): 1. Gifford's support for the candidate is revealed in "Fred Gifford Is Here Today," *La Grande Evening Observer* (December 12, 1923): 1, 5. For the Klan campaign to promote state economic development, see "Raising $300,000 for Development of Mighty Oregon," *Western American* (December 2, 1922): 5. Kubli's search for Klan votes is described in "Klan to Take Hand in Senate Contest," *Oregonian* (December 2, 1923): 19; "Seat in Senate Sought by Kubli," *Oregonian* (December 9, 1923): 1. For the state legislature's attempt to tax church property, see Bone, ed., *Oregon Cattleman/Governor*, 190.

44. For background on Rev. Allison, see Saalfeld, *Forces of Prejudice*, 8, 10, 14–16.

45. See "Cochran May Be Candidate," *La Grande Evening Observer* (April 20, 1924): 1; "G. Cochran Throws Hat into Ring," *La Grande Evening Observer* (April 21, 1924): 1, 5; "Cochran Says He Will Win," *La Grande Evening Observer* (May 15, 1924): 1.

46. The newspaper clipping read at the meeting may have been "The Etiquette of the Stars and Stripes Adopted by Code Conference 1923," *Imperial Night-Hawk* 1 (February 27, 1924): 2–3, 7. Kubli's campaign is addressed in "Kubli Visits The Dalles," *Oregonian* (April 24, 1924): 2; Saalfeld, *Forces of Prejudice*, 40–41.

Conclusion: The Meaning of the La Grande Minutes

1. See "Legion Will Superintend Actual Work," *La Grande Evening Observer* (December 4, 1923): 1; "Will Attempt to Revive 'Y,'" *La Grande Evening Observer* (December 11, 1923): 1; "Y.M.C.A. Is Again Aided by Stange," *La Grande Evening Observer* (December 13, 1923): 1–2; "La Grande Y.M. Is to Be Closed," *Baker Morning Democrat* (April 17, 1924): 2.

2. See "Problem of Water Here Is Reviewed," *La Grande Evening Observer* (March 12, 1924): 1, 5; "Bond Issue Defeated," *La Grande Evening Observer* (May 2, 1924): 1; "Landis Third Commissioner," *La Grande Evening Observer* (November 5, 1924): 1; "Fred Gifford Is Here Today," *La Grande Evening Observer* (December 12, 1923): 1, 5; "Cochran May Be Candidate," *La Grande Evening Observer* (April 20, 1924): 1; "G. Cochran Throws Hat into Ring," *La Grande Evening Observer* (April 21, 1924): 1, 5; "Cochran Says He Will Win," *La Grande Evening Observer* (May 15, 1924): 1; "Cochran Loses Race," *La Grande Evening Observer* (May 17, 1924): 1; "Final Count Now Complete," *La Grande Evening Observer* (May 22, 1924): 1, 5; "Latest Returns," *La Grande Evening Observer* (November 5, 1924): 1; "Coolidge Vote Is Heavy

in Oregon," *La Grande Evening Observer* (November 5, 1924): 6. For Klan support for Cochran, see "Election Post-Mortem," *Oregon Voter* 37 (May 24, 1924): 34.

3. See "Final Vote Now Complete," *La Grande Evening Observer* (May 22, 1924): 1, 5; Walter M. Pierce to Bruce Dennis, May 28, 1923, The Walter Pierce Papers, Coll. 68, Department of Special Collections, University of Oregon Libraries; "La Grande Paper Sold," *Oregonian* (June 28, 1925): 16; "Seat Relinquished by Senator Dennis," *Oregonian* (February 25, 1926): 13; "Death Claims Bruce Dennis, Ex-Publisher, State Senator," *Oregonian* (July 15, 1949): 15.

4. See "Trial of Dr. Willson Is On," *La Grande Evening Observer* (February 26, 1924): 1; "Trial of Dr. Willson Now Nearing End," *La Grande Evening Observer* (February 27, 1924): 1; "Dalles Physician Accused by Girl," *Morning Astorian* (February 28, 1924): 1; "Dr. Willson Found Guilty as Charged," *La Grande Evening Observer* (February 29, 1924): 1; "Willson Gets 3 Years," *La Grande Evening Observer* (March 3, 1924): 1; Obituary, "Dentist Succumbs," *Oregon Journal* (November 1, 1957): 3; *State of Oregon v. E. O. Wilson* [sic], February 5, 8, 11, 1924, June 10, 11, 1925, Records of Circuit Court of the State of Oregon for Union County; "E. O. Willson Found Guilty," *La Grande Evening Observer* (June 11, 1925): 1; Records of Oregon State Supreme Court, 113 OR 450, 113 OR 458, 116 OR 615. Willson was listed in La Grande KKK minutes as a visiting Elgin Klansman. See Minutes, June 6, 1923, Ku Klux Klan, La Grande, Or. Chapter, Records, 1922–23, Oregon Historical Society, Mss. 2604. The Willson affair is discussed in David A. Horowitz, "The 'Cross of Culture': La Grande, Oregon, in the 1920s," *Oregon Historical Quarterly* 93 (summer 1992): 152–53.

5. See Jay Griffiths, "Looking Back: LG Klan Member Reminisces," *Observer* (November 30, 1985): 2; "Harold Raymond Fosner," *Newport News Times* (November 29, 1986): 3; "Prominent Retired Attorney Succumbs," *La Grande Observer* (January 11, 1965): 1; Eberhard's entry in "Who's Who in the Senate," *Oregon Voter* 56 (January 12, 1929): 67–68; "Death Claims Former Solon," *Oregonian* (January 30, 1968): 13; "Prominent Attorney Dies Here," *La Grande Observer* (January 29, 1968): 1.

6. See "Portland, Ore., Klan Holds Naturalization," *Imperial Night-Hawk* 1 (January 23, 1924): 5; "Portland, Ore., Klavern Well Filled on Regular Meeting Nights," *Imperial Night-Hawk* 1 (February 24, 1924): 8; "Klan Initiates Class," *Oregonian* (May 6, 1924): 10; "Royal Riders of the Red Robe Are Guests of Klansmen," *Imperial Night-Hawk* 2 (June 18, 1924): 7; Lawrence J. Saalfeld, *Forces of Prejudice: The Ku Klux Klan in Oregon, 1920–1925* (Portland: Archdiocesan Historical Commission, 1984), 90–92. For the Oregon School Bill, see M. Paul Holsinger, "The Oregon School Controversy, 1922–25," *Pacific Historical Review* 27 (August 1968): 327–41.

7. Walter M. Pierce to B. F. Irvine, May 24, 1923, Walter M. Pierce to A. C. Hampton, June 30, 1923, and Walter M. Pierce to Dr. William T. Phy, August 17, 1923, The Walter Pierce Papers, Coll. 68, Department of Special Collections, University of Oregon Libraries; "Removal Is Demanded," *Oregonian* (August 2, 1923): 7; Arthur H. Bone, ed., *Oregon Cattleman/Governor, Congressman: Memoirs and Times of Walter M. Pierce* (Portland: Oregon Historical Society, 1981), 195–97, 202.

8. See Lem A. Dever to Ward Irvine, July 2, 1923, and Lem A. Dever to Walter M. Pierce, July 27, 1923, The Walter Pierce Papers, Coll. 68, Department of Special Collections, University of Oregon Libraries; "Governor Pierce Surely Will 'Can' This Awful Boob," *Western American* (October 19, 1923): 8; Bone, ed., *Oregon Cattleman/Governor*, 203–8; C. Easton Rothwell, "The Ku Klux Klan in the State of Oregon" (bachelor's thesis, Reed College, 1924), 137–39.

9. See Lem A. Dever, *Confessions of an Imperial Klansman*, 2d ed. (Portland: Lem A. Dever, 1925), 36–39; "Disputed Ticket of Klan Is Out," *Oregonian* (May 6, 1924): 9; "Injunction Suit Waits," *Oregonian* (May 10, 1924): 14; "'Parasites' Held in Back of Suit," *Oregonian* (May 11, 1924): 10; "Stand for M'Nary Is Taken by Klan," *Oregonian* (May 14, 1924): 10; "Injunction Defied by 'Yellow Ticket,'" *Oregonian* (May 14, 1924): 19; "Contempt Charge Fails," *Oregonian* (May 20, 1924): 6. For background on the Good Government League, see "No Indorsement," *Oregon Voter* 36 (February 9, 1924): 22.

10. See Ben Titus, "I Was a Klansman," *Portland Telegram* (November 3, 1922): 1–2, (November 4, 1922): 2, (November 6, 1922): 1, 3; Rothwell, "Ku Klux Klan," 125; "Knights of the Ku Klux Klan Recognize Women's Orders as Auxiliary," *Imperial Night-Hawk* 1 (June 16, 1923): 5; Dever, *Confessions of an Imperial Klansman*, 32. Titus tied Gifford to liquor use in the November 4 installment of his article.

11. See "Astoria Klansmen Are Interested in Secession Action of Pendleton Body," *Astoria Evening Budget* (August 6, 1923): 7; "Gifford Again Is Target," *Oregonian* (December 2, 1923): 19; "Powell Ousted, Claim," *Oregonian* (December 3, 1923): 4; "'Purifying' the Klan," *Oregon Voter* 35 (December 8, 1923): 16–17; "New Society Is Organized," *La Grande Evening Observer* (December 18, 1923): 1; "Luther I. Powell Banished by Klan," *Oregonian* (February 16, 1924): 17; "Lem A. Dever Resigns Post," *La Grande Evening Observer* (December 18, 1923): 1; "Klan Declared Menace," *Oregonian* (November 2, 1924): 12.

12. See "Klan Revolt Rumored," *Oregonian* (June 8, 1924): 16; Bone, ed., *Oregon Cattleman/Governor*, 209; "Political Order Is Incorporated," *Oregonian* (April 1, 1925): 7; "Democrats, Too, Plan New Group," *Oregonian* (April 12, 1925): 1; "Reorganized Klan Sought in Oregon," *Oregonian* (January 14, 1926): 18; "Klan Meets at Salem," *Oregonian* (January 30, 1926): 11; "No Klan Dictation Here, Says Dragon," *Oregonian* (October 31, 1926): 18; "Klan Functions Again," *Oregon Voter* 44 (February 13, 1926): 28.

13. For the fate of Oregon Klan chapters after 1925, see Eckard V. Toy, "The Ku Klux Klan in Oregon," in G. Thomas Edwards and Carlos A. Schwantes, eds., *Experiences in a Promised Land: Essays in Pacific Northwest History* (Seattle: University of Washington Press, 1986), 284. The survival of the Tillamook klavern is described in Toy, "The Ku Klux Klan in Tillamook, Oregon," *Pacific Northwest Quarterly* 53 (April 1962): 60–64; William Toll, "Progress and Piety: The Ku Klux Klan and Social Change in Tillamook, Oregon," *Pacific Northwest Quarterly* 69 (April 1978): 75–85. Klan disruptiveness is discussed in Editorial, "As Others See Ku-Kluxed Oregon," *Portland Evening*

Telegram (March 21, 1923): 6; Editorial, "Regenerating the Ku Klux Klan," *Portland Evening Telegram* (June 5, 1923): 6. For Gifford's attempt to revive the order, see Stewart H. Holbrook, "Grand Finale . . . The Klan Rides Again," *Oregonian Sunday Magazine* (April 18, 1937): 12.

14. See David Chalmers, *Hooded Americanism: The History of the Ku Klux Klan*, rev. ed. (New York: Franklin Watts, 1981), 73, 171–74. The Coburn murder was tied to the Atlanta power struggle between William J. Simmons and Hiram Wesley Evans; for the latter's spin, see "Dr. Evans' Statement on Fox-Coburn Tragedy," *Imperial Night-Hawk* 1 (November 14, 1923): 1. For La Grande newspaper coverage of the incident, see "At the Funeral," *La Grande Evening Observer* (November 14, 1923): 1; "Corridors Full; Await the Verdict," *La Grande Evening Observer* (December 21, 1923): 1; "Phillip [sic] Fox Guilty; Life Term Given Him," *La Grande Evening Observer* (December 23, 1923): 1, 6.

15. See Chalmers, *Hooded Americanism*, 5–7, 304–55; Wyn Craig Wade, *The Fiery Cross: The Ku Klux Klan in America*, rev. ed. (New York: Oxford University Press, 1998), 257–306.

16. See Chalmers, *Hooded Americanism*, 7, 356–406; Wade, *Fiery Cross*, 307–67.

17. See Chalmers, *Hooded Americanism*, 406–23; Wade, *Fiery Cross*, 368–403.

18. See Mark Lienesch, *Redeeming America: Piety and Politics in the New Christian Right* (Chapel Hill University of North Carolina Press, 1993); Michael Barkun, *Religion and the Racist Right: The Origins of the Christian Identity Movement* (Chapel Hill: University of North Carolina Press, 1994); Elinor Langer, "The American Neo-Nazi Movement Today," *Nation* 251 (July 16/23, 1990): 82–90.

19. Eckard V. Toy, "'Promised Land' or Armageddon?: History, Survivalists, and the Aryan Nation in the Pacific Northwest," *Montana, the Magazine of Western History* 36 (summer 1986): 80–82; Jonathan Mozzochi, *Organized White Supremacists in Oregon* (Portland: Coalition for Human Dignity, 1990).

20. Richard Hofstadter, *The Age of Reform: From Bryan to F.D.R.* (New York: Alfred A. Knopf, 1955), 293–96; David H. Bennett, *The Party of Fear: From Nativist Movements to the New Right in American History* (Chapel Hill: University of North Carolina Press, 1988), 1–14, 199–237; Nancy MacLean, *Behind the Mask of Chivalry: The Making of the Second Ku Klux Klan* (New York: Oxford University Press, 1994), xi, 51, 91–96, 98–124, 160–61, 165. For a discussion of negative views of the KKK by historians, see Shawn Lay, "Introduction: The Second Invisible Empire," in Shawn Lay, ed., *The Invisible Empire in the West: Toward a New Historical Appraisal of the Ku Klux Klan of the 1920s* (Urbana: University of Illinois Press, 1992), 1.

21. For the KKK of the 1920s as the first wave of conservative populism, see Leonard J. Moore, "New Insights into the Klan Movement of the 1920s," paper presented before the 58th Annual Meeting of the Southern Historical Association, Atlanta, Ga., November 5, 1992, 10.

22. The racial epithets described herein may be found in Minutes, January 16, 1923, 4; "Klansmen and Their Work during the Last Two Weeks," November 14, 1922, 2;

Minutes, March 17, 1923, 1; Minutes, September 14, 1922, 1; "Along the Main Drag," April 3, 1923, 1; Minutes, April 17, 1923, 1; Minutes, January 9, 1923, 4; Minutes, August 21, 1923, 1; Minutes, February 6, 1923, 3, Ku Klux Klan, La Grande, Or. Chapter, Records, 1922–1923, Oregon Historical Society, Mss. 2604.

23. For "vague discontent," see J. Morgan Kousser, review of *Behind the Mask of Chivalry: The Making of the Second Ku Klux Klan* (New York: Oxford University Press, 1994), *Journal of the History of Behavioral Sciences* 32 (July 1996): 231.

24. W. Fitzhugh Brundage, *Lynchings in the New South: Georgia and Virginia, 1880–1930* (Urbana: University of Illinois Press, 1993), 22–23, 242, 263. Eckard V. Toy has suggested that Klan members "were not always against individual aliens, Roman Catholics, Jews, or Negroes, but feared the abstract, almost incomprehensible, symbol of stereotypes"; see Toy, "The Ku Klux Klan in Oregon: Its Character and Program" (master's thesis, University of Oregon, 1959), 17. Klan racism and nativism are placed in cultural perspective by Leonard J. Moore, "Historical Interpretations of the 1920s Klan: The Traditional View and the Recent Revision," *Journal of Social History* 24 (winter 1990): 341–57, also published as "Historical Interpretations of the 1920s Klan: The Traditional View and Recent Revisions," in Shawn Lay, ed., *The Invisible Empire in the West: Toward a New Historical Appraisal of the Ku Klux Klan of the 1920s* (Urbana: University of Illinois Press, 1992), 24.

25. Leonard J. Moore, "Good Old-Fashioned New Social History and the Twentieth-Century American Right," *Reviews in American History* 24 (December 1996): 562; Christopher Lasch, *The Revolt of the Elites and the Betrayal of Democracy* (New York: W. W. Norton, 1995), 64–65; David Monod, *Store Wars: Shopkeepers and the Culture of Mass Marketing, 1890–1939* (Toronto: University of Toronto Press, 1996), 44, 91–94, 239.

26. For Fosner's claim concerning the Legionnaires and Eberhard's assertion about the Elks, see Minutes, January 23, 1923, 2, and February 6, 1923, 2, respectively, Ku Klux Klan, La Grande, Or. Chapter, Records, 1922–1923, Oregon Historical Society, Mss. 2604. For Klan public activities, see "Celebrated the Charter Arrival," *La Grande Evening Observer* (March 19, 1923): 8; "Knights of the Ku Klux Klan Held Open Air Initiation," *La Grande Evening Observer* (July 26, 1923): 1. Dennis condemned "mob" rule and the "secret" nature of the state Klan and viewed its members as "breeders of trouble"; see Editorials, "And out of the Chaos Came ———," *La Grande Evening Observer* (May 20, 1922): 4; "An Unexpected Horror in America," *La Grande Evening Observer* (December 27, 1922): 4.

27. Shawn Lay, "Conclusion: Toward a New Historical Appraisal of the Ku Klux Klan of the 1920s," in Shawn Lay, ed., *The Invisible Empire in the West: Toward a New Historical Appraisal of the Ku Klux Klan of the 1920s* (Urbana: University of Illinois Press, 1992), 222. See also David A. Horowitz, "The Normality of Extremism: The Ku Klux Klan Revisited," *Society* 35 (September/October 1998): 71–77.

ndex

DAVID A. HOROWITZ, a professor of history at Portland State University, was born in the Bronx, New York, and attended Antioch College and the University of Minnesota. He has written numerous articles on the Ku Klux Klan of the 1920s and is the author of *Beyond Left and Right: Insurgency and the Establishment* and the coauthor (with Peter Carroll) of *On the Edge: The U.S. in the 20th Century.*